Through Other Eyes

EDITED BY DAN HERR AND JOEL WELLS

Through Other Eyes

Some Impressions of American Catholicism
by Foreign Visitors from 1777 to the Present

>>->>><<<-<<<

THE NEWMAN PRESS · 1965 · WESTMINSTER, MARYLAND

Preface

→>)<<←

This anthology presents varied impressions of the Catholic Church in the United States recorded over the course of nearly two centuries by visitors from other lands. The first selection, written in 1777 by an anonymous Frenchman, rumors the hanging of a priest and, in describing the numerous and many sorts of churches in the city of Philadelphia, notes that "the most wretched of all these . . . is that of the Papists." The final selection, written by an English Dominican in 1960, describes a "Church that has 'arrived' to become one of the most characteristically American of institutions."

The Catholic Church in America has come a long way during the period marked off by these two accounts, a distance dramatized by the brief presence of a Catholic in the White House, himself the son of a son of an Irish immigrant. But for years the Catholic Church in America had been despised and, for a time, even persecuted. In these days of the Church powerful— a Church so well established that it can now tolerate and even, in some cases, welcome criticism (the hallmark of maturity)— it seems to us that to fully appreciate where we have arrived it is both important and valuable to see where we have come from.

For some reason, American Catholics are woefully ignorant of the history of the Church in their own land. (Up to a very few years ago, we have been told, no seminary in the country taught a course in American Catholic Church history.) Perhaps it is because this generation is too busy making Church history to look back and appreciate the problems and sacrifices of the past. Whatever the reason, this lack of knowledge and perspective is lamentable at a time when the lessons of the past would make splendid companions in the quest for greater things to come.

This is not to say that American Catholics are not keenly interested in what others think and say of them—a curiosity native to all Americans. When such comment comes from foreign observers, it is enhanced by a certain air of objectivity and impartiality (not necessarily present in fact) which makes it all the more provocative. Over the years the editors have made a casual collection of observations about the Church in the United States, and it occurred to us that others might share our interest. We decided to investigate more seriously the material available in order to present a wide variety of viewpoints and also to construct a sort of informal but chronological history of the growth of the Church in America.

We would be the last to claim the status of professional historians but we have tried to be diligent. Our criteria, we will readily admit, however, embraced two shockingly non-academic factors: selections had to be readable in themselves; and they had to interest *us*. We realize that this means that our anthology will in consequence be exiled forthwith to that great, non-professional plain where roams the general reader. It is our presumptuous hope, though, that a few historians may find it of some passing interest, even if they read it furtively behind a more respectable jacket.

Even the general reader (don't get us wrong: some of our best friends are general readers) will note that the number of selections written in the past twenty years is disproportionately heavy. We have dwelt upon the recent past because with the history of the Catholic Church, as with all of American history, so much has happened at such an accelerated, break-neck rate in the past two decades.

THE EDITORS

Acknowledgments

➺⟫⟪⟬

The editors wish to express their thanks for the assistance so generously granted by the following in the preparation and researching of this anthology: Sister Aurelia, O. P., Sister Peter Claver, O. P., Sister Tobias, O. P., Sister Albertus Magnus, O. P., Dorothy and James Cox, John Delaney, Anthony Delgado, Walter Gray, Philip Gleason, Edmund Wehrle, Rev. E. C. Herr, John Drahos, Louise Wijnhausen, Will Herr, Michael Gill, Elizabeth Wells, John McHale, Patricia Siok and Gloria Adams.

Obviously, none of these fine and helpful people are to be charged with any sins of omission or commission of which this book may be guilty. These must be borne forever upon the corrugated surfaces of our non-academic souls.

Contents

>>><<<

CONTENTS

Through Other Eyes

1

>>)<<<

An Anonymous Frenchman
1777

from *On the Threshold of Liberty*

>>)<<<

The anonymous author of the following brief selections visited in
the American Colonies for a period of five months in the year 1777.
That he was French, Catholic, and had some glorious misconceptions
about the nature of the Revolution which was going on about him
is about all that can be deduced about his identity from the pages of
the journal which he kept during his visit. This journal is dated
1778 and was undoubtedly intended by the author for publication
in France. It is presented in the form of a lengthy letter to a close
friend, but it is likely that this was only a literary posture to enhance
the readability of the manuscript. The author might have spared
himself the device, since his work was not published during his
lifetime, and not at all in its entirety until 1959, when Edward D.
Seeber translated and edited it for publication in Indiana University's
Humanities Series under the title *On the Threshold of Liberty.*
It is reprinted here by permission of Indiana University Press.

>>)<<<

Following the banishment or transmigration of the sectarians
and their complete and successful settlement in the colonies, other
members of the already established sects began to arrive from
France, Germany and Holland, to be received and welcomed by
the government and by their coreligionists as martyrs of the
Roman Church. In a word, hatred of the papists was transformed into generosity for these refugees who, greatly pleased

by the favors bestowed upon them by their narrow compatriots, soon summoned others of their own communion who were still being persecuted. This resulted in new benefactions and afforded motives for hating the Catholics.

This, my friend, explains, if I am not mistaken, the scorn for our sect in general, and the reasons that will prevent these colonists, so long as they recall the origin of their own establishment, from liking the Catholics and from granting them equal prerogatives with the others. You can well imagine how the papists, who for a long time scoffed at and persecuted these good people, are forced in their turn to bear the ridicule, insults, and persecutions of the Anglicans, until they are reduced to the same exigencies that their own cruelties had thrust upon the first tillers of this land to which they were fleeing to escape secret or domestic persecution. Should the Catholics expect, in a country populated through their acts of injustice, to be welcomed, cherished and respected—they who, like the Jews, could not, even though partaking of the bread of the Egyptians, consider them other than rejected by the Divinity and the target of obloquy?

And so, following these principles, they must daily endure the grossest humiliations, either for themselves or for their rites, to the point of being without recognition, respect, or power (I mean as a group). They do not even enjoy a free church in which they can give vent to the enthusiasm which seizes them to damn or to save: each time their pastor preaches in Philadelphia, where they have their only church in the thirteen provinces, a secret envoy of each sect is present to report any unduly harsh remarks made by the priest against alien sects and heresy.

A sorry reward of things in this world!

* * *

In this city (Philadelphia) there are thirty-four religious sects, somewhat less than thirty-four buildings. . . . It is noteworthy that the most wretched of all these churches is that of the papists. Having no cross, steeple, or other distinguishing mark, it looks on the outside just like those of the other sects. The priest is allowed to preach only in English and in German; and once outside the church he can wear only a plain suit, not a cassock, surplice, tonsure, or biretta; he cannot carry the Eucharist in formal procession under pain of death by hanging. Although he is permitted to wear a surplice when accompanying deceased parishioners to the cemetery, he is denied the privileges of other processions and rites held outside. It is apparent that he is completely bereft of the more showy clerical functions to the same degree that his European confreres have full freedom to glory in theirs. Sometime between September 10 and 14 (so they say) the papist cleric was hanged for having declaimed, in a sermon preached in German, against the Congress and the cause of independence.

2

Moreau de St. Mery

1793-1798

from *Moreau de St. Mery: American Journey*

❧ ❦

Moreau de St. Mery was born in Martinique of French parents. He studied law in Paris and returned to Martinique to practice. After eight years he was called to France to assist in codifying French colonial laws. A fervent revolutionist, Moreau was so active that a shift in leadership forced him to flee to America, where he spent five years in exile before returning to France. His report on America, *Voyage aux Etats-Unis de L' Amérique* (translated for the first time in English in 1947 by historical novelist Kenneth Roberts and his wife, Anna) is probably unique in its frankness and its emphasis on the sordid aspects of American colonial life. His attitude toward the Church and American Catholics is, to say the least, anticlerical. This bias is illustrated by the present passage from *Moreau de St. Mery's American Journey 1793-1798,* translated by Kenneth Roberts (Copyright 1947 by Kenneth Roberts and Anna M. Roberts). It is reprinted by permission of Doubleday & Company, Inc.

❧ ❦

What I have said about the harmony which reigns among representatives of the different faiths in no way applies to the Roman Catholics. As I have said, they have three churches in Philadelphia. One, called simply The Chapel, is located interiorly between Walnut Street and a small alley and between South Third and South Fourth streets. It was the first church of this faith in Philadelphia. It is merely a sort of oratory where low masses are said and where, for the convenience of priests who live in that neighborhood, the sacraments can be administered.

In the choir, on the Epistle side of the altar, is a small oil painting about one and a half feet wide by two feet high, representing a brig with a shattered foremast; the Virgin is in the sky, with her Son near her, and seems to be protecting the vessel.

On one of the sides of the picture on the canvas itself one reads Ex Voto and at the bottom of the canvas "Made the 1st of November 1791 by the passengers of the brig Minerva, coming from Cap François to Philadelphia."

The priests of this chapel are Irish and consequently fanatics. They have charge of the parochial duties of the Church of St. Mary of the Irish on South Fourth Street. This church is only an ordinary house with a large door in front and another on the side. Above the altar as altar screen is a representation of the crucifixion of Christ. The pulpit almost touches the altar on the Epistle side. Moreover it has benches and pews and a small organ, as in Protestant churches, and sermons are in English.

The third church is the German Catholic, on the north corner of Spruce and Sixth. Its members withdrew from the Church of St. Mary because Irish domination prevailed there and because the priests are the real administration of it. The German church is newly built and is prettier than the other, if such a word can be applied to either. The pulpit is on the Gospel side of the altar, but too near the choir. Preaching is in German. The altar screen is a frightful daub purporting to show Jesus Christ ascending into heaven and being received by His Father, who holds in His right hand a monstrance with the host. It has benches and a small organ. The custom of Rome is followed in these churches at divine service, but services in the German church are more like those in the churches of the French colonies, which follow the same custom.

The two churches use the cemetery which surrounds St. Mary's, but each church uses a separate portion of the ground. Because of its distance from the German church, the clergy, preceded by the Cross, conduct the corpse to the cemetery after saying prayers for the dead.

The Roman churches are the only ones that display any form of ceremony publicly and in the streets.

The priests of the German church are considered moderates because they are not like the Irish, who will not perform the marriage ceremony unless both parties provide proof of confession, or bury those who have not confessed. Both churches acknowledge the authority of the Roman archbishop, M. Carroll, born in Baltimore.

The Catholic cemetery, like those of other faiths in Philadelphia, is full of monuments and inscriptions no more interesting than were the insignificant humans whose deaths occasioned them.

During the War of American Independence, four Frenchmen were buried there, and marble slabs placed over their graves; but as nobody expected to see any more Frenchmen, these tombstones were taken and used to form the top of the flight of stairs by which people from the German church enter the cemetery from Eighth Street.

On March 5, 1797, the German Catholic church was deprived of its rights by an injunction of M. Carroll, pronounced in the Irish Catholic Church of St. Mary.

The pretended reason for this interdiction was that the parish priest was seizing all surplice fees, even when his vicar did his work, whereupon the churchwardens proposed that he limit himself to the fees he himself could collect, plus half of those that his vicar received, but he refused and was discharged.

The Irish priests of St. Mary made a capital affair out of all this, because the churchwardens of the German church had separated from St. Mary's on the ground that the Irish priests had usurped too much temporal administration.

The only effect of the interdiction was to attract more people to the German church.

3

※※

Mrs. Frances Trollope

1827-1831

from *Domestic Manners of the Americans*

※※

Mrs. Frances Trollope, mother of the English novelist Anthony Trollope, stayed longer—three years, nine months—than most visitors, but her report was no less critical, nor did her prolonged research protect her from bitter attack. She came to the United States in 1827 to start a bazaar in Cincinnati, Ohio. The failure of her bazaar and the resulting financial problems was hardly calculated to make her feel kindly toward Americans. *Domestic Manners of the Americans,* from which these two excerpts are taken, was published in 1832. Few American readers agreed with Mark Twain that Mrs. Trollope "was merely telling the truth. . . . She lived three years in this civilization of ours; in the body of it—not on the surface of it, as was the case of most of the foreign tourists of her day. She knew her subject well and she set it forth fairly and squarely without any weak ifs and ands and buts. She deserved gratitude—but it is an error to suppose she got it."

This passage is taken from the Vintage Book edition which appeared in 1960.

※※

The influence which the ministers of all the innumerable religious sects throughout America, have on the females of their respective congregations, approaches very nearly to what we read of in Spain, or in other strictly Roman Catholic countries. There are many causes for this peculiar influence. Where equality of rank is affectedly acknowledged by the rich, and clamorously claimed by the poor, distinction and pre-eminence are allowed to the clergy only. This gives them high importance in the eyes of the ladies. I think, also, that it is from the clergy only that the women of America receive that sort of attention which is so dearly valued by every female heart throughout the world. With the priests of America, the women hold that degree of influential importance which, in the countries of Europe, is allowed them throughout all orders and ranks of society, except, perhaps, the very lowest; and in return for this they seem to give their hearts and souls into their keeping. I never saw, or read, of any country where religion had so strong a hold upon the women, or a slighter hold upon the men.

*   *   *

I had often heard it observed before I visited America, that one of the great blessings of its constitution was the absence of a national religion, the country being thus exonerated from all obligation of supporting the clergy; those only contributing to do so whose principles led them to it. My residence in the country has shown me that a religious tyranny may be exerted very effectually without the aid of the government, in a way much more oppressive than the paying of tithe, and without obtaining any of the salutary decorum, which I presume no one will deny is the result of an established mode of worship.

As it was impossible to remain many weeks in the country without being struck with the strange anomalies produced by its religious system, my early notes contain many observations on the subject; but as nearly the same scenes recurred in every part of the country, I state them here, not as belonging to the west alone, but to the whole Union, the same cause producing the same effect everywhere.

The whole people appear to be divided into an almost endless variety of religious factions, and I was told, that to be well received in society, it was necessary to declare yourself as belonging to some one of these. Let your acknowledged belief be what it may, you are said to be not a Christian, unless you attach yourself to a particular congregation. Besides the broad and well-known distinctions of Episcopalian, Catholic, Presbyterian, Calvinist, Baptist, Quaker, Swedenborgian, Universalist, Dunker, etc.; there are innumerable others springing out of these, each of which assumes a church government of its own; of this, the most intriguing and factious individual is invariably the head; and in order, as it should seem, to shew a reason for this separation, each congregation invests itself with some queer variety of external observance that has the melancholy effect of exposing all religious ceremonies to contempt.

It is impossible, in witnessing all these unseemly vagaries, not to recognise the advantages of an established church as a sort of head-quarters for quiet, unpresuming Christians, who are contented to serve faithfully, without insisting upon having each a little separate banner, embroidered with a device of their own imagining.

The Catholics alone appear exempt from the fury of division and sub-division that has seized every other persuasion. Having the Pope for their common head, regulates, I presume, their movements, and prevents the outrageous display of individual whim which every other sect is permitted.

I had the pleasure of being introduced to the Catholic bishop of Cincinnati, and have never known in any country a priest of a character and bearing more truly apostolic. He was an American, but I should never have discovered it from his pronunciation or manner. He received his education partly in England, and partly in France. His manners were highly polished; his piety active and sincere, and infinitely more mild and tolerant than that of the factious Sectarians who form the great majority of the American priesthood.

I believe I am sufficiently tolerant; but this does not prevent my seeing that the object of all religious observances is better obtained, when the government of the church is confided to the people, than when it is placed in the hands of every tinker and tailor who chooses to claim a share in it. Nor is this the only evil attending the want of a national religion, supported by the State. As there is no legal and fixed provision for the clergy, it is hardly surprising that their services are confined to those who can pay them. The vehement expressions of insane or hypocritical zeal, such as were exhibited during "the Revival," can but ill atone for the want of village worship, any more than the eternal talk of the admirable and unequalled government, can atone for the continual contempt of social order. Church and State hobble along, side by side, notwithstanding their boasted independence. Almost every man you meet will tell you, that he is occupied in labours most abundant for the good of his country; and almost every woman will tell you, that besides those things that are within [her house] she has coming upon her daily the care of all the churches. Yet spite of this universal attention to the government, its laws are half asleep; and spite of the old women and their Dorcas societies, atheism is awake and thriving.

* * *

Baltimore, is, I think, one of the handsomest cities to approach in the Union. The noble column erected to the memory of Washington, and the Catholic Cathedral, with its beautiful dome, being built on a commanding eminence, are seen at a great distance. As you draw nearer, many other domes and towers become visible, and as you enter Baltimore Street, you feel that you have arrived in a handsome and populous city.

We took up our quarters at an excellent hotel, where the coach stopped, and the next day were fortunate enough to find accommodations in the house of a lady, well known to many of my European friends. With her and her amiable daughter, we spent a fortnight very agreeably, and felt quite aware that if we had not arrived in London or Paris, we had, at least, left far behind, the "half-horse, half-alligator" tribes of the West, as the Kentuckians call themselves.

Baltimore is in many respects a beautiful city; it has several handsome buildings, and even the private dwelling-houses have a look of magnificence, from the abundance of white marble with which many of them are adorned. The ample flights of steps, and the lofty door frames, are in most of the best houses formed of this beautiful material.

This has been called the city of monuments, from its having the stately column erected to the memory of General Washington, and which bears a colossal statue of him at the top; and another pillar of less dimensions, recording some victory; I forget which. Both these are of brilliant white marble. There are also several pretty marble fountains in different parts of the city, which greatly add to its beauty. These are not, it is true, quite so splendid as that of the Innocents, or many others at Paris, but they are fountains of clear water, and they are built of white marble. There is one which is sheltered from the sun by a roof supported by light columns; it looks like a temple dedicated to the genius of the spring. The water flows into a marble cistern, to which you descend by a flight of steps of delicate whiteness, and return by another. These steps are never without groups of negro girls, some carrying the water on their heads, with that graceful tripping gaily with their yet unfilled pitchers; many of them singing in the soft rich voice, peculiar to their race; and all dressed with that strict attention to taste and smartness which seems the distinguishing characteristic of the Baltimore females of all ranks.

The Catholic Cathedral is considered by all Americans as a magnificent church, but it can hardly be so classed by any one who has seen the churches of Europe; its interior, however, has an air of neatness that amounts to elegance. The form is a Greek cross, having a dome in the centre; but the proportions are ill-preserved; the dome is too low, and the arches which support it are flattened, and too wide for their height. On each side of the high altar are chapels to the Saviour and the Virgin. The altars in these, as well as the high altar, are of native marble of different colors, and some of the specimens are very beautiful. The decorations of the altar are elegant and costly. The prelate is a cardinal, and bears, moreover, the title of "Archbishop of Baltimore."

There are several paintings in different parts of the church, which we heard were considered as very fine. There are two presented by Louis XVIII; one of these is the Descent from the Cross by Paul Guirin; the other a copy from Rubens (as they told us) of a study of St. Louis in the Holy Land; but the composition of the picture is so abominably bad, that I conceive the legend of its being after Rubens, must be as fabulous as its subject. The admiration in which these pictures are held, is an incontestable indication of the state of art in the country.

We attended mass in this church the Sunday after our arrival, and I was perfectly astonished at the beauty and splendid appearance of the ladies who filled it. Excepting on a very brilliant Sunday at the Tuilleries, I never saw so shewy a display of morning costume, and I think I never saw anywhere so many beautiful women at one glance. They all appeared to be in full dress, and were really all beautiful.

The sermon (I am very attentive to sermons) was a most extraordinary one. The priest began by telling us, that he was about to preach upon a vice that he would not "mention or name" from the beginning of his sermon to the end.

Having thus excited the curiosity of his hearers, by proposing a riddle to them, he began.

Adam, he said, was most assuredly the first who had committed this sin, and Cain the next; then, following the advice given by the listener, in the *Plaideurs,* "Plaideurs, passons au déluge, je vous prie"; he went on to mention the particular propriety of Noah's family on this point; and then continued, "Now observe, what did God shew the greatest dislike to? What was it that Jesus was never even accused of? What was it Joseph hated the most? Who was the disciple that Jesus chose for his friend?" and thus he went on for nearly an hour, in a strain that was often perfectly unintelligible to me, but which, as far as I could comprehend it, appeared to be a sort of expose and commentary upon private anecdotes which he found, or fancied he had found in the Bible. I never saw the attention of a congregation more strongly excited, and I really wished, in Christian charity, that something better had rewarded it.

There are a vast number of churches and chapels in the city, in proportion to its extent, and several that are large and well-built; the Unitarian church is the handsomest I have ever seen dedicated to that mode of worship. But the prettiest among them is a little bijou of a thing belonging to the Catholic college. The institution is dedicated to St. Mary, but this little chapel looks, though in the midst of a city, as if it should have been sacred to St. John of the wilderness. There is a sequestered little garden behind it, hardly large enough to plant cabbages in, which yet contains a Mount Calvary, bearing a lofty cross. The tiny path which leads up to this sacred spot, is not much wider than a sheep-track, and its cedars are but shrubs, but all is in proportion; and notwithstanding its fairy dimensions, there is something of holiness, and quiet beauty about it, that excites the imagination strangely. The little chapel itself has the same touching and impressive character. A solitary lamp, whose glare is tempered by delicately painted glass, hangs before the altar. The light of day enters dimly, yet richly, through crimson curtains, and the silence with which the well-lined doors opened from time to time, admitting a youth of the establishment, who, with noiseless tread, approached the altar, and kneeling, offered a whispered prayer, and retired, had something in it more calculated, perhaps to generate holy thoughts, than even the swelling anthem heard beneath the resounding dome of St. Peter's.

4

Alexis de Tocqueville

1831=1832

from *Alexis de Tocqueville: Journey to America* and
Democracy in America

Of the many Europeans who attempted to interpret American life,
none achieved the success of Alexis de Tocqueville, a French aristo-
crat who visited the United States in 1831 and whose sympathetic
critique of American democracy, its institutions and its people,
Democracy in America (1835, 1840) is universally considered a
classic study of American society. Since de Tocqueville was a
Catholic, it might be expected that American Catholics would not
suffer from his hands, but he exhibited neither more nor less percep-
tion, objectivity and kindness toward his co-religionists than toward
any other group of Americans. The first selections are from his note-
books, carefully kept during his travels in America. Under the title
Alexis de Tocqueville: Journey to America, they were translated by
George Lawrence and published by the Yale University Press in
1959. They are reprinted by permission of Yale University Press
(Copyright 1959 by J. P. Mayer). The last three selections are from
Democracy in America, edited by Phillips Bradley and reprinted by
permission of Alfred A. Knopf, Inc. (Copyright 1945 by Alfred A.
Knopf).

CONVERSATION WITH MR. MULLAN

Mr. Mullan is a Catholic priest who seemed very ardent in
his devotion. When I met him he was going to Michilimackinac

to give religious instruction to a colony of Catholic Indians newly established at Arbre croche.

Q. *Do you think that the support of the civil power helps religion?*

A. I am profoundly convinced that it is harmful. I know that most Catholic priests in Europe hold the opposite view; I see why they think so. They mistrust the spirit of freedom whose first energy was directed against them. Moreover having always lived under monarchic institutions which protected them, they naturally miss this protection. So they fall into an inevitable error. If they could live in this country, they would not be slow to change their minds. All religious beliefs are on the same footing here. The government neither supports nor persecutes any of them; and without question there is no place on earth where the Catholic faith counts more ardent adherents or more numerous proselytes. I repeat, the less religion and the clergy are mixed up with civil government, the less will they come into political arguments, and the more will religious ideas gain in power.

Q. *Which sects in the United States are most hostile to Catholicism?*

A. All sects are united in their hatred of Catholicism; but only the Presbyterians are violent. It is they too who are the most zealous.

Q. *Do you sometimes find traces of the labours of the Jesuits among the Indians?*

A. Yes. There are tribes which preserve confused ideas of the religion which the Jesuits taught them, and who come back to Christianity very quickly (at Arbre croche there are families who accepted the first principles of Christianity one hundred and fifty years ago, and they still preserve some traces of them), when one manages to reach as far as them. In general the Indian tribes venerate the memory of the Black Robes. From time to time one finds crosses in the wilderness which were put up by the Jesuits long ago.

Q. *Is it true that the Indians have natural eloquence?*

A. Very true. I have often admired the profound meaning and the conciseness of their speeches. Their style has something Spartan in it.

Q. *Do they still make war as ferociously as ever?*

A. Just the same. They burn and torture their prisoners in a thousand ways. They scalp the dead and the wounded. However they are gentle, honest people when their passions are not roused by war. I have seen their war dance. Never have I witnessed a more terrible sight. The warriors who are to dance first make themselves as terrifying as possible by smearing themselves with dyes. In the dance they mimic all the savage scenes which always take place in a war between Indians. Their pantomime sometimes shows them smashing an enemy's head, sometimes torturing him, sometimes scalping him. Some years ago the Bishop of Cincinnati suggested to an Indian tribe (I forget the name which Mr. Mullan mentioned) that they should send him some of their children to educate. I was present at the pow-wow to discuss the matter. Though they were all savages, the meeting, I assure you, was nonetheless impressive for that. They sat round in a circle, each spoke in turn with great seriousness and natural eloquence. An Indian never interrupts a speaker.

Q. *What public authority exists among the savages?*

A. They have their chiefs. Many of them are hereditary, and the family only loses its rights in case of some shameful crime. There is an Indian chief on the banks of the St. Joseph river who claims direct descent from an ancestor who met the first Frenchman in the country.

Q. *Are the Indians of the L'Arbre croche zealous?*

A. (Here Mr. Mullan's expression became extraordinarily animated.) I know no Christian to equal them. Their faith is complete; their obedience to the laws of religion is complete. A converted Indian would let himself be killed rather than break the rules for abstinence. Their life becomes very moral. You saw how eagerly the Indian population of Sault-Sainte-Marie came to look for me when they knew there was a priest on board.

Q. *How is the American clergy recruited?*

A. Up to now most of the priests have come from Europe. We are only beginning to have some native Americans. (Which is much better.) Now we have twelve or thirteen seminaries in the States. In the last forty years Catholicism has made incredible progress among us.

Q. *How are Church expenses paid?*

A. By voluntary gifts. The church pews of each family are the main source of revenue.

Q. *How are Bishops appointed?*

A. The Pope appoints them directly. But it is the custom for him to consult the existing bench of Bishops. He has sometimes been known not to do so, and in those cases his choice has seldom been a happy one.

* * *

BOSTON (30TH SEPTEMBER 1831)

Mr. Coolidge said to me today: We are not afraid of Catholicism in the United States because we are sure that with us it will be so modified that it will have no influence on our political approach. Here we have noticed that the Catholics always vote for the most democratic party. It is true that they are the poorest. Baltimore, where they predominate, is the most democratic toward the Union.

Charles Carroll is a Catholic.

Q. *Do you sometimes feel the absence of government?*

A. No, far from that, what worries us is the fear that it may interfere in matters where its intervention is not indispensable.

* * *

CONVERSATION WITH MR. LATROBE, A VERY DISTINGUISHED LAWYER FROM BALTIMORE (30TH OCTOBER 1831)

'How do the Catholics in America prosper?'

'They are increasing extraordinarily and are pursuing a very skillful policy. The Catholics are the only congregation that is

never divided about doctrine. They march united like a single man. For the last twenty years they have very skillfully diverted all their efforts towards education. They have established seminaries and colleges. The best educational institutions in Maryland are Catholic. They even have colleges in other States. These colleges are full of Protestants. There is perhaps no young man in Maryland who has received a good education who has not been brought up by the Catholics. Although they are very careful not to speak of their beliefs to their pupils, you realise that they always exercise a certain influence. They have also very cleverly directed their chief attention to the education of women. They think that where the mother is Catholic, the children will almost always become such. General[l] are able men.'

'What are the doctrines of the Am question of Church government?'

'They recognise the Pope's right to ꝛ ꞏnd the bishops' right to appoint the parish ꝑ ꞏters of faith they think that only an Ecumenicaꝛ ꞏded over by the Pope has a right to pronounce.'

* * *

CONVERSATION WITH MR. CRANCHE (2ND NOVEMBER 18[3]1)

Mr. Cranche is a Catholic priest and vice-president of the college of St. Mary at Baltimore. Almost the whole of the present generation has passed through this college. It was founded forty years ago by Mr. Dubourg, a French priest. Since then it has had great additions.

Q. *How are the Catholics in the United States governed?*

A. In the United States there is a metropolitan archbishop who resides at Baltimore, and thirteen suffragan bishops. When a bishopric becomes vacant, each of the remaining bishops sends a list of three candidates to the archbishop. It is from among those candidates that the Pope chooses.

Q. *Is that procedure a law or a custom?*

A. A custom. In theory the Pope's choice is free, but he always does select one of the bishops' candidates.

Q. *How are the lower members of the clergy appointed?*

A. All the governmental power is concentrated on the episcopate. In Europe the parish priests can only lose their positions in case of bad conduct. America is regarded as a pagan country where there are no resident clergy, but only missionaries. The bishops choose these missionaries, appoint them and call them back at their pleasure.

Q. *So you have nothing resembling the old French officialites here?*

A. No, we have no sort of ecclesiastical tribunal.

Q. *Is Catholicism spreading in the United States?*

A. Yes, prodigiously.

Q. *But is it spreading through conversions, and have you any idea of the number of converts?*

A. We have not got an idea of the number of converts; but we know that there are a great many.

Q. *I see there are many Protestant children with you. Do they sometimes become Catholic?*

Mr. Cranche, with some animation answered, 'No. At least it is a rare event,' he added. 'We are careful never to say anything to them against the religion of their parents. Two children who talked among themselves about points of controversy with the Protestants would be punished. It is true however that we make them attend our religious services. But their parents know that before they send them to us.'

'But it seems to me that, though you are careful not to talk to your pupils about the Catholic religion, they cannot live like this in a completely Catholic atmosphere without it producing a strong impression on them in favour of your doctrines?'

'The impression is strong enough to take away all their prejudices against Catholicism; not strong enough to convert them. What is more sure of effect is the marriage of a Protestant with a Catholic girl. Such marriages are forbidden in Europe; we favour them here. We have noticed that when the mother is Catholic, the children always and the husband often become Catholics. At Baltimore there are a great number of women's organisations concerned with education. It is not rare to find young girls becoming Catholics.'

'Establishments like yours are multiplying from what I have heard in America?'

'This is the first one; it has 180 pupils. There is another in Maryland which is run on the same plan by the Jesuits, and there is a third in the District of Columbia.'

'What is the opinion of Catholics in America about the power of the Pope and its independence of general councils?'

'It would be very difficult to say. In America as in Europe there are "Gallicans" and "ultramontanes." The latter have the Jesuits as leaders. But up till now these questions are only asked within the circle of those who study theology; the masses have never come into it, and it would be impossible to say what is the view of the majority.'

'Are American Catholics zealous?'

'Yes, I think America is called to become the hearth of Catholicism. It is spreading freely without the help of the civil power, without rousing hatred, simply by the strength of its doctrine and in perfect independence of the State.'

'Do the people subscribe liberally to church expenses?'

'The clergy are not rich, but have what they need.'

'Do you think it is better to meet expenses in this way rather than by enforced contributions?'

'Yes, certainly, in America.'

* * *

CONVERSATION WITH MR. GUILLEMIN, FRENCH CONSUL AT NEW ORLEANS (1ST JANUARY 1832)

Mr. Guillemin is certainly an able man and, I think, of means. All that is exceptional. For incompetence among French agents abroad seems to be the rule. He has been living in New Orleans some fifteen to seventeen years.

* * *

Q. *They say that religion has little sway here over men's souls?*

A. It does not have much, but I think that is partly due to the bad priests they have sent us from Europe. We are flooded with Italians who have nothing in common with the local people, and whose morals are detestable. However, there is no political animosity of any sort against the ministers of the Catholic religion, who, for their part, never meddle in affairs. Recently they broke the windows of a parish priest who refused to bury a suicide in holy ground, but I am sure the people acted very largely in imitation of the scenes at Saint-Germain-l'Auxerrois. From what I see here and in the other States of America, I am profoundly convinced that, in the interests of religion, one ought to make an absolute division between the clergy and the State, and leave religion to exercise the influence proper to it.

Q. *How are the priests paid in Louisiana?*

A. The state does not come into it at all. But the localities generally have landed property devoted to this purpose, besides there are usual receipts, voluntary gifts, pews....

* * *

(22ND JULY)

Entry of the Detroit River. An island: two passages. We take the English channel. House of Fort Maiden. French appearance of the village. Catholic Church. Cock on the church tower. Scottish soldier in full dress on the bank; on the other side two stark naked savages in a canoe, twisting as fast as a whirlpool round our boat. Rings hanging at the nose. Under the trees on the bank, huts of a sort with a fire in the middle. Naked children around. On one side extreme civilisation, on the other the extreme opposite.

We arrived at Detroit at 4 o'clock. A fine American village. Many French names on the houses; French bonnets. We went to see Mr. Richard, the priest in charge of the Catholic church in Detroit. We found him busy teaching at school. His story: brought up by the Irish in Paris; studied theology at Saint Sulpice; ordained priest at the last ordination of 1791; went into exile; came to Detroit; a few years ago was Congress representative for the territory of Michigan. An old man whose religion seems to be ardent and sincere. Desultory conversation, but interesting. The Protestant population begins to be preponderant in Michigan on account of emigration. But Catholicism gains some converts among the most enlightened men. Mr. Richard's opinion about the extreme coolness of the upper classes in America towards religion. One of the reasons for the extreme tolerance; anyhow tolerance complete. Nobody asks you of what religion you are, but if you can do the job. The greatest service one can do to religion is to separate it from temporal power. The slightest nuance of ill feeling towards popular government, intrigues and cabals; the elections are even made by the central government. United States systems for the new States. They are made to get accustomed by degrees to governing themselves. Colony of native Christians at Michilimackinac. Their zeal, their ardour, their education.

* * *

POCKET NOTEBOOK NUMBER 3

Every religious doctrine has a political doctrine which, by affinity, is attached to it. That is an incontestable point in the sense that, where nothing runs contrary to that tendency, it is sure to show itself. But it does not follow that it is impossible to separate religious doctrines from all their political effects. On the contrary, in almost every country in the world one has seen material interests bring about this separation. The Catholics in Canada and in the United States are invariably the supporters of the democratic party. Does it follow that Catholicism leads to the democratic spirit? No. But the Catholics there are poor and almost all come from a country where the aristocracy is Protestant.

(1st October 1831)

ALPHABETIC NOTEBOOK I

There are 35,000 Catholics in New York. There were not 30 fifty years ago. Mr. Power (Vicar-general) claims that the number is daily increasing by conversions. They already form the most numerous community.

What has struck me most in Mr. Power's conversation is:

1st. That he seems to have no prejudice against republican institutions.

2nd. That he regards enlightenment as favourable to the moral and religious spirit.

Conversation of 9th June 1831

Mr. Richard, parish priest at Detroit (Michigan), has been sent by a largely Protestant electorate to Congress, of which for three years he has been one of the most respected members.

As above

The offerings given by the Catholics are enough to pay for the support of the ministers and the upkeep of the churches.

As above

*   *   *

ALPHABETIC NOTEBOOK 2

It is above all the Catholics who were the first, after the foundation of Maryland, to establish practical tolerance in matters of religion. Up to that time all the sects had claimed it for themselves without granting it to others. The Quakers were burnt in England. They took refuge among the Presbyterians of

28

Boston who themselves had fled from persecution in the motherland. And there they were hanged.

Philadelphia, 28th October 1831

NOTEBOOK E

Conversation with Mr. Houston on 31st December 1831.

This man has an extraordinary history. After a stormy and
troubled youth, he finally settled in the State of Tennessee. There
his natural talents and no doubt also his obscure origin won him
the people's votes. He had been elected Governor of the State.

Intolerance

It is something incredible with what rapidity religious tolerance
has made progress in America.

A law at the end of the last century in the State of New York
declares that every Catholic priest who does not leave the territory of the colony within a fixed time, shall be imprisoned for
life and condemned to death if he returns. The historian Smith,
who was writing in 1756, declares that this law was worthy to
last forever.

(K. C.), vol. II, p. 63

I am convinced, Mr. Poinsett said to me today (16th January
1832), that even nowadays in America the Lutherans would burn
the Calvinists, the latter the Unitarians, and the Catholics all the
others, if the civil power was given to any of those persuasions.
There is always deep hatred between them.

Democracy in America

Religion considered as a political institution which powerfully
contributes to the maintenance of a democratic republic among
the Americans. North America peopled by men who professed a
democratic and republican Christianity—Arrival of the Catholics
—Why the Catholics now form the most democratic and most
republican class.

By the side of every religion is to be found a political opinion,

29

which is connected with it by affinity. If the human mind be left to follow its own bent, it will regulate the temporal and spiritual institutions of society in a uniform manner, and man will endeavor, if I may so speak, to harmonize earth with heaven.

The greatest part of British America was peopled by men who, after having shaken off the authority of the Pope, acknowledged no other religious supremacy: they brought with them into the New World a form of Christianity which I cannot better describe than by styling it a democratic and republican religion. This contributed powerfully to the establishment of a republic and a democracy in public affairs; and from the beginning, politics and religion contracted an alliance which has never been dissolved.

About fifty years ago Ireland began to pour a Catholic population into the United States; and on their part, the Catholics of America made proselytes, so that, at the present moment more than a million Christians professing the truths of the Church of Rome are to be found in the Union. These Catholics are faithful to the observances of their religion; they are fervent and zealous in the belief of their doctrines. Yet they constitute the most republican and the most democratic class in the United States. This fact may surprise the observer at first, but the causes of it may easily be discovered upon reflection.

I think that the Catholic religion has erroneously been regarded as the natural enemy of democracy. Among the various sects of Christians, Catholicism seems to me, on the contrary, to be one of the most favorable to equality of condition among men. In the Catholic Church the religious community is composed of only two elements: the priest and the people. The priest alone rises above the rank of his flock, and all below him are equal.

On doctrinal points the Catholic faith places all human capacities upon the same level; it subjects the wise and ignorant, the man of genius and the vulgar crowd, to the details of the same creed; it imposes the same observances upon the rich and the needy, it inflicts the same austerities upon the strong and the weak; it listens to no compromise with mortal man, but, reducing all the human race to the same standard, it confounds all the distinctions of society at the foot of the same altar, even as they are confounded in the sight of God. If Catholicism predisposes the faithful to obedience, it certainly does not prepare them for inequality; but the contrary may be said of Protestantism, which generally tends to make men independent more than to render them equal. Catholicism is like an absolute monarchy; if the sovereign be removed, all the other classes of society are more equal than in republics.

It has not infrequently occurred that the Catholic priest has left the service of the altar to mix with the governing powers of society and to take his place among the civil ranks of men. This religious influence has sometimes been used to secure the duration of that political state of things to which he belonged. Thus we have seen Catholics taking the side of aristocracy from a religious motive. But no sooner is the priesthood entirely separated from the government, as is the case in the United States, than it is found that no class of men is more naturally disposed than the Catholics to transfer the doctrine of the equality of condition into the political world.

If, then, the Catholic citizens of the United States are not forcibly led by the nature of their tenets to adopt democratic and republican principles, at least they are not necessarily opposed to them; and their social position, as well as their limited number, obliges them to adopt these opinions. Most of the Catholics are poor, and they have no chance of taking a part in the government unless it is open to all the citizens. They constitute a minority, and all rights must be respected in order to ensure to them the free exercise of their own privileges. These two causes induce them, even unconsciously, to adopt political doctrines which they would perhaps support with less zeal if they were rich and preponderant.

The Catholic clergy of the United States have never attempted to oppose this political tendency; but they seek rather to justify it. The Catholic priests in America have divided the intellectual world into two parts: in the one they place the doctrines of revealed religion, which they assent to without discussion; in the other they leave those political truths which they believe the Deity has left open to free inquiry. Thus the Catholics of the United States are at the same time the most submissive believers and the most independent citizens.

It may be asserted, then, that in the United States no religious doctrine displays the slightest hostility to democratic and republican institutions. The clergy of all the different sects there hold the same language; their opinions are in agreement with the laws, and the human mind flows onward, so to speak, in one undivided current.

I happened to be staying in one of the largest cities in the Union, when I was invited to attend a public meeting in favor of the Poles and of sending them supplies of arms and money. I found two or three thousand persons collected in a vast hall which had been prepared to receive them. In a short time a priest in his ecclesiastical robes advanced to the front of the platform. The spectators rose and stood uncovered in silence while he spoke in the following terms:

"Almighty God! the God of armies! Thou who didst strengthen the hearts and guide the arms of our fathers when they were fighting for the sacred rights of their national independence! Thou who didst make them triumph over a hateful oppression, and hast granted to our people the benefits of liberty and peace! turn, O Lord, a favorable eye upon the other hemispheres; pitifully look down upon an heroic nation which is even now struggling as we did in the former time, and for the same rights. Thou, who didst create man in the same image, let not tyranny mar thy work and establish inequality upon the earth. Almighty God! do thou watch over the destiny of the Poles, and make them worthy to be free. May Thy wisdom direct their councils, may thy strength sustain their arms! Shed forth thy terror over their enemies; scatter the powers which take counsel against them; and permit not the injustice which the world has witnessed for fifty years to be consummated in our time. O Lord, who holdest alike the hearts of nations and of men in thy powerful hand, raise up allies to the sacred cause of right; arouse the French nation from the apathy in which its rulers retain it, that it may go forth again to fight for the liberties of the world.

"Lord, turn not thou thy face from us, and grant that we may always be the most religious, as well as the freest, people of the earth. Almighty God, hear our supplications this day. Save the Poles, we beseech thee, in the name of thy well-beloved Son, our Lord Jesus Christ, who died upon the cross for the salvation of all men. Amen."

The whole meeting responded: "Amen!" with devotion.

* * *

How Religion in the United States Avails Itself of Democratic Tendencies

I showed in the first part of this work how the American clergy stand aloof from secular affairs. This is the most obvious but not the only example of their self-restraint. In America religion is a distinct sphere, in which the priest is sovereign, but out of which he takes care never to go. Within its limits he is master of the mind; beyond them he leaves men to themselves and surrenders them to the independence and instability that belong to their nature and their age. I have seen no country in which Christianity is clothed with fewer forms, figures, and observances than in the United States, or where it presents more distinct, simple, and general notions to the mind. Although the Christians of America are divided into a multitude of sects, they all look upon their religion in the same light. This applies to Roman Catholicism as well as to the other forms of belief. There are no Roman Catholic priests who show less taste for the

33

minute individual observances, for extraordinary or peculiar means of salvations, or who cling more to the spirit and less to the letter of the law than the Roman Catholic priests of the United States. Nowhere is that doctrine of the church which prohibits the worship reserved to God alone from being offered to the saints more clearly inculcated or more generally followed. Yet the Roman Catholics of America are very submissive and very sincere.

* * *

The Progress of Roman Catholicism in the United States

America is the most democratic country in the world, and it is at the same time (according to reports worthy of belief) the country in which the Roman Catholic religion makes most progress. At first sight this is surprising.

Two things must here be accurately distinguished: quality makes men want to form their own opinions; but, on the other hand, it imbues them with the taste and the idea of unity, simplicity, and impartiality in the power that governs society. Men living in democratic times are therefore very prone to shake off all religious authority; but if they consent to subject themselves to any authority of this kind, they choose at least that it should be single and uniform. Religious powers not radiating from a common center are naturally repugnant to their minds; and they almost as readily conceive that there should be no religion as that there should be several.

At the present time, more than in any preceding age, Roman Catholics are seen to lapse into infidelity, and Protestants to be converted to Roman Catholicism. If you consider Catholicism within its own organization, it seems to be losing; if you consider it from outside, it seems to be gaining. Nor is this difficult to explain. The men of our days are naturally little disposed to

34

believe; but as soon as they have any religion, they immediately find in themselves a latent instinct that urges them unconsciously towards Catholicism. Many of the doctrines and practices of the Roman Catholic Church astonish them, but they feel a secret admiration for its discipline, and its great unity attracts them. If Catholicism could at length withdraw itself from the political animosities to which it has given rise, I have hardly any doubt but that the same spirit of the age which appears to be so opposed to it would become so favorable as to admit of its great and sudden advancement.

One of the most ordinary weaknesses of the human intellect is to seek to reconcile contrary principles and to purchase peace at the expense of logic. Thus there have ever been and will ever be men who, after having submitted some portion of their religious belief to the principle of authority, will seek to exempt several other parts of their faith from it and to keep their minds floating at random between liberty and obedience. But I am inclined to believe that the number of these thinkers will be less in democratic than in other ages, and that our posterity will tend more and more to a division into only two parts, some relinquishing Christianity entirely and others returning to the Church of Rome.

5

Michael Chevalier

1833=1835

from *Society, Manners and Politics in the United States*

While many European visitors simply came to see how life was lived in this new country, many business men and professional men were sent here to learn about new American techniques which were beginning to attract attention throughout the world. Michael Chevalier, a young French engineer, was sent to America by his government to study communications and transportation in the United States. He stayed for two years, 1833 to 1835, and later wrote a formal report on his findings. During his travels he wrote a series of letters about his impressions for a French magazine. The following selections are taken from *Society, Manners and Politics in the United States*, edited by John William Ward. (Copyright 1961 by John William Ward.) Reprinted by permission of Doubleday & Company, Inc.

American society is essentially and radically a democracy, not in name merely but in deed. In the United States the democratic spirit is infused into all the national habits and all the customs of society; it besets and startles at every step the foreigner who, before landing in the country, had no suspicion to what a degree his every nerve and fiber had been steeped in aristocracy by a European education. It has effaced all distinctions except that of color; for here a shade in the hue of the skin separates men more widely than in any other country in the world. It

37

pervades all places, one only excepted, and that the very one which in Catholic Europe is consecrated to equality, the Church; here all whites are equal, everywhere, except in the presence of Him in whose eyes the distinctions of this world are vanity and nothingness. In Roman Catholic countries, the churches, vast structures, are open to all without distinctions; each takes his seat where he pleases; all ranks are mixed together. In the United States the churches are very numerous and very small, being built by jointstock companies. They are appropriated to the exclusive use of the proprietors, with the exception of one free-seat for the poor, each one's share of property being designated by an enclosed space or pew. The whole floor of the church is thus occupied by pews and the gallery is generally divided in the same manner, though a part of the latter is generally open and free to all. Each pew is sold and transferred like any other property; the price varies according to the town, the sect, or the situation. The proprietors pay an annual tax for the support of public worship, lighting and warming the church, and the minister's salary, the amount of the tax being proportioned to the value of the pew. Sometimes the church itself owns the pews and the rent covers the expenses of the public worship. According to this system, the place occupied by the worshipers depends on their wealth, or at least, on the price they are able or willing to pay for their pews. In this regard, Catholics in the United States have followed the example set by the Protestants.

Strange inconsistency! Or rather solemn protest, attesting that the principle of rank is firmly seated in the human heart by the side of the principle of equality, that it must have its place in all countries and under all circumstances!

* * *

When the Yankee came to settle in the New World, it was not for the purpose of founding an empire but to establish a church. He fled from a land which had shaken off the yoke of the Babylon of the Pope, only to fall under that of the Babylon of episcopacy. He left behind him Satan, his pomp, and his works; he shook from the soles of his feet the dust of the inhospitable land of the Stuarts and the Anglican bishops; he sought a refuge in which he might practice his own mode of worship and obey what he believed to be the law of God. The Pilgrims, having landed on Plymouth Rock, established liberty according to their own notion; it was a liberty for their own use exclusively, within whose embrace they felt perfectly at ease with themselves without caring if others were stifled by it. It might have been expected that, proscribed themselves, they would at least have admitted religious toleration; but they did not grant it the narrowest corner and even now it is far from having elbow room among them. Originally, the right of citizenship was extended only to Puritans like themselves; the State and the Church were confounded; it was not until 1832 that they were definitely and completely separated in Massachusetts. The Jew and the Quaker were forbidden to touch the soil under the severest penalties and in case of return under pain of death. At present, if the law tolerates the Roman Catholic, public opinion does not, as the burning of the Ursuline convent in 1834 and the scandalous scenes exhibited at the trials of the incendiaries testify. Still less mercy is shown to unbelief; witness the trial of Abner Kneeland for blasphemy on account of his pantheistic writings.

* * *

And, unfortunately, while society, driven about by the waves, at the mercy of chance and without a compass, is exposed to disasters which the control of religion alone can prevent, religion makes no effort to resume the helm and recover her authority. In the midst of nations which rush toward every risk, Catholicism stands still, silently shrouded in her mantle, with arms folded and eyes bent on heaven. The Church bore all the shocks of the revolutionary storm with heroic resignation; she meekly submitted to be scourged with rods, like the Just One; like him she has been fixed to the Cross and has opened her mouth only to pray for her executioners. But the sufferings of the Just saved sinners and changed the face of the world; nothing betokens that the recent sufferings of the Catholic Church will have any saving power. From the tomb where it was laid for dead, we see it bring back no scheme for the restoration of suffering, longing humanity.

The Roman Church is what it was four hundred years ago; but within that period the world has become quite another thing; it has made great progress and freed itself from the past with the firm purpose of never turning back. If civilization, then is about to assume a new form, as everything forbodes, religion, which is at once the beginning and end of society, the keystone and the cornerstone—religion must also recast herself. Would it be the first time that Christianity has modified her forms and rules to adapt herself to the instincts and the tendencies of the nations she has sought to bless?

Here in the United States religion has presided over the progress of the lower classes. Puritanism has been the starting point of the democratic movement. The Puritans came to America, not in quest of gold, nor to conquer provinces, but to found a Church on the principle of primitive equality. They were, as I have said before, new Jews; they wished to govern by the laws of Moses. In the beginning the state was completely swallowed up by the Church; they divided themselves into religious congregations in which all the heads of families were equal, in conformity with the Mosaic law, over which the elders and the saints presided and in which all earthly distinctions were abolished or contemned. Under the influence of their religious views one of the first objects of their care was to establish schools in which all the children should be educated together and in the same manner. Although unequal in respect to property, all adopted the same habits of life. The physical exertions to which all were obliged to devote themselves in common in order to defend themselves from famine and the savages strengthened their habits and feelings of equality. Now, New England, which is inhabited exclusively by the sons of the Puritans and in which their traditions and their faith are still kept unchanged, has ever been, and is yet, the focus of American democracy.

Thus American democracy has been enabled to organize and establish itself. On the contrary, all our efforts to found a democracy in France in 1793 would have been vain, even had we not been unfitted for democratic habits, because we wished to build on irreligion, on the hatred of religion. Manners and feelings must prepare and inspire the means of social improvement; the laws must express and prescribe them. Politics and religion, then, must join hands in this difficult task. Politics, as well as religion, must be transformed for the furtherance of civilization and the safety of the world.

I admire the results which the political system of the United States has produced in America. But it seems to me impossible that the institutions by which the condition of the people has been so much bettered here can be naturalized among us. There must be harmony between the political and religious schemes that are suited to any one people. Protestantism is republican; Puritanism is absolute self-government in religion and begets it in politics. The United Provinces were Protestant; the United States are Protestant. Catholicism is essentially monarchical; in countries which are Catholic, at least by recollections, habits, and education if not by faith, a regular democracy is impracticable. The anarchy of the former Spanish colonies fully proves to what bitter regrets Catholic nations expose themselves when they attempt to apply to themselves the political institutions of Protestant countries.

6

>>)《《‹

Captain Frederick Marryat

1837–1838

from *A Diary in America*

>>)《《‹

A good case can be made for the proposition that Captain Frederick Marryat was the most unpopular of all our controversial English visitors. Most of these visitors did not let loose their critical attacks until they had returned safely home. Captain Marryat, however, suffered from foot-in-mouth disease almost from the time he arrived and so managed to irritate and often infuriate Americans that his journeys were sometimes marked by violence, including a near-lynching, and he was the unfortunate witness to his hanging in effigy and the burning of his books. To the surprise of no one, his *A Diary in America,* from which these excerpts are taken, denounced not only specific American customs and institutions but also the basic concept of democracy. Much of what he wrote about America was absurd, but as a successful novelist—sea stories were his forte—he was blessed with a discerning eye and a pleasing style. Even today his diary is readable and entertaining.

>>)《《‹

An energetic and enterprising people are naturally anxious for an investigation into cause and effect, a search into which is, after all, nothing but curiosity well directed, and the most curious of all men is the philosopher. Curiosity, therefore, becomes a virtue or a small vice, according to the use made of it. The Americans are excessively curious, especially the mob; they cannot bear anything like a secret,—that's unconstitutional. It may be remembered, that the Catholic Convent near Boston, which had existed many years, was attacked by the mob and pulled down. I was enquiring into the cause of this outrage in a country where all forms of religion are tolerated; and an American gentleman told me, that although other reasons had been adduced for it, he fully believed, in his own mind, that the majority of the mob were influenced more by curiosity than any other feeling. The Convent was sealed to them, and they were determined to know what was in it. "Why, sir," continued he, "I will lay a wager that if the authorities were to nail together a dozen planks, and fix them up on the Common, with a caution to the public that they were not to go near or touch them, in twenty-four hours a mob would be raised to pull them down, and ascertain what the planks contained." I mention this conversation to shew in what a dextrous manner this American gentleman attempted to palliate one of the grossest outrages ever committed by his countrymen.

*   *   *

At present Massachusetts, and the smaller eastern states, are the strong-hold of religion and morality; as you proceed from them farther south or west, so does the influence of the clergy decrease, until it is totally lost in the wild states of Missouri and Arkansas. With the exception of certain cases to be found in Western Virginia, Kentucky, and Ohio, the whole of the states to the westward of the Allegheny mountains, comprising more than two thirds of America, may be said to be either in a state of neglect or darkness of professing the Catholic religion.

Although Virginia is a slave state, I think there is more religion there than in some of the more northern free states; but it must be recollected that Virginia has been long settled, and the non-predial state of the slaves is not attended with demoralizing effects; and I may here observe that the black population of America is decidedly the most religious, and sets an example to the white, particularly in the free states.

44

It may be fairly inquired, can this be true? Not fifty years back, at the time of the Declaration of Independence, was not the American community one of the most virtuous in existence? Such was indeed the case, as it is now equally certain that they are one of the most demoralized. The question is, then, what could have created such a change in the short period of fifty years?

The only reply that can be given is that, as the Americans, in their eagerness to possess new lands, pushed away into the west, so did they leave civilization behind and return to ignorance and barbarism; they scattered their population, and the word of God was not to be heard in the wilderness.

That as she increased her slave states, so did she give employment, land, and power to those who were indifferent to all law, human or divine. And as, since the formation of the Union, the people have yearly gained advantages over the government until they now control it, so have they controlled and fettered religion until it produces no good fruits.

Add to this the demoralizing effects of a democracy which turns the thoughts of all to Mammon, and it will be acknowledged that this rapid fall is not so very surprising.

But, if the Protestant cause is growing weaker every day from disunions and indifference, there is one creed which is as rapidly gaining strength; I refer to the Catholic Church, which is silently but surely advancing.* Its great field is in the west where, in some states, almost all are Catholics or, from neglect and ignorance, altogether indifferent as to religion. The Catholic priests are diligent, and make a large number of converts every year, and the Catholic population is added to by the number of Irish and German emigrants to the west, who are almost all of them of the Catholic persuasion. . . .

* Although it is not forty years since the first Roman Catholic See was created, there is now in the United States a Catholic population of 800,000 souls under the government of the Pope, an Archbishop, 12 Bishops, and 433 priests. The number of churches is 401; mass houses about 300; colleges, 10; seminaries for young men, 9; theological seminaries, 5; novitiates for Jesuits, monasteries and convents, with academies attached, 31; seminaries for young ladies, 30; schools of the Sisters of Charity, 29; an academy for coloured girls at Baltimore; a female infant school; and 7 Catholic newspapers.

It is true, as Mr. Tocqueville observes, that the Catholic Church reduces all the human race to the same standard, and confounds all distinctions—not, however, upon the principle of equality or democracy, but because it will ever equally exert its power over the high and the low, assuming its right to compel princes and kings to obedience, and their dominions to its subjection. The equality professed by the Catholic Church is like the equality of death, all must fall before its power; whether it be to excommunicate an individual or an empire is to it indifferent; it assumes the power of the God-head, giving and taking away, and its members stand trembling before it, as they shall hereafter do in the presence of the Deity. . . .

At present Catholicism is, comparatively speaking, weak in America and the object of that Church is to become strong; they do not, therefore, frighten or alarm their converts by any present show of the invariable results, but are content to bide their time, until they shall find themselves strong enough to exert their power with triumphant success. The Protestant cause in America is weak, from the evil effects of the voluntary system, particularly from its division into so many sects. A house divided against itself cannot long stand; and every year it will be found that the Catholic Church will increase its power; and it is a question whether a hierarchy may not eventually be raised which, so far from advocating the principles of equality, may serve as a check to the spirit of democracy becoming more powerful than the government, curbing public opinion, and reducing to better order the present chaotic state of society.

Judge Haliburton asserts that all America will be a Catholic country. That all America west of the Alleghenies will eventually be a Catholic country, I have no doubt, as the Catholics are already in the majority, and there is nothing, as Mr. Cooper observes, to prevent any state from establishing that, or any other religion, as the Religion of the State; and this is one of the dark clouds which hang over the destiny of the western hemisphere. . . .

l think that the author of Sam Slick may not be wrong in his assertion that all America will be a Catholic country. I myself never prophesy; but, I cannot help remarking that even in the most anti-Catholic persuasions in America there is a strong Papistical feeling; that is, there is a vying with each other, not only to obtain the best preachers, but to have the best organs and the best singers. It is the system of excitement which, without their being aware of it, they carry into their devotion. It proves that to them there is a weariness in the church service, a tedium in prayer, which requires to be relieved by the stimulus of good music and sweet voices. Indeed, what with their anxious seats, their revivals, their music and their singing, every class and sect in the states have even now so far fallen into Catholicism that religion has become more of an appeal to the senses than to the calm and sober judgment.

7

Sir Charles Lyell

1845

from *A Second Visit to the United States of North America*

->>)<<-

President of the Geological Society of London and author of *The Principles of Geology*, Sir Charles Lyell, F. R. S., first visited the United States in 1842. He returned with his wife in 1845 to record every detail of a vertical journey that took them from Halifax to Savannah. A great recorder and cherisher of fact, Sir Charles kept a complete diary—including a table worked out to show the number of revolutions made by the screw of his Cunard Line's ship of passage. His diary was published in this country by Harper & Brothers, under the title *A Second Visit to the United States,* from which the following passage is taken.

->>)<<-

All these 11,000 schools [in the State of New York] have been organized on what has been styled in England, even by respectable members in the House of Commons, the infidel or godless plan, which generally means nothing more than that they are not under the management of the clergy. The Roman Catholic bishops and priests command a vast number of votes at the elections in New York, yet they failed, in 1842, to get into their exclusive control that part of the public school money which might fairly be considered as applicable to the teaching of children of their own denomination. Their efforts, however, though fortunately defeated, were attended by some beneficial results. It is obviously the duty of every government which establishes a national system of secular education, to see that no books are used in the schools, containing sectarian views, or in which the peculiar opinions of any sect are treated with marked contempt. The Catholics complained that some of the works put into the hands of children, especially those relating to English history, were written with a strong Protestant bias, and that, while the superstitions of popery and the bigotry of Bloody Mary were pointedly dwelt upon, the persecutions endured by Romanists at the hands of Protestant rulers were overlooked, or slightly glanced at. The expunging of such passages, both in the State of New York and in New England, must have a wholesome tendency to lessen sectarian bitterness, which, if imbibed at an early age, is so difficult to eradicate; and children thus educated will grow up less prejudiced, and more truly Christian in spirit, than if the Romish or any other clergy had been permitted to obtain the sole and separate training of their minds.

8

❧❧❧❧

Alexander Mackay

1846-1847

from *The Western World*

❧❧❧❧

A barrister in London's Middle Temple, Alexander Mackay had made one previous visit to this country before undertaking the journey of 1846–1847, which he described in a three-volume work published in London in 1850 under the ambitious title *The Western World*. Mackay's journey was made for the express end of gathering material for this book (which proved to be popular, running to several editions) and he set out from Boston to make a complete circuit of every state in the Union. He evidently was well-connected in Washington and in the Congress and took advantage of these contacts to arm himself with all the latest statistics. Though he tends to wordiness and experiences some difficulty in concealing his good opinion of himself, his book is nonetheless one of the most interesting of its kind, largely because he did not hold to the strict diary form and because he wrote with a sense of humor somewhat rare in nineteenth-century Englishmen of his calling—or any other.

❧❧❧❧

Their [Catholics] numbers are not great, as compared with the Protestants; but they are nevertheless a sect of considerable power in the Union. In 1848 they had about 850 churches— nearly 900 priests, and 1,175,000 communicants. It would not be correct, however, in comparing their aggregate number with that of the other sects, to take the number of communicants as the basis of comparison; inasmuch as with the Roman Catholics almost every adult is reckoned a communicant, which is far from being the case with the adherents of the Protestant denominations. The Catholics are a strong body in all the large towns; and in some parts of the country they have rural districts, of considerable extent, under their sway. Until the purchase of Louisiana, in 1803, Maryland was, in point of numbers, the leading Catholic State in the Union, as she is yet in point of influence. As the American has not yet out-numbered the French population in Louisiana, it follows that the majority of the white inhabitants of that State are Roman Catholics.

It is to her colonial origin that Maryland owes the pre-eminence which she has so long maintained as the chief seat of Roman Catholic influence in the Union. After other sects had fled from the Old World to the New to escape persecution, the Catholics, in some instances, found that they too were in want of a place in which they could worship God according to their consciences. They accordingly emigrated in great numbers to the State of Maryland, named after Queen Mary, and being for some time a proprietary colony belonging to the Lord Baltimore, whose name its chief town still bears. The Roman Catholic colonists set an early example of religious toleration, which was but ill requited by the Protestants, as soon as they attained a numerical superiority in the State. The number of Roman Catholics in the State is now daily diminishing, as compared with that of the Protestants—the hold which Catholicism now has on Maryland consisting chiefly of the adhesion to it of many of the older families of the State. The Catholic cathedral at Baltimore has already been adverted to, in the brief description given of that city. The only other ecclesiastical edifice in the Union, dedicated to Catholicism, which deserves the name, is the cathedral at New Orleans.

It is not so much on account of its present number of adherents, or the influence which it now exerts, that Catholicism in the United States demands the attention of Christendom. It is in view of its future prospects, that it assumes an attitude of rather formidable character. Nowhere on earth is the far-seeing policy of the Church of Rome at present so adroitly displayed as on the American continent. Indeed from the earliest epoch of colonization we find her aiming at the religious subjugation of America. For a time success seemed to crown her efforts. The whole of South America, Central America, and the greater part of North America, together with all the islands on the coast, were divided between the crowns of Portugal, France and Spain. England, for many years after her first attempts at colonization, possessed but a comparative narrow strip of land between the Atlantic and the Alleghenies, and extending along the sea-board from Arcadia to Georgia. New France swept round the English colonies, from the mouth of the St. Lawrence to that of the Mississippi, whilst the Spanish Floridas intervened between them and the Gulf of Mexico. Within this wide embrace, with the ocean in front, lay the group of Protestant colonies belonging to England. It was not sufficient for the Church of Rome that she hemmed them in on three sides by her territory. The wide domain which owned her sway was but thinly peopled, whilst the English colonies were rapidly filling with population. Protestantism was thus fast attaining on the continent a more extensive moral influence than its competitor. It was then that a Roman Catholic colony was planked in its very midst, on the shores of the Chesapeake, the policy of the church having had no little influence on the moral destinies of Maryland. But the tide had set in too strongly in favour of the rival system, and it soon overpowered all opposition to it. Since that time Catholicism in Maryland has acted more on the defensive than otherwise—its object having chiefly been to maintain itself as a centre and rallying point for Catholicism in the Union, with a view to future operations in new and vaster scenes of action.

The ground has now for many years been broken, and these operations have long since actively commenced. The Roman Catholic church has, in a manner, abandoned the comparatively popular States of the sea-board, and fixed its attention upon the valley of the Mississippi. In this it has discovered a far-seeing policy. Nineteen-twentieths of the Mississippi valley are yet under the dominion of the wilderness. But no portion of the country is being so rapidly filled with population. In fifty years its inhabitants will, in number, be more than double those of the Atlantic States. The Church of Rome has virtually left the latter to the tender mercies of contending Protestant sects, and is fast taking possession of the great valley. There, opinion is not yet so strongly arrayed against her, and she has room to hope for ultimate ascendency. In her operations, she does not confine herself to the more populous portions of the vallay, her devoted missionaries, penetrating its remotest regions, wherever a white man or an Indian is to be found. Wherever the Protestant missionary goes he finds that he has been forestalled by his more active rival, whose coadjutors roam on their proselytizing mission over vast tracts of the country, into which the Protestant has not yet followed him with a similar object. Catholicism is thus, by its advance-guards, who keep pace with population whithersoever it spreads, sowing broad-cast the seeds of future influence. In many districts, the settler finds no religious counsellor within reach but the faithful missionary of Rome, who has thus the field to himself—a field which he frequently cultivates with success. In addition to this, seminaries in connection with the church are being founded, not only in places which are now well filled with people, but in spots which careful observation has satisfied its agents will yet most teem with population. Ecclesiastical establishments too are being erected, which commend themselves to the people of the districts in which they are found by the mode in which they minister to their comforts and their necessities when other means of ministering to them are wanted. The Sisters of Charity have already their establishments amid the deep recesses of the forest, prescribing to the diseased in body, and administering consolation to the troubled in spirit, long before the doctor or the minister makes his appearance in the settlement. By this attention to the physical as well as to the moral wants, the Roman emissaries, ere there are yet any to compete with them, gain the goodwill of the neighborhood in the midst of which they labour, and proselytism follows hard upon a lively sentiment of gratitude. Circumstances have favoured the Church of Rome in the development of this policy. When both the St. Lawrence and Mississippi, with most of their tributaries, were in the possession of France, a belt of ecclesiastical establishments accompanied the chain of military posts, which, extending westward from the coast of Labrador to the lakes, descended thence to the mouth of the Ohio, and then spread north and south on both banks of the Mississippi. The basis was then laid for the future operations of the Church. It is nearly a century since France lost Canada, since which time a gap intervened between the Church's establishments in its eastern section and those dotting the province of Louisiana. But down to the year 1803, the whole of the west bank of the Mississippi, and both banks in the neighborhood of its mouth, were in the hands of the French, the advanced posts of the Church spreading and multiplying between St. Louis and New Orleans, whilst the eastern or Protestant bank of the river was yet an unbroken wilderness. The present operations of the Church of Rome, therefore, in the valley, cannot be regarded as an invasion of that region, her object now being to profit by the advantages which she so early secured. Were the Protestant sects to confront her as actively as they might, in the great field which she has thus selected for herself, they might even yet check her growth and limit her influence. But they seem to be either unaware of, or indifferent to, the danger with which they are menaced. They are seeking to rival each other in the older states, whilst their common rival is laying a broad foundation for future influence in that region, which will soon eclipse the older states, in population at least. Both in St. Louis and New Orleans, some of the best seminaries for young ladies are Catholic institutions, and not a few of those who attend them become converts to the Church. But it is in the remote and yet comparatively unpeopled districts that the probabilities of her success in this respect are greatest. She has thus, in the true spirit of worldly wisdom, left Protestantism to exhaust its energies amongst the more populous communities; and going in advance of it into the wilderness, is fast overspreading that wilderness with a network which will yet embrace multitudes of its future population. How can it be otherwise when, as settlements arise, they find at innumerable points the Church of Rome the only spiritual edifice in their midst? Were she to secure the valley, she would gain more in America than all she has lost in Europe. The stake is worth striving for; and Protestantism would far more consult its own interests by directing its efforts less to the Niger and more to the Mississippi.

9

Ole Monch Raeder

1847-1848

from *America in the Forties: The Letters of*
Ole Monch Raeder

A Norwegian scholar who had won some distinction in the fields of
jurisprudence and political science, Ole Monch Raeder was sent to this
country by his government to prepare a report on the Jury System of
the United States. Arriving in New York in the summer of 1847,
he traveled fairly extensively before his departure in October, 1848.
The following selection is taken from a series of letters in which he
recorded his impressions of America for publication in a Christian
newspaper. The "West" to which he has reference is Wisconsin.

This extract is taken from *America in the Forties: The Letters
of Ole Monch Raeder,* translated and edited by Gunnar J. Malmin
and published, in 1929, by the University of Minnesota Press.

It has often been stated that the Catholic church makes many
proselytes out here in the West and there is undoubtedly considerable truth in the contention, as is seen from the rapidly
increasing number of Catholic churches and congregations. Its
greatest progress, however, is made not among the whites but
among the Indians. Catholic missionaries made their way into
the wilderness hundreds of miles from civilization as early as
two hundred years ago, Claude Allouez having established a
mission on Lake Superior even before Penn founded Philadelphia.

They gave wonderful proof of their zeal and devotion to the cause of religion. The Catholic church thus has a sort of historic claim to this part of the world, based on the untiring efforts of its priests, a right which it is now trying to assert by employing its best forces. Its progress among the whites is considerably hindered by the peculiar, almost ridiculous, prejudices people have against the church politically. Many people fully believe that the Catholics have a secret organization of a dark and bloody nature, a sort of gunpowder plot through which they hope to blow up the republican form of government. This is said to be particularly dangerous in Pennsylvania. As far as the Norwegians are concerned, I have not heard that any of them have been converted to Catholicism.

10

Reverend James Shaw
1854-1866

from *American Resources: Twelve Years in America*

✦✦✦✦

Rev. James Shaw was a Methodist minister from Ireland who visited the United States twice for extended periods between 1854 and 1866. During these visits he travelled 35,000 miles through nine states and Canada, preaching and lecturing, but most of his time was spent in various Methodist churches in Illinois. He came to America both because the Irish climate did not agree with his health and because he considered the United States a "foreign mission." When he returned to Ireland in 1866, he reported at length on his "life, labor and travels" in *American Resources: Twelve Years in America,* from which the excerpt is taken.

✦✦✦✦

The Roman Catholic Church in America stands at the head of all the un-evangelical churches, as the oldest and largest. Her increase latterly in the United States is almost exclusively confined to the Catholic emigration from the old countries, Ireland furnishing about the largest contingency. Scarcely any native Americans belong to that church, and her converts from Protestantism have been still less. In the large cities and railroad and river towns she builds large churches, erects nunneries and monkeries, and schools attached, by which she tries to give her own children and others a higher and a lower education. In the smaller towns and country places, there are scarcely any Romanists to be found,

59

and there they have lost millions of their people. *The National Intelligencer* gives the following statistics: Archbishops, 7; bishops, 35; priests, 2,215; churches and chapels, 3,884; schools and academies, 1,404; pupils, 80,000; convents and monasteries, 362; orphan asylums, 150, with 9,000 children. The Catholic population may be set down, in round numbers, at 3,000,000; yet the half of these could not obtain church accommodation from the number of churches they have built. There is no doubt at all but they have lost enormously in the United States. Bishop England, in a letter to Rome, said that 50,000 were lost in his diocese alone. Priest Mullen, writing from New Orleans, to the *Irish Tablet,* Dublin, in April, 1852, states that, after examining the statistics of Catholic emigration to America, from different countries, that at that time they had lost of their population in America, 1,980,000. Since then, they must have lost nearly another million, so that the number lost to that church of her people, up to the present time, is about 3,000,000. There are very few of the second and third generation of Catholic emigrants, who remain connected with that church at all. On a small circuit the writer travelled in Illinois, he found about fifteen familes of Irish Catholic origin, who had become devoted Methodists. The same will apply to the number that join Baptist and Presbyterian churches. In travelling extensively through the country, I have met hundreds of families who had thus left Romanism for Methodism.

A few facts have produced these results:

1) There is a moral and political atmosphere thrown around the Church mind that is death to his system. The freedom of thought; the equality of man before law, human and divine; the right of private judgment; and accountability to God, meets him everywhere. To an American mind, no thought is more revolting or absurd than that "the priest can forgive sins." Often, when pressed with this question, the tongue has denied what the conscience was trained to believe, and Patrick has often found himself in a dilemma between the two. The whole genius and spirit of the political system is opposed to popery.

2) A few years ago, the hierarchy with the priests endeavoured to obtain the public school funds, and appropriate them to the support of Roman Catholic schools, over which the priests had exclusive control. This led to a severe conflict, in which the priests and their adherents were defeated, several Catholic rioters being shot down in the streets.

3) Another conflict arose in the church itself between the people and the bishops, in which the latter endeavoured to obtain the control of all the church and ecclesiastical property, by deeding the property to themselves. The people objected, and laws were passed by the several legislatures requiring the deeds of ecclesiastical property to be vested in laymen for the benefit of the churches.

4) The part the clergy took some years ago, in controlling and directing the votes of their people, led to the formation of "the American Party," which was extremely hostile to popery; so that at the time I landed in America, popery was everywhere the object of hatred and contempt.

5) The rioting propensities of this part of the population is remarkable—there being few riots committed in the United States in which they are not implicated—even in connection with the most solemn events. Scarcely can they attend a funeral of their own people without either racing, drinking, or fighting coming home. The American people cannot understand the mixing things sacred and tender with the profane and savage. Yet, popery in America is of a much milder form and more enlightened type than in Europe. Although popery has lost in America fully as many people as she has now attending her mass-houses, yet the greatest danger to the American people will come from this source, and the next great conflict there will be with this political system.

11

➤➤〉〈《

Henry Sienkiewicz

1876=1878

from *Portrait of America: The Letters of Henry Sienkiewicz*

➤➤〉〈《

England and France did not furnish all of our visiting critics, as
might easily be assumed. Visitors came from all over the world,
and many reacted in print. Too frequently their reports, for one
reason or another, were not translated into English, and Americans
were deprived of or spared their views. One of the more interesting
visitors of the nineteenth century, Henry Sienkiewicz, wrote extensively for Polish newspapers of his two-years' sojourn in America
(1876–1878) but it was not until eighty years later his "letters" were
made available to English readers. The selections that follow are
from these newspaper articles. Sienkiewicz came to the United States
at the age of thirty as the spearhead of a group (which included
the actress Helen Modjeska) intending to establish a socialistic colony
in California. The colony failed and Sienkiewicz returned to Poland
to achieve fame as a short story writer and novelist, author of that
durable and dashing romance, *Quo Vadis,* and winner of the Nobel
Prize for literature in 1905. He took a dim view of many aspects
of American life (including American women, whom he proclaimed
were unattractive: "Without breeding and distinction in appearance,
their despotism becomes all the more intolerable"). Unlike many
Europeans, however, he expressed enthusiasm for the future of this
"young, courageous and energetic" country.

This extract is from *Portrait of America*: *The Letters of Henry
Sienkiewicz,* edited by Charles Morley, and published by Columbia
University Press, New York, N. Y. Copyright 1959. These excerpts are

taken from pages 13–15, 28–29, and 282–291, and are reprinted here by courtesy of Columbia University Press.

->>)<<-

A goodly majority of these unfortunate people [New York slum dwellers] are Irish, of whom there are said to be almost ten million in the United States. They are easily recognized by their dress, or, rather by the remnants of their national garb, and by their blue eyes, beautiful blond or dark hair, strong physique, and typical Gaelic liveliness of speech and gesture. These traits so sharply differentiate the members of this nationality from the Anglo-Saxons that it is practically impossible to mistake them. Addicted to drinking, gambling, and all sorts of excesses, and possessing a fiery temperament, these people would certainly commit many more crimes were it not for their religious devotion which never deserts them. All of them are very devout Catholics, and for future heavenly bliss they patiently endure all kinds of earthly woe and affliction.

In the Western states there are likewise many Irish, but they do not suffer the same misery as those in New York. Some of them have achieved a good livelihood, others considerable fortunes, and still others even millions. They set an example of clannish solidarity; they help one another, they always flock together, and they vote alike, i.e., as the priests tell them. They never forget their nationality, or their motherland; they love Ireland and hate England, even in the tenth generation. They constitute an element America must already reckon with and will have to reckon with even more in the future.

The reason for this lies in the exceedingly rapid increase in numbers of this people. The Irish are as prolific as rabbits, while the native Americans are exactly the opposite. While American families have two, or at most three children, pious Irish parents, who regard children as God's special blessing, bring them into the world like poppy seed: "each year brings forth a prophet," as the saying goes, and the years follow in rapid succession.

This extraordinary fecundity has thus far been beneficial to America, whose territories need to be populated in the national interest. The Irish are already playing an important role in the United States and in addition are necessary and advantageous to the States in ways Americans perhaps are not even aware of, or, being aware, do not appreciate. The Irish contribute a certain element of idealism to this thoroughly materialistic society, thereby maintaining a desirable measure of equilibrium. I can imagine how my positivist colleagues are smiling at this moment; nevertheless, I stand by my opinion. A preponderance of idealistic tendencies is harmful to any society; it gives rise to dreams, political Don Quixoterie, expectation of divine intervention, longing for spring in the midst of winter, but in springtime, only laziness, poverty, and weakness. All of this is unquestionably true, but it is also true that all onesidedness is harmful. The Chinese, for example, are a people lacking all elements of idealism. Among them realism has been developed to the highest degree and has so permeated the national character that it has obstructed all progress and the formulation of powerful ideas for which European peoples are willing to sacrifice their lives. The Chinese, by destroying their national imagination, have at the same time destroyed all initiative, not only in the realm of social relationships, but also in technology, science, and art; in short, they have lost creativeness, the child of imagination.

Perhaps their character predisposed them to the course they have followed. Inherent traits, however, are not the sole determining factor, for, just as they may influence the nature of a civilization, so the latter in turn may affect national characteristics either favorably or adversely. In my opinion, the American people, despite their many truly great virtues, are likewise creating a very onesided civilization in which the Irish character serves as an antidote both necessary and beneficial to the welfare of American society.

But the Irish, too, have their weaknesses. They are lazy,

especially in the first generation. Incomparably more boisterous than the Americans, they are given to indulging in political disturbances. Thus they constitute a very dangerous element, especially in a republic. Moreover, since they are entirely in the hands of their priests, they may in time form a strong clerical party. Such a party is harmful in any state because it considers its own particular objectives as surpassing all others in importance. In the United States such a party might with the passage of years disrupt that harmony which now prevails among the various religious denominations.

Europeans have many false impressions about Americans and their country. I have referred to religion; allow me, therefore, in passing to speak of this aspect of American life. American society is generally considered the most religious in the world. Agnostics are few, religious regulations are strictly observed, and on Sundays and holidays a dead silence descends upon the cities and villages—stores are closed, cabs and omnibuses run only occasionally, theaters are dark, public places are deserted; in short, nowhere else have I seen such gravity and solemnity. But upon closer examination we see in this solemnity the influence of unreasoning habit rather than a living, fervent, conscious faith. The American people are extraordinarily matter-of-fact. No one troubles himself about things which have no connection with reality of material benefits or which cannot be grasped and calculated. Such questions as the origins of the universe, the existence of the Creator, the immortality of the soul, all of which are agitating the minds of European youth, professors, philosophers, and the intelligentsia—these ideas, which so often lead first to philosophical bankruptcy and then to widespread doubt among the people, here carry no weight at all. No other people are less capable of philosophical reflection than Americans. Tangible activity prevails over abstract contemplation. Occupied with commerce, industry, and agriculture, they do not inquire about the validity of religious formalities. Thus, when Sunday comes, the American goes to church because such is the custom;

he reads his Bible for the same reason; he stays at home because everybody stays at home. But who can tell in all of this outward observance of the Sabbath whether mechanical routine and empty formality do not predominate over genuine piety?

On the other hand, the great number of sects and the competition among them and the struggle with an ever growing Catholicism color religious feelings with a partisanship which, it must be admitted, produces a purely secular stimulus. The communicants of an old sect try to maintain and extend it; therefore, they must set an example to others. A faction always ties followers to itself, and, as a result of the entanglement of their general and individual interests, it creates partisans who eventually find themselves attached by so many ties that they are neither willing nor able to separate themselves, even though they may have become indifferent to the main principle.

On the other hand, every American regards religious liberty as the jewel in the Constitution of the United States, and, wishing to demonstrate this freedom, he feels obligated to observe assiduously all the rites of the sect to which he belongs. However, my original contention that Americans possess only the outward semblance of deep religious sentiment still stands. Hence they remain unresolved, and religious matters will continue to be dictated by habit and tradition.

*   *   *

The main force, however, which maintains some degree of moral unity among the Poles is the Church and the Polish priests. The Church gathers around itself the leading workers or peasants and is constantly creating new parishes. The priest marries, baptizes, and buries, but above all, teaches. Not only do these functions provide a source of income for the priest, but they also enable him to wield political influence, for he controls the votes of his flock. That such a state of affairs may be displeasing to some does not prevent its existence. It is even possible that this preponderance of purely clerical influence engenders a certain exclusiveness and diminishes the size of the Polish-American community by excluding, for example, the Protestants of whom there are many among the Prussian Silesians and Mazurians. On the other hand, one must admit that the Church brings together the Polish masses, creates from them a social entity, does not allow them to become scattered and to disappear unnoticed among foreign elements; and, finally, the Church provides the only refuge for those new arrivals whose fate I described at the beginning of this sketch.

In the founding of new settlements the clergy play a very important role. It frequently happens, especially in the larger American cities, that the workers suddenly display a desire to exchange their life in the factories for the plow and the pioneer's ax. The reason for this is economic depression with its accompanying unemployment. Although difficult at first, the settler's life is more secure than that of a laborer. He can stake out a land claim with payment over a period of ten years at $1.50 per acre, or acquire it likewise on installment payments from the railroad. After surviving the initial hardships, the settler eventually comes to possess his own property and to earn a decent livelihood.

But, of course, a solitary individual cannot settle on the prairie far from people. Cooperative action is necessary here. A sizable group of people must be ready to set out together and to work as a unit. Families that intend to establish a settlement usually select one or more representatives who go out in advance to view the land. These men negotiate contracts with the railroad companies, endeavor to secure the best possible terms, and, finally, subdivide the acquired territories. In settling on government lands such intermediaries are not so necessary, for government land actually belongs to no one and legally may be settled upon without previous agreements with anyone. Once the $1.50 per acre is paid in the nearest land office, or even after the first installment is paid, the land is regarded as private property.

Thus, when occupying land, it is necessary simply to make sure that someone else does not already have a claim to it—otherwise no difficulties exist. But settlers usually prefer lands belonging to railroad companies, since locations along railroad lines have greater prospects of development in the future. In such instances, the role of the emissaries is exceptionally important, for everything depends on the kind of terms that are included in the contract with the railroad management. For example, the management may promise a new station to the growing colony, it may sell the land at a higher or lower price, it may spread out the payments over a very long period—all of this depends on the skill of the emissaries as negotiators.

Almost without exception priests serve as such envoys for our colonists, and were it not for them, settlements like Radom, Czestochowa, and others would never have arisen, for peasants would not know how to handle these matters. The clerical plenipotentiary has this further advantage over the secular that the latter might be bribed into accepting the worst possible land and the least desirable terms for the settlers and thereupon wash his hands of the whole affair and depart; conversely, the priest usually remains with the settlement, becomes its father-confessor, and is thus directly affected by the fate of the colony. This is entirely natural and I had an opportunity to be convinced of this superiority of the clerical leaders over the secular during my sojourn in the United States.

Two new Polish settlements were being founded at that time. A secular leader bought land in Arkansas, named the prospective colony Warren Hoino, and by portraying it in truly golden colors, succeeded in assembling over a hundred families. The whole enterprise was strongly supported by Dyniewicz's *Chicago Polish Gazette,* a bitter rival of the *Polish Catholic Gazette,* edited by the clergy. The latter, or rather its partisans, decided to oppose the venture, fearing that the *Chicago Polish Gazette* might gain in popular favor by backing so important an undertaking. On their initiative the proposal was made to establish simultaneously another Polish colony in Nebraska to be called New Posen. Since interested participants were not lacking, lands were soon bought and New Posen passed from the realm of fancy to that of reality.

Each newspaper now began to praise its own colony and could not find enough derogatory terms to describe the settlement of its rival. New Posen was accused of being situated in a treeless region which lacked materials for building homes and which was devastated from time to time by locusts. There was some truth in this accusation. Nebraska is one gigantic prairie where even to this day the Pawnee Indians roam and where trees are found only along the Platte River and its tributaries. The locust does, indeed, frequently lay waste to this remarkable prairie. On the other hand, the fertility of the virgin soil rewards the settlers for all their misfortunes. In refuting the accusations the *Catholic Gazette* stated that the lands in Arkansas were covered with oaks whose clearance might take so long that the settlers would first die of starvation. It was further alleged that the terms of the contract were unfavorable, that the purchased territories had only a thin layer of black earth, and, finally, that the Arkansas River annually flooded the whole region, causing deadly fevers and other diseases which decimated the population. Both sides sent out commissions to determine the true state of affairs, but being highly partisan, these commissions declared pro and con according to the views of each group.

In the end, the situation in Warren Hoino took a turn for the worse. Arkansas is, indeed, famed for the fertility of its soil, and the abundance of its forests is an added attraction for any colony. Yet I came to the conclusion that, despite these favorable attributes, the colony founded there had no real future. Apparently the land was purchased rashly, without foresight, and subdivided so as to please various private interests; and even the administration of the funds was not above reproach. Most of the settlers who had already gone to Warren Hoino returned posthaste, raising a cry that they had been duped. Others, having spent all of their money for the journey and not wishing to remain in the colony, found themselves in truly desperate straits. The expedition to Warren Hoino was termed an expedition to Siberia. In short, it appears that much blame may be attached to the secular promoters of the new colony. Meanwhile New Posen, which at first glance did not appear to have as many possibilities for successful development, was established from the very beginning on a firm foundation and as far as I know, its prospects for the future are improving daily.

I have devoted a few lines to the history of these two colonies in order to give my readers an example of the manner in which new colonies are founded and, at the same time, to show the importance of the role and activity of the Polish priests in the United States. The care and conscientiousness with which the New Posen affair was conducted may undoubtedly be attributed to the intention of the clerical negotiators to settle in the colony and create a parish. Thus, whatever would concern New Posen would concern them, and their own future success would depend upon that of the colony. I do not mean to imply that personal interests alone gave assurance of the honesty of their actions; but it is an axiom that the general interest is always and everywhere the more vigorously defended the more closely and directly it is tied to the personal interests of those at the helm.

From what I have said thus far it is clear that the clergy are largely responsible for such organization as exists among the Poles residing in America. To be sure, the existing organization is insufficient. Colonies are scattered throughout the breadth of the United States and know very little about each other. The newspapers published in Chicago lack news reports from the multitude of Polish colonies, making it difficult to compile any accurate statistical data. Truthfully speaking, no one knows how many Poles there are in the United States. The figures cited in the Polish press are not based on any accurate calculation; they are always exaggerated, for the editors wish to give the impression that their newspapers are widely read and are the organs of large political parties. On the one hand, this brings them paid commercial advertisements, the main source of their income; on the other hand, it gives them a certain political importance during elections.

*   *   *

Above and beyond their religious and social functions, the clergy are principally concerned with preserving Polish national identity. This is likewise the objective of Polish newspapers, secular societies, and veterans' groups—in short, of all Polish institutions in America.

Unfortunately, however, all their efforts are in vain. In my opinion, despite the most noble endeavors on the part of their leaders, American Poles will sooner or later become denationalized and be completely assimilated by the Americans. Stronger elements than the Polish have been unable to resist the influence of the Anglo-Saxon language and civilization. No one attempts to Americanize you or to force anything upon you. Each national group is free to set up newspapers, schools, and even an army. In the latter case the government intercedes only to the extent of furnishing the rifles.

And yet American influence is irresistible. Foreigners who come to America and who obtain citizenship live under American laws, take part in public life, and sooner or later transform themselves into Americans in spirit. After that, it is only a matter of time before the acceptance of the English language becomes an inexorable necessity. All of the national groups living side by side must, of course, use a common language; otherwise, a Pole in Haywood would never be able to understand his Portuguese neighbor. Then, too, English is the common social, commercial and official language. In addition, Poles, Italians, Czechs, Spaniards, etc., who come to the United States do not have in their tongues the numerous expressions which serve to define purely local American concepts, relationships, and conditions. English expressions soon force their way into these linguistic gaps and fissures, and the decay of the native speech inevitably sets in. One might say that the English language is wafted in the wind and somehow is inhaled involuntarily by those who arrive from Europe. It is like a flood, gradual to be sure, but moving forward without interruption. In the purely German settlement of Anaheim in southern California, the parents spank their children because the latter insist on speaking English with one another. And yet this community, situated in the midst of a predominantly Mexican population, does not even have direct contact with the Anglo-Saxon element. I saw this same influence of English language and manners on the German youth of Cincinnati, the strongest German hearth in the whole United States. As for the Poles, even their clergy, even their newspaper editors and reporters, have been unable to resist the persuasive effects of English; and yet these are people who are well educated and who consciously defend themselves against this ascendancy. I would say that under the influence of the English language there is being created here a separate Polish-American dialect whose common words are Polish, while all aspects of American life differing from that of Poland, such as commerce, society, government, customs, and agricultural methods, are described by English terms and expressions.

* * *

As the number of Polish immigrants in the United States declines, the denationalization of those who came earlier will gain momentum. Furthermore, all immigrant groups are composed primarily of men who, unable to find enough women of their own nationality, take wives from among the local inhabitants. Thus, I am unacquainted with a single Pole, married to an American woman, whose children know the Polish language. I do not exclude even the intelligentsia. This is inevitable. Such children are unable to read Polish books and newspapers.

But even if they learn Polish, it will no longer be their mother tongue. Exclusively Polish settlements, such as Radom or Czestochowa, and especially those founded on the prairie far removed from large cities, as New Posen in Nebraska, will hold out longer, perhaps even very much longer, but with the passage of years even these will succumb to the common fate. It should be added that people who are poor invariably come under the influence of those who are rich and the native Americans are richer than the Poles. Thus everything conspires against the best intentions of the Poles. This small segment of the Polish nation will sooner or later by the irresistible force of circumstances become absorbed within the foreign element. A shoot grafted on another trunk is transformed into another kind of tree.

We must remember only the first generation lives here and it will hold out. Whether on the shores of the Great Lakes or the Pacific Ocean those who have been born in the fatherland will not forget it and will remain faithful to it. Settlers in Illinois and in Texas preserve lumps of Polish earth as if they were relics. These they place in the coffin under the head or over the heart of the deceased. The Polish peasant loves his homeland more than he realizes. Today on the prairies of Nebraska and Arkansas many a Polish peasant pauses to ponder and frequently to weep as he strikes his scythe against the whetstone, for the sound reminds him of his native village. Or somewhere under the hot skies of Texas when the church organ resounds and the people begin to sing "Holy Father," their eyes fill with tears and their peasant thoughts wing their way back across the ocean like sea gulls and return to the thatched huts in their native Poland.

But what of the second, third, and fourth generations? What of the children born of German, Irish, or American mothers? Sooner or later they will forget. They will change everything, even their names, which English teeth find too difficult to chew and which interfere with business. How long this will take is difficult to say. But just as Poland disappeared, so will this same, sad fate inevitably befall her children who, today, are scattered throughout the world.

12

Richard Frederick Clarke, S. J.

1882-1887

from *"Roman Catholics in America"*

Born in England in 1839, Richard Frederick Clarke was educated at the Merchant Taylors' School and St. John's College, Oxford. After taking his B. A. degree he served for two years as an assistant master at Radley School. In 1864 he took his M. A. degree at Oxford and received Anglican Orders. However, he became increasingly interested in Catholicism and severed his connections with the Anglican Church and with Oxford to enter the Church in 1869. Two years later he entered the Jesuit Novitiate at Manresa and was ordained a priest in 1878. From 1882 until 1893 he was editor of the respected English Jesuit periodical *The Month* and became well-known as a writer, preacher, retreat master and spiritual director. In 1883 and 1884 he visited both Ireland and America. He recorded his impressions of both countries in a series of articles for *The Month*. The one in which Father Clarke treats of American Catholicism follows in its entirety.

If the Church is destined to triumph in America, if her progress is undoubted, the emigrant ship which carries across the Atlantic the surplus population of Catholic Germany, or the struggling peasantry of Ireland, is doing a good work in the spiritual as well as in the natural order. It is hastening on the triumph of Catholicity in America. It is providing for future generations not only a home of material prosperity, where they shall be free from the poverty and misery to which they were subject in Europe, but a home where hereafter religious freedom in its true and Catholic sense shall gain the victory over the direct and indirect disadvantages to which in most countries in Europe the Church is subjected.

But if on the contrary the progress of Catholicity in the States is more apparent than real, if in each successive generation, the loss to the Church is far greater than the gain, if faith seems to fade away under the unfavorable influences, both positive and negative, which it encounters in American cities, then emigration is a misery and misfortune, even though the emigrants should build up splendid fortunes and achieve the most glorious material success. A necessary misery and misfortune perhaps, if it is the result of an inevitable law, but a very unnecessary and a thrice mischievous one if, in defiance of sound economic laws, it is fostered by a policy which seeks to turn into a vast grazing field the land which under happier and Catholic influences would be covered with smiling farms and flourishing villages and towns increasing in numbers and in wealth.

In order to estimate the progress of the Catholic religion in the United States there are three questions for us to answer.

1. What is the proportion of Catholics to the whole population of the States? Have they increased in proportion to the increase of the general population during the last fifty years?
2. Is this increase due to internal development or to immigration?
3. Are there reasons to hope that under the present course of events the proportion of Catholics to the rest of the population will continuously increase?

The first of these questions is easily answered. The total number of Catholics in America is now about six and a half millions, or 13 per cent of the whole population. In 1835 the Catholics amounted to about half a million or 3 per cent. So far our statistics are eminently satisfactory. Catholics have increased more than four times as fast as the non-Catholics around them. If the proportion of increase continues for another fifty years, the Catholics of America will find themselves in a majority of the inhabitants of the country.

And here before I proceed, I must bear my personal testimony to the splendid growth of Catholic organization throughout the States. Not a city where Catholic churches are not springing up on every side, not a diocese where priests are not increasing in numbers, within fifteen years the number of churches throughout the States has almost doubled, and the increase in the clergy is equally encouraging. Everywhere there is a religious activity which must impress the traveller. Everywhere works of charity are liberally supported. Everywhere new convents are being founded, and the various religious orders are extending their influence and founding new houses. Christian Brothers are devoting themselves to the self-denying work of education. Sisters of Mercy, Sisters of Charity, Nuns of the Sacred Heart and of Notre Dame, are winning over the American mind to respect, admire and value them. In the diocese of New York there are over seventeen hundred religious women. In each of the dioceses of Philadelphia, St. Louis and Cincinnati there are over one thousand. The magnificent Cathedral of New York bears witness to the generosity of the Catholics of the city. The other great cities have cathedrals which, if they do not rival that of New York, are handsome, spacious and costly. Colleges and schools are being multiplied on every side, and the higher education is making steady progress.

The congregations in the Catholic churches are also a most consoling sight. Go into the church attached to the College of St. Ignatius in Chicago, or into the Cathedral of the little city of Detroit on Christmas morning, and you will see a sight to gladden the Catholic heart. It is a cold frosty morning, and the wintry wind sweeps through the snowladen streets: a morning to keep all comfort-loving souls at home, at least until the hour of mid-day draws near, and the obligation of hearing Mass enforces their presence at the mid-day Mass. But at present it is far from mid-day, it is still night, and chimes of joy are ringing through the frosty air. For an hour past a stream of pious worshippers have been wending their way to the house where God dwells. There is a Solemn Mass at 5 a. m., and men, women, and children are flocking thither. We enter the church soon after five has struck. It is crowded to overflowing. Those present are to be numbered by thousands rather than by hundreds. The church is all ablaze with light, and a perfect crowd of acolytes and torchbearers in scarlet and purple cassocks throng the sanctuary in picturesque assembly. Sweetly rings the *Adeste Fideles* from the choir, and a perfect roar of voices at the end of each verse echoes the *Venite adoremus*. Look at the congregation— there are no mere sightseers there, save a handful of Protestants standing round the door and gazing all a-gape at what is indeed a glorious sight. At length the bell rings the *Domine, non sum dignus*. The stream, the throng of communicants includes nearly all of that enormous congregation. Not women chiefly, scarcely a majority of the pious female sex—but old men, men in the prime of life, men in their early manhood, youths and boys, and innocent children. Three priests come in to assist the celebrant in giving Communion, and he, as the Mass has already been a long one, administers to a few railfulls and then returns to the altar. But the assistants go on with that work of love which seems as if it would never end. On and still on follows the unceasing stream of those who come to receive their God. On and still on, though the Mass is over, and the long procession has wound its way out from the sanctuary—on and still on, though another Mass has now begun—on and still on, until once more the *Domine, non sum dignus* is said, and a fresh stream of communicants mingles with those who have been patiently waiting their turn ever since the High Mass began. It is a sight to gladden the heart of every Catholic, a sight to give joy to Angels and Saints in Heaven, a sight, too, which may be witnessed in almost every large city in America, a sight which makes him who sees it feel inclined to say that there is in God's providence, the almost certain hope of a glorious future for the Church in America, and that perhaps by God's mercy we shall one day see the provinces of that mighty Continent become the Kingdom of God and of His Church.

Or go again into one of the parishes in the heart of New York City, and seek out the Church of the Immaculate Conception on Fourteenth Street. Ask the zealous and indefatigable pastor to show you the school attached to his mission. In a building hard by the presbytery, which is quite perplexing to the stranger by its innumerable numbers of class rooms and countless passages and staircases and floors, you will find between two and three thousand children assembled. Christian Brothers and Sisters of Charity superintend the work, and quite a crowd of trained secular teachers assist them. All is beautifully organized, the children bright and happy, intelligent and well-looking, ready to answer questions in any of their lessons, and especially in their Catechism. What a privilege to bring up those two thousand children and more in the love and fear of God, to save them from the streets and from the public school! Most of the older children are total abstainers. They are for the greater part of Irish parentage, and their parents belong to the working class. There is a scattering of other nationalities—a stray English child or two and half a dozen little Italians and a few Germans. One or two (not of the Irish) are Protestants, but not likely to remain so long in an atmosphere like this. We feel inclined to say as we pass from room to room: Here is the hope of America in the future: from schools like this will proceed the sinew and muscle of a Catholicity which will go on gaining ground from year to year.

Yet in spite of encouraging scenes like these, in spite of the ever increasing prominence of the Church in America, I am sorry to say that I am unable to take as cheerful a view of the present or as hopeful a view of the future as first impressions seemed to justify. The further I penetrated into the country, the more I saw of one great city after another, the more I found myself compelled by the stern logic of facts to set aside my too brilliant expectations respecting the victory of Truth over error in that great continent. I may be wrong in my conclusions; I hope with all my heart my fears are ill-founded, and that I am too much inclined to look at the dark side of the question. But I am sure that my readers desire only the sincere expression of my honest opinion. It is folly to cry peace, peace, where there is no peace.

I will now proceed to explain the basis of my hopes and fears.

An American paper has recently made an estimate of the number of Catholics who ought to be found in America. The foreign born residents in 1880 amounted to over six and a half million, of whom about half are Catholics. The foreign born residents at the same date, plus their American born children were fifteen million, which would give seven and a half million Catholics of foreign parentage residing in the States four years ago. Add to these the native American population, which in 1835 amounted to little over half a million, and according to the average rate of increase would now be between three and four times that number;[1] and also the Catholic settlers since 1880 who amount to about half a million more. We say nothing of the converts, who amount to a very considerable number, though we do not venture any estimate of it, or the children of mixed marriages, to whom the Church has a right, and who at least ought to be brought up as Catholics, if the Catholic parent is faithful to his or her duty. Even apart from these, the total number of Americans who ought to be Catholics must amount to nearly ten million, and these included, to a good many more.

Now what are the actual numbers? According to the Catholic Directory, there are at present in America, not ten million Catholics and more, but only six million and a half. Mr. Mulhall, in his *Statistical Dictionary,* arrives at very nearly the same re-

[1] In 1840 the Catholic population was estimated by Archbishop Hughes at one million. As the calculation made in 1835 was based on the Church accommodation, which was then miserably insufficient, it is probable that the Catholics at that time were more numerous than would appear from the situation.

sults, and we may therefore regard the statistics of the Directory as fairly accurate.[2]

What does this mean? It means that hundreds of thousands, not to say millions, in America, who ought to be Catholics, have voluntarily relinquished, or been robbed of their inheritance of Faith! Some of them have drifted away from the belief of their childhood on the fatal tide of worldly interest, or ambition, or passion; some of them through no fault of their own have been swallowed up in the flood of hostile influences or by the bigotry of Protestant proselytism. Some were taught from their childhood to hate the religion of their forefathers; others lapsed into indifference in the absence of all opportunities of practising their religion; some were led astray by the specious teaching of the sceptic; others were brought up in schools and colleges where the name of God was unknown and religion was a tabooed subject. In one way or another two or three million or more of the Church's children have now become her enemies, or if not her open enemies, yet are torn irrevocably from her bosom and are deserters from the standard of faith.

Not that the change came all at once. Rarely did those who had been brought up in Kerry or Mayo fall away themselves from their religion. Rarely indeed did the Catholic emigrants from Rhineland or Tyrol lose the faith of their dear fatherland. Too many indeed ceased to practise their religion; but only one here and one there abandoned the name of Catholic and ceased to give in their adherence to the Divine Teacher. But away from church or priest they grew indifferent: fainter and fainter burned the light of faith: little by little they lost their appreciation of the priceless treasure of Catholic belief. The supernatural became subordinated to the natural: material prosperity became more important in their eyes than any spiritual

[2] I have seen this estimate disputed more than once in Amercian Catholic papers as insufficient. I hope it may be so, but the coincidence of the two independent calculations, and Mr. Mulhall's unrivalled accuracy as a statistician, make me inclined to believe that the number is not very much below the truth.

advantages for themselves and their children. When it was a question of a Catholic or Protestant education for their children, they considered rather which of the two would be most likely to further their worldly success. The natural result of this was that the children grew up untrained in their religion. The catechism was relegated to Sundays, or perhaps not taught at all. The same indifference of the parents made them careless to guard the purity of their children, and the second generation became notorious for their abandonment of the Faith, for their immorality, and in some cities for their degradation, lawlessness and crime. When they became fathers and mothers, their children proved even worse than the parents, not perhaps in their outward conduct or in their relations to society, but in their complete and entire loss of Faith. I know that there were many exceptions to this rule, and I have heard it stated on good authority that when the children fell away the grandchildren in many cases returned to their allegiance by some happy law of hereditary reversion. But this was not sufficiently often the case to prevent the wholesale defection which has reduced the number of American Catholics to a number very far short of what they would have been, had they not been weighted by the disadvantages of which I am going to speak.[3]

What are the causes of this lamentable defection? In former times the scarcity of priests was sufficient to account for it, and even now there are many districts where the number of priests is altogether below that which is necessary in order that the wants of the people may be duly provided for. For the country in general we find the proportion of priests to people is a little more than 1:1,000. This would be sufficient if we had not to subtract from the missionary priests a large number who are sick or infirm, and a larger number still who are engaged in teaching or other special work. Colleges, seminaries, asylums,

[3] I have heard an American priest assess the defections in former years at 90 per cent; and though I hope and believe that his estimate was altogether too large, even at the worst times, yet he was a man whose long experience gave weight to his almost despairing estimate of the history of the past.

hospitals, convents, subtract from the available parochial priests a very considerable proportion, and the actual number of those engaged in mission work cannot be much above 1:2,000 of the population. When we remember the enormous extent of territory over which the six million Catholics are scattered, and that in many thinly populated districts a priest has hard work to minister to five hundred or seven hundred souls, it is clear that there is some reason for this belief.

But this is an evil which by God's mercy is diminishing day by day. It may have been a cause of much decay of faith in the past, but it can scarcely be said to be so in the present. There are other causes at work far more destructive of the souls of Catholics than the difficulty of finding priests.

One of the chief dangers to faith throughout the country arises from the engrossing devotion of the nation in general to mere material and temporal interests. America is in point of material prosperity far ahead of other nations. Her most prominent men are men who have realized enormous fortunes or who have by their determined and persevering industry worked their way upwards. There are exceptions to this rule; General Sherman is a man who won his position by his military genius; General Butler was brought into notice by his energy and success as a commander of the Northern troops. Literary men, poets and novelists, historians and humorists, have, by the force of their genius, taken their places among the first ranks of the American nation, and indeed of their compeers in every nation.

But in general the spirit of America is keenly commercial, and the activity of the nation is directed into the channel of an ever-increasing devotion to business pursuits. It is the result of the circumstances of the country, of her unbounded resources, and unlimited field for fresh activity, and the rich return with which she is ready to compensate the man who devotes himself to the development of the treasures that lie around him. Perhaps the exhilarating climate, stimulating to activity of body, and still more of brain, tends to the same end. Now it is quite true that in commerce there is nothing essentially unfavourable to the Catholic spirit. The commercial has some advantages in point of religion, which are lacking alike to peer and peasant. But in a Protestant nation where five out of six are Protestants, where the whole tone is Protestant, and the very atmosphere is opposed to the supernatural, this commercial activity is so exclusively the object of men's lives, that it becomes almost a matter of course that every other consideration should give way to it, and that the Catholic population living among Protestants should be carried away by the stream. The young Catholic in store, office or bank drinks in the prevalent idea that worldly success is the main end of life, and his hold on the supernatural becomes weakened, and perhaps in the end he loses it altogether. This world's interests become absorbing, and he seems to have no time or thoughts left for the interests which concern the world invisible, and so the invisible becomes ever more and more out of sight, and at last he declares that he looks up to heaven and finds there nothing but thick darkness.

Add to this another important consideration. In many cities of America to be a Catholic involves a certain social inferiority. It is not the case everywhere: in some parts there still lingers among the Catholic population the memory of their ancestors, driven forth by persecuting England or revolutionary France. Once English nobles or French aristocrats, their children still retain a sort of hereditary dignity. The old Catholic families of Maryland, Missouri, and Michigan still have their representatives among the best families of Baltimore, St. Louis, and Detroit. In New Orleans this is still more the case. But in most American cities there is no such aristocratic flavour about the Catholic name. Most of the Catholics are immigrants from Germany or Ireland, and belong to the poorer, if not the poorest classes in their native land. In Philadelphia, Boston, New York, Chicago, Cincinnati, to be a Catholic in nine cases out of ten means to belong to the lower class. In Chicago this is more the case than it was some twenty years ago. I was informed on the best authority that at that time there was more land in Catholic hands than there is now. Somehow or other, the most enterprising American Protestant has ousted the Catholic landholders of that rising and industrial city. The result of all this is that a great many weak-kneed Catholics, whose business qualities have enabled them to attain a good position in the various cities, have deserted their faith for social reasons. They had not the courage to endure the sort of reproach that is involved. They feared it might be a hindrance to their desire to make their way into the best society. Some have even changed their Irish names into something more fashionable and more American. Not that America in general has social prejudices; but it was only natural that certain associations should cling to the name of Catholic where most of the labourers are Catholics, most of the "helps" or servant girls are Catholics, while among those who held a good position and were rich, among those who were well-educated and refined, very few were Catholics. Where this was the case it was impossible that the name of Catholic should not be regarded generally as a mark of inferiority in the social and intellectual scale. This necessarily is a serious obstacle to its success.

There is another element of American character respecting which I have often asked myself whether it was on the whole prejudicial to Catholicity or not. The independence and self-reliance of American character is in many respects an admirable trait. There is so much self-respect in every class. The class of "rouchs" which in England is a very large one, scarcely exists at all. Ruffians there are enough and to spare in the big cities, thieves and bullies and men who live by violence and dishonesty. But one never encounters the boys and young men who are ready to insult the passer-by just for the fun of the thing, and who are the curse of some parts of London on a Sunday evening. It is one of the best traits in America that there is not that barbarous spirit of lawlessness which now and then breaks out in Europe. When there is a riot in America it is a display of popular indignation against some real abuse. It is a protest of the law-makers against those who have in their opinion set aside and violated the law. The Cincinnati riots were an expression of the wrath of the people against the judicial corruption or inefficiency which allowed murderers to escape unpunished. But while there is no lawlessness, this is because the laws are the people's laws. It is the uncrowned King respecting his own sceptre. Now the Church's laws have a different origin. Though in one sense they are the people's laws, yet they are imposed at the same time from above, by an authority which cannot be called in question by its subjects. American notions respecting law have to be set aside when applied to ecclesiastical law. The American view of obedience to civil law is that the law is the people's law framed by the people's representatives for the people's good, and therefore, I as a sensible, self-respecting man, must obey it whether I like it or not. I am free to criticise the law, and get it abolished if I can, but according to the Constitution of the United States (which I regard as the most perfect of all constitutions) I am bound to submit to the will of the majority of the people, and I do so as a self-respecting American citizen. But can I apply the same sort of argument to matters ecclesiastical? Is it a safe attitude in respect of the Church's laws to criticise them and wish to get them abolished? Are they *my* laws at all in the same sense in which the laws of my country are my laws, framed by me through those who represent me in Congress or in State Legislature?

Hence, arises a tendency to resent, in the church's legislation, her attitude of independence and irresponsibility to her members. The American is not used to it. It is altogether a foreign notion to the American mind. In the civil order, law is the voice of those subject to the law, and they can change it when they see fit. In the spiritual order, law is in no way dependent on the voice of those subject to the law, and they cannot change a little of it at their pleasure. This makes it much more difficult for them to submit; their independence of mind has a tendency to force its way into a sphere where independence is inadmissible.

But there is a far more serious influence at work in the great cities of America, which tends to first weaken and then destroy faith. It is an evil which increases day by day. It is an evil which has more power than any other to sap the foundations of faith in the mass of the people. It is an evil which for many reasons I would fain pass over, but which I cannot pass over in any analysis of the influences hostile to the spread of the Catholic religion in the States. It is an evil which seems to be gaining ground all over the world, and which threatens in time to wreck modern society altogether, as it wrecked the society of Rome and Greece. Of all the influences which are separating America from the Church there is none so fatal as the vice and corruption of the large cities, and especially the vice and corruption prevalent among the young. It is a subject most painful—I had almost said most heartrending—to one who loves the souls for which Jesus Christ shed His blood upon the Cross; it is a subject, too, in which few can realize the wholesale degradation of the younger generation save the physician of souls or of bodies, the priest or the doctor, to whom the sinner is led by the soul stricken with remorse or the body enfeebled by disease. I am not concerned with any comparison between the morality of England and of America. They are both bad enough, God knows. What else can we expect in big cities where the mass of the population is Protestant, and where the lower classes in general are left to grow up without restraint, without religious teaching, without any idea of what sin is and what is its foulness in the sight of God and of the Court of Heaven? There is another comparison with which I am concerned. From the simple innocence of their peasant homes, from the watchful care of the village pastor, from the holy and sweet influences of Catholic teaching, Catholic atmosphere, a country the most Catholic of all countries in the world, from the almost primitive simplicity of morals which the land of St. Patrick has never lost, and through God's mercy will never lose—hundreds and thousands every year emigrate or are emigrated to the shores of Canada and the States. By an unhappy fatality they crowd into the big cities, and there are sucked into the vortex of misery and sin. The very advantages of country and climate are turned by the devil to work his diabolical ends. The facilities for independence at an early age on account of the

demand for labour—rich food in abundance instead of the pota-
toes and porridge of Ireland—the exhilarating climate—the
habits of self-government—the freedom of intercourse between
the sexes—all work to the prejudice of morality.

Here I must turn aside for a moment to what is regarded
by outsiders as one of the unreasonable prejudices of the Irish
Episcopacy and the Irish clergy—I mean their hatred of emigration. Those who are ignorant of the facts of the case—those who
have not been behind the scenes—those who think first of material prosperity and regard the welfare of the soul as of little
account—those who judge of the matter sitting at their ease at
home, or who really are touched with the story of Irish distress
and congested misery—wonder at the unalterable ineffaceable
hatred that the Irish pastors bear to the transportation of their
flocks across the Atlantic, and why it is they would sooner see
them half-starved at home than prosperous in the cities of America. I think I can throw some light on this extraordinary prejudice.
A traveller in Donegal not long since asked a parish priest of
a large village there respecting the general morality of the country, and was assured by him that the serious sins committed in his
parish from one year's end to the other could be counted on the
fingers of one hand. Another traveller asked a priest in one of
the largest of the American cities a similar question, and the
answer he received was that all the city through there were few
boys of thirteen or fourteen who had not already lost their innocence. Out of our Catholic young men, said an American
Bishop, I believe nine out of ten are practical infidels, or at least
neglect the practice of their religion altogether. This loss of faith
is in almost every case the result of previous moral corruption.
Pittsburgh, where there is a large Catholic population, is said to
contain more bad houses, in proportion to the population, than
any other city in the world, and the age at which boys begin to
frequent them is scarcely credible. Cincinnati is not much better,
and in Chicago I heard the saddest accounts of the unblushing
effrontery of open vice.

13

>>><<<

George Santayana

1912

from *Character and Opinion in the United States*

>>><<<

Born and raised in Spain until the age of nine, George Santayana was educated in and lived in the United States for forty years. During much of this time he was at Harvard University, both as a student and as a renowned professor. But neither in thought nor in fact did he ever become an American. As a result, his comments on the American scene, though friendly and unusually perceptive, were characterized by the objectivity of a foreign visitor. Although his parents were nominally Catholic and Santayana was always friendly to the Church, his philosophy—as expressed in such works as *Interpretations of Poetry and Religion, Scepticism and Animal Faith,* and *The Realms of Being*—is decidedly not Catholic oriented. His most popular book was a novel, *The Last Puritan*. The following selection is taken from *Character and Opinion in the United States,* published by George Braziller in 1920, eight years after Santayana had left the United States to reside permanently in Europe.

>>><<<

While the sentiments of most Americans in politics and morals, if a little vague, are very conservative, their democratic instincts, and the force of circumstances, have produced a system of education which anticipates all that the most extreme revolution could bring about; and while no one dreams of forcibly suppressing private property, religion, or the family, American education ignores these things, and proceeds as much as possible

as if they did not exist. The child passes very little into a free
school, established and managed by the municipal authorities;
the teachers, even for the older boys, are chiefly unmarried
women, sensitive, faithful, and feeble; their influence helps to
establish that separation which is so characteristic of America
between things intellectual, which remain wrapped in a feminine
veil and, as it were, under glass, and the rough business and
passions of life. The lessons are ambitious in range, but are made
as easy, as interesting, and as optional as possible; the stress is
divided between what the child likes now and what he is going
to need in his trade or profession. The young people are sympathetically encouraged to instruct themselves and to educate one
another. They romp and make fun like young monkeys, they
flirt and have their private "brain-storms" like little supermen
and superwomen. They are tremendously in earnest about their
college intrigues and intercollegiate athletic wars. They are fond,
often compassionately fond, of their parents, and home is all
the more sacred to them in that they are seldom there. They
enjoy a surprising independence in habits, friendships, and opinions. Brothers and sisters often choose different religions. The
street, the school, the young people's club, the magazine, the
popular novel, furnish their mental pabulum. The force of example and of passing custom is all the more irresistible in this
absence of authority and tradition; for this sort of independence
rather diminishes the power of being original, by supplying a
slenderer basis and a thinner soil from which originality might
spring. Uniformity is established spontaneously without discipline, as in the popular speech and ethics of every nation.
Against this tendency to uniformity the efforts of a cultivated
minority to maintain a certain distinction and infuse it into
their lives and minds are not very successful. They have secondary
schools for their boys in which the teachers are men, and even
boarding-schools in the country, more or less Gothic in aspect
and English in regimen; there are other semi-foreign institutions
and circles, Catholic or Jewish, in which religion is the dominant

consideration. There is also the society of the very rich, with cosmopolitan leanings and a vivacious interest in artistic undertakings and personalities. But all these distinctions, important as they may seem to those who cultivate them, are a mere shimmer and ripple on the surface of American life; and for an observer who sees things in perspective they almost disappear. By a merciful dispensation of nature, the pupils of these choice establishments, the moment they plunge into business or politics, acquire the protective colouring of their environment and become indistinguishable from the generic American. Their native disposition was after all the national one, their attempted special education was perfunctory, and the influence of their public activities and surroundings is overwhelming. American life is a powerful solvent. As it stamps the immigrant, almost before he can speak English, with an unmistakable muscular tension, cheery self-confidence and habitual challenge in the voice and eyes, so it seems to neutralise every intellectual element, however tough and alien it may be, and to fuse it in the native goodwill, complacency, thoughtlessness, and optimism.

Consider, for instance, the American Catholics, of whom there are nominally millions, and who often seem to retain their ancestral faith sincerely and affectionately. This faith took shape during the decline of the Roman empire; it is full of large disillusions about this world and minute illusions about the other. It is ancient, metaphysical, poetic, elaborate, ascetic, autocratic, and intolerant. It confronts the boastful natural man, such as the American is, with a thousand denials and menaces. Everything in American life is at the antipodes to such a system. Yet the American Catholic is entirely at peace. His tone in everything, even in religion, is cheerfully American. It is wonderful how silently, amicably, and happily he lives in a community whose spirit is profoundly hostile to that of his religion. He seems to take stock in his church as he might in a gold mine—sure it is a grand, dazzling, unique thing; and perhaps he masks, even to himself, his purely imaginative ardour about it, with the pretext that it is sure to make his fortune both in this life and in the next. His church, he will tell you, is a first-rate church to belong to; the priests are fine fellows, like the policemen; the Sisters are dear noble women, like his own sisters; his parish is flourishing; and always rebuilding its church and founding new schools, orphan asylums, sodalities, confraternities, perpetual adoration societies. No parish can raise too much money for any object, or if there are temporary troubles, the fact still remains that America has three Cardinals and that the Catholic religion is the biggest religion on earth. Attachment to his Church in such a temper brings him into no serious conflict with his Protestant neighbors. They live and meet on common ground. Their respective religions pass among them for family matters, private and sacred, with no political implications.

14

>>><<<

Hilaire Belloc

1923-1937

from *The Contrast* and *"Belloc Surveys
the American Church"*

>>><<<

Hilaire Belloc, English essayist, poet and apologist for Catholicism,
was a frequent visitor to the United States. Although he disapproved
of much of what he found here, he could not ignore the attraction
of America. For him the New World was "wholly alien" to the Old
and he was both fascinated and repelled by this new land. Belloc was
a controversialist and, as could be expected, his views on America
and Catholic life in America were not calculated to lull readers into
agreement. Both because Belloc was primarily a journalist, rather
than a creative writer, and because many of his political and social
views were already outdated when he proclaimed them, his writings
have slowly passed into oblivion since his death in 1953. Two views
of American Catholics are presented here: a selection from *The
Contrast,* a comparison of the New World with the Old, written in
1923 and published by Robert M. McBride & Company, of New
York, the following year. "Belloc Surveys the American Church,"
is reprinted with permission from *America,* The National Catholic
Weekly Review, 920 Broadway, New York, N. Y. 10010.

>>><<<

... The United States present a religious contrast to Europe,
and especially to England, in the fact that their religious experience is isolated; that the reaction of Catholic culture upon
Protestant is hardly felt; that certain consequences of religious

difference which we in Europe had known for generations and allowed for were, in the United States, hitherto unknown, have but recently appeared, are still novel and as yet not fully analysed. Of these by far the most important—so much the most important that it covers all that is worth noting in the field—is the necessary conflict between the civil State and Catholic Church where the two are not identified.

The Catholic Church is in its root principle at issue with the civic definition both of freedom and of authority. For the purpose of the State, religion is either a universally admitted system, or a matter of individual choice. But by the definition which is the very soul of Catholicism, religion must be for the Catholic, first, a supreme authority superior to any claims of the State; secondly, a corporate thing, and not an individual thing; thirdly, a thing dependent upon Authority, and not upon a personal mood; fourthly, a guarantee of individual freedom in all that is not of Faith.

Harnack uttered a profound truth in what he intended to be a sneer, when he said that men either had their own religion or somebody else's religion. The religion of the Catholic is not a mood induced by isolated personal introspection coupled with an isolated personal attempt to discover all things and the Maker of all things. It is essentially an acceptation of the religion of others; which others are the Apostolic College, the Conciliar decisions, and all that proceeds from the authoritative voice of the Church. For the Catholic, it is not he himself, it is the Church which can alone discover, decide and affirm. Moreover, the Catholic regards that which is so decided and affirmed as good and salutary, forming the only home of the human race, outside which are but puerilities or despairs, and he regards that which denies or combats such Authority and such affirmation as evil in its consequences and destructive to the dignity and right ordering of man. Lastly, the Catholic instinctively feels his right of personal choice in all that is not defined by creed: e.g., in the matter of food and drink.

Now it is clear that between this attitude and the attitude of a non-Catholic State which proposes "tolerance" (that is, the definition of all religion as an individual concern), there is conflict. For "tolerance" means indifference to those acts and doctrines which the State treats as private, coupled with enforcement of certain acts and doctrines which the State insists upon treating as universal.

I am not here concerned with the evident falsehood of this word tolerance. I use it because it is the current word for this particular attitude, which every State, not identified with Catholicism, must take up.

I repeat, tolerance means to-day, in the mind of the modern statesman, and particularly in the mind of the American citizen, the enforcement of certain doctrines and practises, and, side by side with these, a complete freedom in such doctrines and practices as lie outside those limits.

For instance, the American State enforces the doctrine of private property; the doctrine and practice of monogamy—not of monogamy in the sense of tolerating only one living wife, but in the sense of not tolerating two legal marriages with one person at the same time. It also forbids the purchase and transport of wine, but not those of Mrs. Stopes' books, etc.

Up to the present day the position of the Catholic in the United States has insecurely fitted in with this modern conception of tolerance, through the fact that the dogmas taken for granted by the State, and enforced in practice, were mainly Catholic dogmas; and that the action of the State, where its dogmas differed from Catholic dogma, was mainly negative and permissive.

But such a state of affairs cannot be permanent; and to prove that it cannot be permanent I will give two examples.

It may well come about, at any moment, that the State shall pass a law compelling those who have the guardianship of human beings incapable beyond a certain degree to see to the removal of those human beings. The State may take it for granted as a universal doctrine, to be held and enforced upon all citizens, that the preservation of imbecile or imperfect life, much more its continuance from one generation to another by the propagation of children, is destructive to society; and it may order that these unfortunate beings be placed in what is called, in our modern scientific jargon, the lethal chamber.

Now for a Catholic to act in this fashion is, by Catholic definition, murder; and what is more, any action supporting, or even permitting this thing, is also from the Catholic point of view murder. If A. is a Catholic receiving an order to put out of life the imbecile B., he not only commits murder if he obeys, but he commits murder if he hands over the imbecile B. to the State official C., whom he knows will so act. More, he will be committing murder if he does not do everything in his power to prevent the official C. from carrying out the law.

I have chosen this extreme and violent example because it is particularly illuminating; nor can anyone say that it is fantastic, seeing what things are proposed to-day and what ideas are becoming familiar.

But I can give much nearer instances. A law forbidding a minister of religion to marry two people unless they were certificated by medical or other authority would not, and could not, be obeyed in the Catholic community; nor could a law in any way artificially restricting the birth of children.

If an actual example be demanded, we have one before our eyes in a proposal which has already arisen in the matter of education in the United States. It has already been proposed and may at any time become law, in certain parts of the United States, that a parent should be forbidden to send his child to any but one particular type of school agreeable to the State, and shall be compelled to send his child to that school. The State here affirms the doctrine and practice that a certain religious atmosphere is, or should be, universal to the human race; or, at any rate, to all its citizens; which religious atmosphere is other than the

Catholic. Such a law no Catholic would obey; for, by Catholic definition, it is the parent who should decide upon the education of the child, not the State.

In general, that conflict with which Europe is acquainted to the full, and which has filled the history of two thousand years, from the time of Nero to our own, is inevitable.

Now we in Europe, being so familiar with this, taking it for granted, and knowing that the conflict is always potentially present, arrange for it in various ways; by certain compromises and anomalies in one time; by vigorous persecution in other times; by accepting corporate union between the faith and the civil power. In all these ways the strain is resolved or postponed, and an equilibrium, stable or unstable, preserved. But no one can know the United States without admitting that when the conflict shall there arise, an equilibrium will not be established or preserved, for the conflict will be novel and will seem monstrous. On the one side you have a plain affirmation that the law is the law and must be obeyed, and indignant surprise on the rejection of what seems so obvious and universal a rule. On the other, you will have, as you have had throughout history, resistance to and denial of that rule.

The chief political problem presented by religion has, then, still to be solved in the New World. What the result will be certainly no foreigner could attempt to predict, and probably no American citizen who has recognized that problem from his reading of history, or from his instinctive reaction against the presence of the Catholic Church, can foretell one either. But presented the problem certainly will be, and in one or other of the many fashions, stable or unstable, more or less tragic, it will have to be solved.

I must close with this suggestion, putting it so that it shall be as inoffensive as possible, though I fear there must always be some note of offence in it. The new and separate spirit which has made America, which creates a spiritual condition peculiar to that Continent, may produce, perhaps will soon produce, at any rate tends to produce, some quite unique experiment in the field of religion.

We have had islands, as it were, of such experiment in more than one case; but seeing the way in which great waves spread suddenly over that field of a six score millions, seeing the rapid intensity and unity of their action, I cannot but think that the future holds some rapid, and to us of Europe startling new, American growth: a new body and organization of the domain of religion. Not an isolated, fractional experiment, but a great national or cultural invention. A new Religion. Should such a transformation come, then the conflict with Catholicism of which I have spoken must arise immediately and in its severest form.

*　*　*

A plan has been in my mind for many years past to write a survey of the Catholic position in various countries. I have never carried out this plan because it seemed to me increasingly difficult, as I surveyed it, without the detailed knowledge of a great many conditions such as few Europeans can possess, and certainly not myself. But during a recent visit to America extending over four months, wherein my duties led me into contact mainly with Catholic families and institutions (I had gone to lecture at Fordham, the great Catholic University in New York), I found myself able to obtain an outline—if no more than an outline—of the Catholic situation in the States.

Anyone writing of an international matter carries in his mind the contrasts as well as the similarities of the various situations he is describing. Thus, if you were dealing with such an international force as Communism today you would have to point out that it had hardly any strength in England, and why; how in France it was found in the transport service and the industrial towns but not among the bulk of the agricultural population; why it had been such a menace in Germany; how and why it appealed to certain sections of the Russians, and so on. In the same way a discussion of the Catholic situation in any modern nation involves quite as much recognition of the differences between nations as of the similarity in the claims made everywhere by the Catholic Church.

The first difficulty in discussing Catholicism in the United States—or anywhere else, for that matter, except where there are very small minorities of Catholics living in societies almost wholly non-Catholic—is to be clear as to what one means by the term "Catholics."

It may be used of practising Catholics alone, and a practising Catholic may be defined as one who communicates not less frequently than once a year and presumably goes to Mass weekly. But that is a narrow definition; the Catholic body in any mixed society is wider than that. It includes, at least, nearly all those who have been baptized Catholics, or at any rate all those who have been instructed in their religion or been familiar with the practice of it by others during their childhood. It may include (and in my judgment should include, if one is discussing the effect of Catholicism on the whole of a society) even those who have had no instruction, perhaps not even baptism, but who have lived as part of a Catholic family, in a society mainly Catholic, and are in sympathy with the Catholic tone and traditions.

Between the widest of these limits and the narrowest there must be everywhere a very considerable margin. You see that margin at its widest in such a country as France, where the national atmosphere is traditionally Catholic, where there is widespread indifference, where, at the same time, a great number of specifically Catholic ideas are deeply rooted, and yet certain most active political organizations (such as the Masonic "Grand Orient") are violently opposed to the whole Catholic scheme and use all their energies to destroy it.

That is one end of the scale. At the other end of the scale you have a nation like the Poles in Poland itself. Excluding certain important minorities in the country, which certain minorities live within the geographical boundaries of Poland, but are not Polish, the Poles are a homogeneously Catholic people.

Now in this scale American Catholicism lies very far "to the right," that is, the proportion of the total Catholic community which is also practising and actively Catholic is exceedingly high. There is a good historical reason for this. The Catholic Church came into America from without. The original society of the United States was not only overwhelmingly Protestant, but overwhelmingly anti-Catholic. But the philosophers of the eighteenth century, to whom we owe the American Constitution, held it as a sort of dogma that no religious difference between citizens should affect their political status, and this very strong feeling, though it cannot be defended in strict reason, made the spread of an alien spirit possible.

The Catholic immigrants who poured into the United States during the nineteenth century, when economic expansion was clamoring for new workers, were at first mainly Irish; to these were later added Germans, Poles, Italians, and in certain parts of the country a small proportion of French Canadians. Both because they were foreigners by origin, and also because their religion was not that of the majority, still less that of the people who owned property and dominated social life, the discipline in the Catholic body had to be strict, or it would have been swamped. As it is, there has been a heavy, if unknown, proportion of leakage. There is certainly an element of leakage today, though estimates differ widely on its extent; but now the Catholic body as a whole throughout the United States is both held in strict discipline and highly organized. That is the first thing that strikes a foreigner in this country if he will be at the pains to study its real conditions.

The next thing to note about Catholicism in America is its urban quality. It has been pointed out in a recent study of American statistics that American society as a whole may be divided into three fairly equal zones. There is the agricultural body, including local populations up to, say, 2,500 souls. These are not exactly villages nor market towns, for these typical European institutions do not exist in America, but they are small agglomerations of shops and crafts and professional people standing in wide neighborhood to a farming population. The next zone above this, about equal in numbers, has been called "middle town." It includes all the small towns of from 2,500 to 3,000 population, and at the other end the larger towns of say 50,000. The third zone is the zone of the very large American towns. The population of each zone is about the same as each of the other two, each forming about one-third of the population.

Now the strength of Catholicism is in the large towns and it is at its weakest in agricultural America. This has some simple and highly defined political consequences. It gives the Catholic views more emphasis because it speaks in great numbers just in those centers where opinion and expression tell most. But at the same time it permits the opponents of the Catholic Church to challenge her on the ground of national tradition. The great cities are far more cosmopolitan than the countrysides. There are wide districts in the United States where the farmers and the professions depending upon them form the bulk of the population and where Catholics are absent or in very small number.

These things being so, we might say that while American Catholicism, if you looked at it statically, that is, if you looked at it here and now without taking into account its past and its future, comprises a powerful minority of the nation, certainly a fifth of the white population under the widest definition of Catholicism, and at least a sixth under the most strict definition, is also urban, and specially strong in the greatest cities. It is most active in the larger nerve centers of the nation. One could add to this that a very high sense of unity and cohesion had been given to the Catholic body, superior perhaps to any similar body in the world.

But nothing human can be looked at statically alone. We must consider any human phenomenon in the dimension of time as well, and I propose in a following article to consider how the development of this thing is shaping, or the probabilities of it, for no man can do more in estimating the future than consider the possibilities.

How does the future of Catholicism in America appear to be shaping? Let us look at the facts. Immigration, the constant source hitherto of Catholic increase, has been cut down from the wide torrential river which it was before the Great War to an insignificant trickle. Mere numerical increase of the Catholic body in the United States for the future can only come from either a higher birthrate or from conversion, or both.

As to a higher birth-rate, *a priori* one might expect this to be a considerable factor in Catholic increase; but only the future will show whether in point of fact the superior Catholic birth-rate will tell heavily. It must be remembered also that the very fact that the discipline and cohesion is so strict tends to make the indifferent or the discontented man alienate himself from his family tradition. Still, taking it all round, it is presumable that the mere numerical increase of Catholics will in the near future continue to be appreciable, from the religious insistence upon family life.

As to converts, so far the numbers are not there, any more than they are here, sufficient to be of great and immediate effect. But it is to be remembered that in America, even more than in Europe, and certainly more than in England, the rapid break-down of all other philosophies except the Catholic may make for a big movement towards Catholicism, not by individual conversions, but by mass conversions; it is a factor to be watched in the future. This applies, of course, not only to America but to the whole world. Probably within the lifetime of young men now under thirty, you will see the white world divided into Catholic and anti-Catholic, with the anti-Catholic known for his anti-Catholicism and not for any particular sect or proclaimed beliefs. It is difficult to imagine that in such a situation the tendency to conversions on a great scale can be checked. As it is, the Catholic Church is everywhere becoming the sole champion of certain parts of traditional morality which numbers of people who have never associated the idea with Catholicism desire to preserve. One has only to mention the private property of the small man, the authority of the family and the permanence of marriage to see the truth of this.

There is another factor, apart from the numerical factor, which may make for the expansion of Catholicism in the States during the next lifetime. That is the economic factor.

It is a sad thing to have to say it, for it is not flattering to human nature, but it is a truth, that the influence of wealth in every department of human effort, religion not excluded, is overwhelming. A body in which there are very few rich people is, number for number, hopelessly outweighed by a body in which there is a large proportion of rich people. Now in the old days the proportion of large fortunes among Catholics in the United States was very small. Even the proportion of moderate professional fortunes was small compared with the total number of Catholics. The reason was obvious. The old proprietors of the soil and the old commercial fortunes had been founded under conditions almost entirely non-Catholic. Indeed, America was the only great white country the past of which contained no Catholic memories to speak of. But the immigrant, especially the Irishman, enriched himself as time went on, Catholics appeared more and more among the successful in the great professions and, perhaps, to a lesser degree in commerce.

Today, comparing one's experience with that of the first days in which I knew America, nearly fifty years ago, the increased weight of Catholic wealth, not only collectively but in the shape of private fortunes, is very striking. If one could strike a curve, as one can in some simple social matters, one might predict with firm confidence a steadily increasing influence for America in numbers and in social force generally, until with the absence of any other positive philosophy to oppose her the Church there might triumph.

But there is a powerful consideration on the other side to make us pause before we come to such a conclusion.

The American national tradition as a whole is opposed to

the Catholic culture. No matter how much the doctrinal force of the original American Protestantism decays the old feeling that Catholicism is alien survives, in spite of that decay.

The feeling is not at all like the feeling here in England, where the whole of the national history since the Cecils led the great social revolution three and one half centuries ago, treats Catholicism not only as something foreign but as something hostile. All our official teaching in school and college, our fiction, our press, is full of that conception. Our national heroes are the anti-Catholic figures, and the chief Catholic figures in European history during the last three hundred years stand out as the enemies of England. There is nothing of that in the United States, but there are a number of deeply rooted national traditions which appear strongly in local feeling, connecting the American spirit with non-Catholic or anti-Catholic ideas.

A very good example of the way in which the traditional idea and the actual modern circumstances clash is to be found in the city of Boston. What the exact figures are I do not know and, perhaps, they are not obtainable. But it is evident to any traveler who keeps his eyes open that the proportion of Catholics in Boston and its outliers is very high. At a guess I should say it was a considerable majority, and remember that the Catholic population there as everywhere in America holds together. But when you say "Boston" or "Boston spirit" nothing of this appears. To hear men speak, especially men who are active in the town and who are proud of it, one might imagine Boston to be a mainly Unitarian city, or at any rate one wholly colored by a non-Catholic and even anti-Catholic inheritance.

The proportion of all these factors differs from one great center to another. But everywhere in the great American cities, especially of the North, there is something of the same situation: the Church very strong financially and numerically, and still somewhat increasing, perhaps about to increase rapidly in a new generation; but tradition, national and local, still attached to the old days before Catholics were either wealthy or numerous.

15

≫≫≪≪

Padraic Colum

1927

from *"America Today and Tomorrow"*

≫≫≪≪

Padraic Colum, Irish dramatist and lyric poet, was one of the leaders of the Irish literary renaissance. His name will forever be associated with those other Irish literary giants, Yeats, Lady Gregory and A. E., with whom he was associated in the Irish National Theatre, as well as with James Joyce, a lifetime friend. Both Padraic Colum and his wife visited the United States frequently and at length. The following comments are part of a book review which appeared in *Studies XVI* (Sept., 1927) and are reprinted by permission of the Editor of *Studies* (Dublin). Mr. Colum was commenting on a book by André Siegfried, whose views on American Catholicism are also to be found in this collection.

≫≫≪≪

An enormous quota of immigrants lose touch with the Church from the moment of their landing in America. I remember a group of Czechoslovak families whose case, I think, must be typical: they live not thirty miles from Saint Patrick's Cathedral, and the younger members of the families have not, I think, seen the face of a priest for years. These people are farmers and rural labourers in a district where the Catholic place of worship is at some distance: the older people make an effort to go to Mass at Christmas and Easter, but never think of trying to go at any other time. The children went to the local schools, which are, of course, secular with the normal Calvinistic tendency. They attended

Protestant Sunday Schools. They will probably get married in Registry offices, and the young men will be drawn into the Masonic Lodge. When this sort of happening is in New York State, one can imagine what losses there are in States west of the Mississippi, in Oregon and Washington. Many of the Kleagles and Grand Dragons of the Ku Klux Klan have Irish names.

Disintegration goes on at both levels of the Catholic community. There are Catholics in society, but there is no Catholic society in America. 'One has to be very rich to get away with being a Catholic in this country,' a clever observer of American society once remarked to me, meaning by that that a millionaire could afford to go to Mass with the servants, but anyone out of the millionaire class who had some social pretensions could hardly afford to do it. In America the Church is not looked upon as native, and the Catholic groups except in a few places—Baltimore and New Orleans, for instance—have no social prestige. The people whose convictions are not deep go the way their neighbours are going. The people whose convictions are deep are troubled all the time by this social pressure. 'Where can my sons just out of the university meet Catholic girls of good family and education?' 'Where can my girls now out of college meet Catholic young men whose people are like the people we know?' Catholic people who are wellplaced and important are always asking these questions. They know that at any gathering their sons and daughters will meet one Catholic amongst a hundred non-Catholics.

On the other hand, among thoughtful people in America, there is a growing interest in Catholic personalities, Catholic faith and Catholic philosophy. To certain of the intellectuals who have been thwarted by Calvinism and bored by Pragmatism, Catholicism exhibits a norm that is both rich and human. It is significant that in that remarkable satire upon the predatory Puritanism of the American village community, *The Spoon River Anthology,* one of the few characters who are looked upon as having any illumination in their lives is the priest, Father Molloy. The best known of the American publicists, Walter

Lippman, has recently published an essay praising the Catholic idea of the state. It is true that the most powerful opposition to the candidature of Governor Smith for the presidency is due to the fact that he is a Catholic. But it is also true that the fact that he is a Catholic gives warmth and colour to the conception of the man held by thousands of people outside the Church and outside Governor Smith's own party.

And Catholicism in America could improve its position by appealing more and more to an elite in America. To do that it would have to create within itself an intellectual elite. At present it is true that in the United States Catholics do not pull their weight intellectually: amongst them there is no group of artists, critics, philosophers, and scientists who have the prestige or anything like the prestige of Catholic groups in France or Germany. Catholicism in America, it can be said, has had to struggle to maintain and organize itself. But that struggle has ceased to be a difficult one, and the time has come when a more vigorous intellectual life, a more sound cultivation should show itself in Catholicism in America.

Writing in an Irish publication one can be frank about the Irish influence upon the Church in America. If the Irish did not establish the Church in the United States, they certainly have kept it alive there. But our people, coming from a country in which the intellectual and artistic tradition of Catholicism had been broken, did not attempt to re-create these things in the United States—they had the faith, and that they deemed, was sufficient. Had Catholic leadership in the United States been in the hands of the French or the Germans the churches, no doubt, would look better, and the organs of opinion would have more regard for tradition and ideas. The Irish leadership has not endowed the Church intellectually or artistically. But no matter for that! There can be but few Catholics in America who want to do anything else but bless the fact that the Church there has had an Irish leadership. That leadership has been democratic and expansive, and it has helped to form a church that is really of the people.

16

-->>><<<--

Robert Francis Wilberforce

1931

from *"The Church in America: An English View"*

-->>><<<--

Robert Francis Wilberforce, English diplomat, barrister and man of
letters, studied life in America thoroughly before he wrote about it.
He was a member of the British Delegation to the Washington
Conference of 1922 and served two extended tours with the British
Information Services in New York, as director of the British Library
of Information and as Cultural Officer. A Catholic, Mr. Wilberforce
also served the British Foreign Office at the Vatican. His comments
on the Church in the United States, first published in *The Catholic
Survey* of London, appeared in this country in *The Catholic Mind*.
They are reprinted with permission from *America*, The National
Catholic Weekly Review.

-->>><<<--

One of the difficulties in approaching the United States from
any angle is that one is dealing with a continent and a country
at the same time. Politically we are dealing with a country, and
a country which since the second part of the 19th century, that
is to say, since the Civil War, has shown a growing tendency
towards centralization. Politically it is preeminently a nation,
and probably the most powerful nation in existence today, for
the British Empire, continuing that decentralizing process, inherent in its very nature and arising largely from geographical
necessity, has become a loosely bound system of states with vary-
ing views on foreign policy. Thus the United States has in this
century definitely taken the place occupied by the British Empire

in the 19th as the most powerful sovereign state. I say most powerful and not the greatest, as views of greatness will differ and each will apply his own standards. But so far as the position of nations can be judged by such criteria as population, natural wealth and, above all, the potential power which a nation possesses, to impose its will upon the world, by such criteria as these, the United States must be counted the most powerful nation of the present day.

The paradox, however, is that national as it is politically and in its sentiment towards the world, nevertheless its immensely diverse population and its enormous variety of languages, the huge influx of races from Continental Europe, from Russia, and to a less extent from Asia, gives it a social complexity in striking contrast to its political unity. Literally millions of immigrants have entered the United States since the beginning of the 19th century, with results which have been duly noted by almost as many observers who have from time to time published their impressions of the country. But perhaps the most amazing result of all has passed unnoticed. It is that, in spite of these formidable invasions, the original English-speaking stock America, threatened time and again by successive waves of foreigners, has none the less maintained its political supremacy and imposed its language, laws and culture upon millions whose background and racial origin are wholly alien. So much so, that even one generation is enough to turn a Scot from Aberdeen, and Russian Mujik, a Neapolitan peasant, a Swedish farmer, a Dutch business man and last, but not least, a German professor into something which, without attempting to analyze it too closely, we yet can never fail to recognize as an American citizen. Can history afford any parallel to so rapid a process of naturalization? It would be difficult to find one. But stranger still this transmutation is effected with as little apparent effort or consciousness as Nature herself displays in changing the color of certain animals to meet their environment.

And here the question may be asked what has all this to do with the Church in America. It has this to do with it, that to understand the problem and the character of the Church in America we must bear in mind the considerations just set forth.

The irresistible, even if unconscious, influences which have moulded successive racial groups into the American model were not exercised without the ruthless destruction of those foreign characteristics with which they arrived in the country. The ruling classes in America, it must be remembered, until the middle of last century, were almost entirely English and Protestant. English by race, law, and custom. Protestant in religion and outlook. The interesting Catholic settlement of Lord Baltimore in Maryland was a conspicuous exception. But, generally speaking, throughout the Northern and Southern States, when the Americans separated themselves politically from Great Britain at the end of the 18th century, they retained intact their English inheritance in law, custom and religion. Thus, when immigrants with a culture intensely Catholic, say a Bavarian or Italian, arrived on the shores of the United States, they found themselves thrust into an environment where, not only their language and civilization were regarded as something bizarre by the general public but, much more serious, where it was taken for granted that their religion was absurd and superstitious. Isolated by the necessity of obtaining employment here, there, and everywhere, very soon scattered and removed far from the possibility of attending Mass or of practising their religion; unable to organize for the defence of the Faith; handicapped by ignorance of the new language, these unfortunate people in large numbers must either have lost the Faith themselves or failed to hand it on to the next generation. For so great is the power of environment on the isolated individual and so strong is his fear of ridicule when called upon to support alone a strange custom in opposition to the group in which he lives that, humanly speaking, the earlier

Catholic immigrants, who arrived in small groups, would undoubtedly have been divested of their religion in the same way as they lost their former national characteristics. And there is evidence to show that this indeed happened. The process consisted in the reiteration of the statement that there was something alien to American culture in the Catholic religion. This belief was spread and accepted with such persistency that there exists, even today in some American circles where prejudice obscures judgment, a survival of this strange fiction, namely, that it is impossible to be at one and the same time a true Catholic and a true American. One can easily imagine with what effect this was brought to bear upon the immigrant aspiring to American citizenship, and how strong the character of those must have been who successfully resisted it. In a word the forces against the Catholic immigrant up to the middle of the 19th century were overwhelming and, humanly speaking, as has just been said, the majority must have become Protestant Americans and the Church in America would consequently be today only a small and inconspicuous body. How comes it then that on the contrary it is today the most influential and most flourishing religious community in the country? The answer, of course, is that the ways of God are inscrutable. But one can trace to some extent the instruments which He uses. In this case it was the arrival of the Irish which saved the situation. The enormous Irish immigration to America since the middle of last century is a very interesting chapter in American history. Though immigration from European countries had continued since the beginning of that century and earlier, it was only in small numbers that the previous immigrants had arrived. The arrival of the Irish after the middle of the 19th century was the first example of mass immigration. With unbelievable rapidity and thoroughness the Irish immigrants and their offspring proceeded to organize the Church in America. They encountered the same disintegrating forces, which immigrants from other nations had met. But they had two advantages. Unlike immigrants from Continental Europe they had not the obstacle of language to overcome; and, still more important, their number gave them a strength and cohesion which was of inestimable value.

With a tenacity not to be excelled, and with that pugnacity which is one of their special characteristics, the Irish fought their way forward over unbelievable obstacles and prejudices and succeeded in a surprisingly short time not only in identifying themselves with America, but also carrying with them, as they went, the Catholic religion, which they planted triumphantly in the very heart of American life.

When, therefore, other racial groups arrived in America in larger and larger numbers they, unlike earlier immigrants, found the Church already firmly established in the country. That in the circumstances was of incalculable value, and it is a debt which the Catholic Church, not only in America, but throughout the world, will always owe to the Irish race.

The Church in America is often criticized for being too highly organized, but it must be remembered that without organization Catholics would have been lost. Organization, which is today of secondary importance, was not so very long ago and, in some parts of America is still today, an essential of their very existence. This may be the reason why American Catholics are so much more inclined than we are in England to act in groups.

It is a familiar sight in the Cathedral of New York and everywhere to see the police and other public officials corporately attending Mass and receiving Holy Communion. The spirit of community action seems to be natural and to be aroused with the minimum of effort. It is often an inspiring spectacle, when, for instance, the Eucharistic Congress was held in Chicago, to see the number of organized societies and groups which participated.

This article might easily have been devoted exclusively to a discussion of Church organization in America. Striking figures could be marshalled illustrating the size and importance of the dioceses: the Catholic population, the number of schools, colleges and religious institutions, the large circulation of the numerous Catholic reviews and periodicals; the work of the National Catholic Welfare Conference and its many committees. But these are matters on which information can be obtained in any reference book, or certainly in the *American Catholic Directory*.

There are today over 100 Archbishops and Bishops governing the Church in America, and some of the dioceses cover an area larger than that of France and Germany combined. Other dioceses, chiefly comprising the urban populations of the Eastern Seaboard, though smaller in extent have so large a membership that their importance almost equals the Metropolitan Sees of Paris, Warsaw and other Catholic capitals. The Archbishops of four of the chief American cities have been created Cardinals, thus indicating the importance which the Holy See attaches to the Archdioceses of New York, Boston, Philadelphia and Chicago.

Finally, the latest census reveals a Catholic population of over 20,000,000, whilst the number of religious houses continues to increase in proportion to the Catholic population. It is also a matter of record that over 39,000 Americans were received into the Church last year. But the statistics of the Church's organization and growth in any part of the world, however imposing they may be, are merely a picture of the framework for the inner spiritual life—the only true measure of strength. One can gauge this in America no more than in other countries. Much, however, can be surmised from what is seen. One is struck by the devotion at Daily Mass in the various churches throughout the country. One is astonished to see the number of clerks and office workers daily receiving Holy Communion at the midday Mass in the Cathedral of New York. It is significant that there is a growing attendance at various retreat houses. The number of vocations to the secular clergy and religious orders for men and women is very large. Such things as these, though they touch perhaps only a small part of the Catholic body, are indications of a deep spiritual life. There are, of course, obvious dangers, which threaten the Church in America as there are elsewhere. Perhaps one is its very prosperity. But that is tempered greatly by the fact that this prosperity is by no means uniform. There is no diocese in America which is not constantly reminded of that fact. At one point the Church is strong and wealthy, so strong and firmly rooted that one has the impression of living in a Catholic country. A day's journey takes one to a state with churches sparsely scattered through immense areas, very few priests, and many of them living in great poverty. In short, you find yourself in an essentially missionary country. This is a contrast which is often disregarded in speaking of the prosperity of the Church in America. Moreover, there is the complexity of rites—communities living in various parts of the country under the central jurisdiction of their own bishop. Again, there is the unimaginably difficult negro question, which is now pressing with greater and greater urgency on the Catholic Church.

I shall not touch upon the many problems in the intellectual field which confront American Catholics. They are the same which we have to meet in England. But, speaking with all the diffidence which one should feel in criticizing a foreign country, it seems to me that the great majority of American Catholics are only just beginning to realize the intellectual problems with which we are beset today. At the beginning of this article it was observed that America had now become the most powerful nation in the world. That position is reflected, so far as American Catholics are concerned, in the position which they occupy vis-à-vis their fellow Catholics throughout the English-speaking world, where their numbers and influence have given them at least a temporary leadership. One has only to compare the relative position of English and American Catholics in Rome today and twenty years ago to realize the significance of this remark.

It is a position of immense responsibility calling for a broad international outlook. It can only be adequately fulfilled if a larger number of American Catholics accustom themselves to take a keener intellectual interest in the affairs of the Church. I do not mean to imply that the intellectual is in any sense on a par with the spiritual life. An intellectually alert Catholic body is not necessary to religion, but it is a very useful attribute, particularly in the present age. There are many interesting study movements in social, economic and international affairs developed through the National Catholic Welfare Conference. But, generally speaking, I have gained the impression that the Church in America is still parochial in character and outlook. When one considers the intellectual activities of Catholics in England, and when one reflects that we in England number scarcely as many as the Catholics of New York, one realizes what a vast opportunity American Catholics have in that direction.

I would not, however, end this article on a note of criticism. I should like to end with the statement of my belief that in a comparatively short time, owing to the steady increase of Catholics in the British Empire and the United States, the English-speaking element in the Church will be the strongest in numbers and influence. Many close ties at present unite the English-speaking world, but the strongest of all will then be added in the unity of faith held by the majority of each country, a unity which we shall feel all the more strongly if, as it seems more than probable, we shall have to exercise it for the protection of the Church's rights in other parts of the world. Before this century ends it may see the English-speaking Catholics occupying that preponderant numerical position which for so many centuries has been held by the Latin races. May we in that case offer as great a spiritual contribution to the Church as they have in the past! There could be no nobler ambition than that.

17

❧❧❧

Robert Speaight

1938

from *"America Today"*

❧❧❧

Since the days of Shakespeare, actors who were also favored with literary talent have been few. Robert Speaight is a distinguished English actor, a teacher, a critic and a novelist. Educated at Oxford, Mr. Speaight first achieved fame in a drama of World War I, *Journey's End.* He played leading roles at the Old Vic and acted in many Shakespearian productions, including the title role in *Hamlet.* His greatest triumph, however, was in the role of Becket in T. S. Eliot's *Murder in the Cathedral,* which he played for more than 800 performances both in England and the United States. His reflections on "America Today" were written for *The Tablet* on his return to England from touring in this play. He has been a frequent visitor to America and has taught Modern Poetry and English Literature at the University of Notre Dame. He became a convert to Catholicism in 1930.

❧❧❧

There are three possible attitudes for a man to adopt who is visiting America for the first time—simplicity, superiority, or sophistication. The first of these is silly, the second is impertinent, but the third is essential. For the truly sophisticated man is the man with a sense of tradition, and without this sense, you will merely stumble through America. You will see neither the excellences nor the jokes.

Boston, for instance, is reputed to be "English" in character.

"There is Berkeley Square, and Grosvenor Square, and Louisburgh Square," your old-time Bostonian will proudly boast; and certainly the architecture of Queen Anne is a link between Beacon Hill and Queen Anne's Gate. There are Bostonians whose pedigrees can match it; I have sat in a room with seventy or eighty odd Bostonians whose every suit had been evidently tailored in Savile Row; I lunched with a distinguished historian at Harvard and found that we had a close mutual acquaintance in the hallporter of a certain hotel in Mayfair of an overwhelmingly conservative character; I looked out every morning on to the famous "Common" ringed by the statues of "worthies" whose military, humanitarian and sculptural virtues would have graced a London park, and one of whom bore an ominous resemblance to Mr. Gladstone. But, for all this, Boston, which is regional— I dare not say provincial—in character, seemed to me more American than New York, where the cosmopolitan luxuries were already familiar, and where the Statue of Liberty mounts guard over the Metropolis of money.

Boston, they will tell you, is a Catholic city. It has a Cathedral and a Cardinal and a lot of Irish. The Cardinal was away, but then American Cardinals are always going away; the Cathedral I, shamefully, never discovered; and of the Irish I caught no glimpse and heard no accent. Boston, they will also tell you, is a Puritan city. This is apparent in its culture—and a very great culture it has been, though I should hesitate to ask the Pilgrim Fathers what they thought of Mr. T. S. Eliot or Mr. Henry James. But if Mr. Eliot is your passion in modern poetry, and Henry James is your passion in modern fiction, there is a great deal to enlighten and to amuse you in Boston. Both have trodden, in themselves and their ancestry, one of the great trade routes of literature—from Plymouth to Massachusetts, and from Massachusetts to Paris or Florence. It does not matter which, for once you have crossed the Atlantic, the unity of Europe is a greater reality than the United States of America—even though Europe may be at war and America be at peace within itself. But Boston is tenacious of its past. A Unitarian lady, in persuading me to visit the King's Chapel, told me that they still used the Book of Common Prayer and retained everything in it—except the Trinity!

But these are the conservative rather than the traditional things of Boston. For genuine tradition you must consult, as always, the poor. Go down to the Italian quarter and consider the wedding cakes in the confectioners' windows. You will pass many treasured and traditional things on the way, including the Old State House, but nothing so truly traditional as these. They are there for sale, but not for show; and for the satisfaction of a European sense. Here, mounted on tier upon tier of dazzling confectionery, are brides and bridegrooms plighting their troth, framed in the baroque portal of a church; leaving for their honeymoons in aeroplanes or motor-cars; receiving the benediction of a priest; dressed in all the ridiculous regalia of their nuptial pomp. They proclaim, in their own extravagantly operatic way, the domestic assurances round which European civilization has been built and which America has neglected at her peril.

Before leaving Boston, I was asked, in an interview on the radio, what had impressed me most during my stay in the city; and I replied that these wedding cakes would be my dearest and most abiding memory. And, indeed, now that I am in England, they serve as a text on which to hang the speculations, which are the result of one's interest and one's ignorance alike. Which way is America going? How far is Catholicism likely to modify the general trend? Considering the vast influx of Catholic immigrants from Ireland, Italy and Poland, one is certainly surprised how little stamp they have left on the visible culture of the continent. The American tradition, at any rate in the north and west, is wholly Protestant and Puritan. This is seen in a dozen ways. In the ascendancy of commerce, in the contempt for wine, in the puerile business of "publicity," in the absence of architecture, in the sentimentalizing, and, therefore, the ruin of marriage, in the traffic of ideals. You will search through the best journals of New York without finding the least insight into the nature of the Spanish struggle. The evident truth is that in Spain two ways of life, and, therefore, two philosophies, are irreconcilably opposed to one another, is everywhere unperceived, because urban America has no knowledge of that culture—historical, rural and military—which the Nationalist movement is trying to preserve. A Christianity of the catacombs is quite intelligible to the modern, idealistic America; what he cannot understand is the Christian culture of the Mediterranean with its moral laxities and mental laziness contradicting its heroisms and holiness and historical pride. He cannot grasp the presence of Christianity to concrete cultural forms.

It is not difficult to point to the birth-rate and say that the materialist America of the Puritan inheritance will die by a slow process of suicide. But the energy of the spirit may enter it again by ways as cruelly apocalyptic as the Pilgrim Fathers and breed a reaction just as fierce in its irreligion and just as ignorant in its ideals. I am quite sure that American culture can only be saved by Catholicism, but I would put no limit to the strange gods which will bring America to its knees. There is a sense in which the chief peril of a Protestant country is an excess of religious feeling in an absence of religious faith. America, like so much of England, prefers Democracy to God. Even American Liberals, of high intelligence, like Dorothy Thompson, are beginning to see Red. When you have churches and pastures and the souls of your children to fight for, like the Spanish Nationalists, you know, at least, where you are. But Democracy is a delusive, and in the big modern commercial State, a quite meaningless abstraction.

No, the true American conversion will come by way of the wine on the table and the wedding cakes in the windows, more than by the missioner in the pulpit and the feature journalist in the press. It is only the sacramental view of life, of which the wedding cakes and wine are symbols, which will conquer the materialism and the money. There are many rich houses in America which will drug you with cocktails before you dine, and leave you thirsty during your dinner; and there are many poor presbyteries where you will always find wine on the table. These are small matters, but still they are symptomatic. For, just as the consideration of wedding cakes leads one to the consideration of weddings, so the consideration of wine leads one on to the vineyard and to that high, simple civilization of which the vine is the crowning glory, and onward again to that religion of which it is the Sacrament and to that Person of which it was the simile.

What I found attractive in America, apart from what amused or excited me, was the leaven of Catholicism in the American people, bringing their humour and friendliness and sincerity to a graceful fruition. I hope I shall not be misunderstood when I say that I saw it as a civilizing, even more than as a spiritualizing force—though, indeed, you cannot separate the two. To come out of the world of the theatre, and visit a great Catholic University for men, like Fordham or Notre Dame, or a great Catholic college for girls, like St. Mary's, or Rosary, or Mundelein—the skyscraper on the shores of Lake Michigan—is to meet a new America. It is, I believe, the America of the future, and it is not without significance that some of its ideas have percolated to the White House. In these academies you will find efficiency without hustle, friendliness without familiarity, culture without pedantry, spirituality without pietism. You will find an America remembering its European roots and untouched by European decadence. You will find a Catholicism shaking hands a little more easily with the present day than the Catholicism of England and France. And you will discern a fascinating paradox. The principles of equality and justice, of human dignity and freedom, which animated the Republican Fathers, are today only guaranteed by that philosophy which they, in their invincible ignorance, rejected, by those dogmas which they despised. Where, one asks, would Jefferson stand today? Would he be able to separate the shibboleth from the reality? Would he have the lucidity to recognize the transcendental reasons why he had been so triumphantly in the right? It is a provocative question. But that lucidity, which is no small part of spiritual illumination, is the great and necessary gift of American Catholics to their country, for without it the "American dream" will remain like a receding horizon in the minds of the American people.

18

>»)«<

H.-J. Duteil

1947

from *The Great American Parade*

>»)«<

One of the most prominent and outspoken lay-Catholic leaders of France, and a frequent contributor to Catholic journals of that country, H.-J. Duteil set forth the following bitterly critical impression of the Church in the United States in his book *The Great American Parade*—a run-away best seller in France. The present selection is from the English edition, *The Great American Parade,* translated by historian Fletcher Pratt (© Twayne Publishers, Inc.). Used by permission of Twayne Publishers, Inc.

>»)«<

The American Catholic Church is more disciplined than the Protestant Churches but its clergy has placed no greater emphasis on mysticism and humility. The poor country priest of France and Italy, with his worn soutane who, after a day of apostleship, catechisms, and visits to the dying, goes back to his humble peasant residence in his worn sandals, where his only luxury is a "curé's garden," a few dahlias and some bees; this man of God, this secular Franciscan, of whom even unbelievers say, "He is a good man!" does not exist, and cannot exist in the United States.

The choice between humility and comfort must be made; the American Catholic clergy has opted for gold-rimmed spectacles— the number of American Catholic priests wearing gold-rimmed spectacles is unimaginable—arrogance, ecclesiastical pride and well-pressed clothes, beer parties and bingo games in the churches.

Well, then, no holy men and for that matter, no saints—although the United States does have one saint, Mother Cabrini, recently canonized.

It would seem that the first duty of an American Catholic is a blind veneration of the clergy. Like the Italian peasant who doubts whether the Virgin Mary or Jesus Christ himself is as powerful as his local saint, the American Catholic believes in the infallibility of his parish priest; he is certainly a greater man than St. Thomas, St. Jerome or St. Augustine. For that matter, the names of these three saints are unknown to the greater number of Catholics in the New World; they are particularly aware of Notre Dame de Lourdes because of the Hollywood film about Bernadette Soubirous.

American Catholic literature is insignificant. It hardly rises above the level of patronage. The great French Catholic writers who have maintained Catholic thought in literature for sixty years, the Barbey d'Aurevillys, the Bloys, the Huysmans, the Verlaines, the Péguys, the Jammes, even the Bernanos would exclaim with indignation over the average American Catholic; he is habituated only to authoritarian stupidities.

The Protestants would also be horrified by such writers. Only American intellectuals knowing the exterior world and practising Jews could comprehend them.

The Catholic mass in the United States is principally made up of the Irish, who jealously control all church offices and bar the avenues of ecclesiastical power to the poor Poles and Slovaks, the Hungarians, Italians, the miserable Portuguese of the New England fisheries, many Germans and finally the French-American group. Thanks to some of the Franco-Americans, Irish, Italians and Germans, the American Catholic church is very rich, although for many Protestants, Catholicism is a mark of low birth. "When you are visiting my family," said a rich Bostonian to his French wife, "I wish you wouldn't go to the Catholic Church, because only servants go there!"

We repeat: No holy men and no saints. Nevertheless, every

year on Shrove Tuesday a considerable crowd invades the Church of the Holy Redeemer in New York. A little before the war the number of visitors reached 7,000. This crowd gathered to give its homage to a saint. That is, he had not yet been canonized, but they all hoped he would be. From time to time someone murmured: "Where is the figure of the martyred cop?" There is a statue of a man prone, as though he had been wounded. It is actually a statue of St. Datien, but thousands of New Yorkers are convinced that they filed past the real image of a policeman named Frederick Smith, who was killed in this church at midnight on October 26, 1897, by bandits who were robbing the poorbox. In justice to the Redemptorist Fathers, to whom this church belongs, they have tried to restore the truth, but without success; the number of devotees for the "martyred policeman" seems to be on the rise.

But come, not the slightest evidence of sanctity? To fill this gap, there was fortunately a nine year old boy of the Bronx. He was playing in an empty lot next door, among sordid houses of dirty brick, when the Virgin Mary appeared to him. This is the account the boy gave to the *Bronx Home News* at the beginning of November, 1945: "I saw the Virgin Mary with long blond hair and a kind of light around her. She wore a blue dress which turned to pink and stood behind a golden table and four chairs." The young lad, who had recently seen the film about Bernadette Soubirous, added that his vision was altogether different than that in the movie. Following this event, the crowd estimated by the police at 25,000 people, marched past an altar built among the brickbats by the boy and his little friends. These 25,000 people passed, one by one, to touch with their hands the little boy, sitting in his chair like a saint in a niche. Asked what he wanted, he replied, "Vanilla ice cream"; it was given to him. Hardly an ecclesiastic sense of values.

The power of the Catholic Church in the United States is considerable, especially in certain municipalities. Nevertheless it does not seem that the Catholics—or the Protestants either—had the slightest influence on American policy during the recent conflict. No protest prevented the total and perfectly useless destruction of the monastery at Monte Cassino by the American forces, the monastery which was one of the holiest places of Christianity. The only bombs that fell on Rome were American bombs; a fact which provoked the vigorous but ineffectual protest of Monsignor Joseph P. Hurley, Bishop of St. Augustine in Florida: "The news of the bombing of Rome—by our own soldiers—has pained me beyond expression. Every decent Christian thought and sentiment within me cries out that we have made a tragically mistaken decision in the higher moral strategy of this just war. . . . Let Washington not be deceived by the obscene chorus of approval which is registered in the regimented press."

But while Washington is listening politely to Cardinals, Bishops, magistrates, professors, philosophers, presidents of associations and virtuous women, Washington is paying no attention to what they say. They are very sympathetic and respectable people, but abstract and without pragmatic value. The words and threats which influence Washington are those of people whose ideas can have repercussions on the material level — military commanders, industrialists, practical scientists, technicians, union bosses and so on.

It seems that Stalin quoted Napoleon to Winston Churchill, when he said that the Pope would not be happy about some Allied decision, "And how many divisions does the Pope have available?" Without saying it, Washington thinks along the same lines as Stalin.

Sometimes there are dissensions among the laity of the Catholic Church, which is much more jealous of its independence than the Protestant Church. Such was the case when Mayor LaGuardia of New York decided to supress bingo games in the churches. Since the authorities had stopped such games run by private citizens, the Catholic churches benefitted by a new influx of people. It was not rare to see a big banner across the front of a church, saying "BINGO TONIGHT." The game took place in one of the attached rooms, the catechism chapel, the sacristy or basement, and it usually lasted from 8 to 11 in the evening. The play was often rather high. An ecclesiastic presided, and the church took a dime out of every pot. Most of the players were women.

When the mayor launched his prohibition, saying this was the law and it would be enforced, he told the newspaper men that he rested his case on the Bible, the Gospel according to St. Matthew, Chapter V, verses 17 & 18: "Think not that I am come to destroy but to fulfill. For verily I say unto you, till Heaven and Earth pass, one jot or one tittle shall in no wise pass from the law, till all be fulfilled."

The *New York World Telegram* of December 4, 1942 says that when it inquired of eight Catholic Churches in Brooklyn whether the bingo games should continue, it was answered in the affirmative, and it was added that no prohibition had come from the diocesan authority. The diocesan chancellery said that it had no declaration to make regarding bingo. The civil authorities ultimately triumphed. But what a row! Thousands of letters for and against came to the newspapers. Here are a couple of characteristic ones:

Bronx: Do you realize, my dear Mr. Mayor, what will happen if you stop church bingo games in New York City? You will deprive churches and charities of much of their maintenance; you will put many people back on relief, and you will cut into sales of War Bonds and Stamps. And how do you think the people of New York will feel if you take one of their chief pleasures away from them?

(Signed) M.S.

But here is another point of view:

Brooklyn: Kindly, Mr. Mayor, pin a medal on any cop who has the courage to put a stop to a professional racket named bingo. I am one of many married men who, since you began suppressing bingo, is beginning to enjoy home life again. My children are getting more attention, and I am getting my meals on time, and many thanks to your gallant coppers.

Family Man

19

>>>×<<<

John Epstein

1947

from *"The Church in the United States"*

>>>×<<<

Diplomat, author and holder of a distinguished World War I
military record, John Charles Epstein served as Britain's Assistant
Secretary to the League of Nations 1928–1938, and was Director of
the British Society for International Understanding in 1939. A
convert to Catholicism, he was received into the Church in 1919.
The journey through the United States which he used as the basis
of the following commentary took place in 1947. This article appears
by courtesy of *The Tablet,* of London.

>>>×<<<

At the invitation of the editors of the Catholic weekly *America,* I recently had the good fortune to spend two months in
travelling through the U. S. from coast to coast. To one accustomed to the small scale of Catholic life in England and, on the
other hand, to the homogeneity of the Catholic body in most
European countries, it takes time to sense the realities of the
Church's life in America. The first impression is of size. In
almost any town there appears, at short notice, an audience of
1,000 to 2,000 Catholics to hear a comparatively unknown Englishman lecture. The average church is, by our standards, large;
on Sundays packed, and with more than the sprinkling faithful
at the weekday Masses to which we are accustomed. On the
outskirts of any large town there seems to be one if not two

colleges, each of 500 to 700 serious young ladies studying for degrees with the aid of nuns, priests and, generally, a lay faculty. The Catholic men's universities and colleges, ranging from 500 to 10,000 undergraduates each, are even more impressive.

Almost everywhere the Church seems to be growing rapidly. At Syracuse, N. Y., I was confronted with a large, eager audience, half men, though the Catholic Women's league had organized the meeting, who rose like a bird to a quotation from Chesterton's *Lepanto* and peppered me with questions about Eastern Europe and Spain; no one had succeeded in pulling wool over *their* eyes. There I learned that a new college for men, Des Moines College, was in process of formation by the Society of Jesus. They had not waited for buildings, but already had about 300 young men, mostly veterans, attending lectures in hired halls, and, presumably, sleeping wherever they could. In Southern California, the Catholic population has risen in 20 years to half a million from a fifth of that number; and all the churches, colleges, houses of retreat, and seminaries which one sees, but for the few lovely old yellow mission buildings of Spanish days, seem brand new. In Salt Lake City, the Mormon Vatican, the Catholic cathedral, boldly put up in prominent position 30 years ago by the enterprising bishop with a flock of barely 4,000 to his crook, is now the center of a diocese of 20,000. Here I spoke to a meeting of the Converts' League at the invitation of the wise and eloquent Bishop Hunt, himself a convert.

To reduce these impressions of size, vitality, and expansion to figures: there are 150 dioceses, grouped in 21 ecclesiastical provinces, with a Catholic population of 24 million, at a conservative estimate, and 38,000 priests. Despite the free state education, nearly 8,000 Catholic parishes maintain their own nun-staffed elementary schools, where the fees are either very low, and scaled to encourage large families, or nonexistent, cost being met by the parish. There are between 1,500 and 1,600 Catholic high schools, 131 universities and university colleges for men, and 638 such colleges for girls.

I had the privilege of visiting a good many of them. The men's colleges, like all institutions of university standard in the U. S., are filled to bursting with ex-servicemen, profiting from the GI Bill of Rights to study for degrees at the expense (mostly) of the nation. There are 153,809 Catholic undergraduates now instead of 91,444 in 1939–40. They even overflow into girls' colleges. At Seton Hill, Greensburg, Pa., I found 50 war veterans studying with 500 girls. The nuns thought it an excellent idea; so, no doubt, do the veterans. At Georgetown, the oldest Catholic University, with its charming quadrangle and colonial pump house, I found three undergraduates sleeping in a room meant for one. The same problem of accommodation is acute everywhere: at many places army huts have been fitted as dormitories. Fordham, at New York, now has a student population of 8,150. De Paul university, Chicago, is largest, with 11,506. Notre Dame, of football fame (the football team is called "the Irish" in the sport news, but largely consists of Poles) has 4,500. As I walked through St. Louis to my evening lecture, the windows in the many-storied university buildings were ablaze with light; for here lectures in several of the schools are given on the shift system, morning, afternoon, and evening; it is impossible to accommodate more than a fraction of the students taking a particular subject in any one hall. Here the student population has almost doubled; 9,000 against 3,830 before the war. St. Louis, Mo., is "the Rome of the West," with 700,000 Catholics out of a population of a million. Its Catholic university straddles the center of the town; the college church stands at the center crossroads and seems to be full of people going to confession at all hours of the day.

As to the quality of Catholic life, and especially of higher education, I found much humility, and a tendency among parish priests, university teachers, and the educated laity to disparage the effect of large classes. They seemed to think that American Catholic colleges lacked the depth and quality of English university teaching; but I am not so sure. Clearly, with such a mass of students individual tutoring is impossible; the veteran or the boy from high school is left to sink or swim. But never have I seen undergraduates in an English university working as hard as the young Americans are. Any college library on the hottest afternoon is packed with students, lately demobilized, sitting on every chair, table or window ledge on which the human frame can be lodged, and swotting for all they are worth.

So much for the strength of the Catholic body in the U. S. as it appears to the naked eye. Why, then, is its influence not more apparent in the public life and foreign policy of the country? The Catholics are close upon a fifth of the population; they form the largest single religious society, well over a third of all who profess attachment to any religion, and their schools, colleges, and charitable institutions outnumber such establishments of all the other denominations put together. Yet it is only rarely, and under stress of war or economic crises, that a President or secretary of state is found to do or say anything which corresponds to specifically Catholic desires. President Roosevelt, some years ago, warned by an adviser that some policy of his would alienate the Catholic vote, replied, "There is no Catholic vote."

While this is perfectly consistent with the practice of the Catholic religion, it operates against anything like the formation of an *imperium in imperio* by the Catholic body comparable to that of American Zionism; it operates against aggressive minority action of any kind; it inclines the Catholic laity to vote Republican or Democrat, as a matter of course, according to local feeling or interests, rather than to make their religion an issue at elections. It means that the mode of action or influence of the Catholic laity, when it *is* aroused, is more that of a leaven in American society as a whole than that of a distinctive sect or section; and, as American Catholics, and many of their fellow citizens as well, become more and more educated in the realities of international life—and that education is proceeding far more quickly and thoroughly in the U. S. than it is here—that influence grows steadily greater.

To start with my own experience. Here was I, a foreign Catholic, entirely unknown except for a book called *The Catholic Tradition of the Law of Nations,* which I compiled ten years ago for the Carnegie Endowment for International Peace, and which is out of print anyway. Yet I found myself invited to more Catholic colleges, universities, and forums than I could pack into about seven weeks' traveling between Montreal and Los Angeles, San Francisco and Baltimore. I had to speak everywhere on the substance of the Christian doctrine of international ethics and its application to the problems of the day: the United Nations in theory and in practice; war in the atomic age; trusteeship; the impact of Soviet power on Europe and the world; the reconstruction of Western Europe; the German question. Large popular audiences wanted the broader picture; before highly educated groups, such as the great Jesuit seminary of the Maryland and New York provinces at Woodstock or the diocesan seminary at Rochester, I had to speak to the best of my ability the language of the moral theologian, and lecture on the ethics of intervention, with special reference to Spain and Eastern Europe. But what was far more important than the phenomenon of many thousands of Catholics listening to that kind of thing was the volume and quality of the questions. I adopted the plan of having them written down, and returned to New York City with a suitcase full of them. A few, of course, were funny, but the vast majority were very intelligent questions indeed, and revealed far greater knowledge of such matters as the food situation in Germany and Italy, the real nature of Soviet policy, the actual political conditions in Poland, Yugoslavia or Hungary, the realities of the Spanish question, or the moral defects of the United Nations Charter, than, I believe, you would find in any comparable English gatherings.

How did such knowledge find its way to places and people all over the great continent? In the first place, nearly all American daily papers carry more uncensored world news than the English dailies, nor do radio commentators practice the *disci-*

plina arcani of the BBC. Then there is the wide-awake and sometimes passionate interest of Americans of various European origins in the plight of their mother countries, which has no equivalent here.

But Christian charity has been the great educator. There is not a Catholic parish nor college which has not had repeated appeals from the pulpit for relief in kind for the suffering of Europe; and each such appeal has been buttressed with facts, figures, and descriptions of social, economic, and political conditions, mainly supplied by the National Catholic Welfare Conference and its foreign correspondents. I heard one such appeal in December at Omaha. It was the day when a nation-wide campaign for clothes and shoes to be sent to Germany, Poland, and other afflicted countries was launched in all the Catholic churches. We learned that 53 million cans of food had already been given for relief purposes in Europe by American Catholics and distributed, but that the cold of the impending winter made clothing more immediately urgent. Graphic descriptions were given of the way in which German Catholic children in the Ruhr and Rhineland could not go to school for lack of shoes. All this has made the practicing American Catholic Europe-conscious as never before.

So much for the ways in which American Catholics are learning and feeling about foreign affairs *as* Catholics, with some indication of the practical consequences. What of their influence as U. S. citizens within the general body of public opinion? First of all, the Catholic intelligentsia in the widest sense, including the large proportion of the Catholic people who have benefited or are now benefiting from the great system of Catholic higher education, and those who form the lively Newman clubs, which exist in all non-Catholic universities, is as much fired with the ideal of "One World" as are most other thoughtful Americans. The emphasis in all this discussion, about world government and organizing the world for peace, is less sentimental in Catholic circles than elsewhere; it concentrates upon the primacy of the moral law, and is wide awake to the reality and power of sin. This is a tonic contribution to the formation of a national conscience in the matter.

Now that the question of working out an International Bill of Rights in the Human Rights commission of the United Nations is coming up, we find plenty of evidence of Catholic cooperation in the drafting of the bill drawn up by the American Federation of Labor and submitted to the United Nations (as the federation, being a recognized consultative body on the Social and Economic council, has a right to do). In short, just as Catholics have a *negative* enthusiasm in common with the prevailing trend in the U. S. today, namely the hatred of communism, so (what is more valuable) they are coming to have a *positive* aim in common with the best and most typical of their fellow citizens, namely the achievement of peace on the basis of justice and liberty.

20

---※≫≪※---

Harold J. Laski

1948

from *The American Democracy*

---※≫≪※---

Harold Laski, a brilliant English political scientist was well known in America. He came to the United States to teach at Harvard in 1917—leaving three years later after a controversy over the Boston Police strike—lectured at Amherst and Yale, visited here often and was much praised and condemned for his views in the American press. He achieved fame and influence as Professor of Political Science at the London School of Economics and later became the Chairman of Britain's Labour Party. A confirmed socialist, although not a communist, his Marxist philosophy made him a controversial figure. This philosophy is apparent in his classic study of American institutions, *The American Democracy*. Mr. Laski wrote his study "out of a deep love for America" in an effort "to make intelligible to Europeans and above all to Englishmen, why America arouses that deep love."

The following selection is from *The American Democracy: A Commentary and Interpretation* by Harold J. Laski. Copyright 1948 by The Viking Press, Inc. and reprinted by their permission.

---※≫≪※---

It is interesting to observe how little in one way, and how much in others, the Roman Catholic Church has been influenced by the environment of America. Historical circumstances have made the United States so profoundly a Protestant country that it is always difficult not to feel that the Catholic Church is permanently on the defensive; even its aggressive policies, as in Boston in the era of Cardinal O'Connell, or in Brooklyn, New York, in the vulgar attacks of the followers of Father Coughlin, have about them the exaggeration of men who are not quite sure of, or satisfied with, their place in the secular scheme of things. It is not, indeed, beyond the mark to say that Know-Nothingism, the Ku Klux Klan, the political revolt of the Solid South against the candidature of Governor Smith in 1928, are all parts of the important fact that, beneath the surface of things, the Catholic Church is not fully recognized as having achieved a real fusion with Americanism. Partly that is because the history of immigration, much of it an immigration the impact of which is known to many Americans still alive, made the Catholic Church the active defender of minority groups; and partly it is also the fact that, in protecting them, the Church sought to safeguard them against the results of an Americanization which invariably tended to the relaxation of their religious ties. This had the deeply interesting result of giving the Catholic priest an authority over his flock which has remained more living and more intense than any which the ministers of other churches dare seek to secure. The Irishman or the Italian, the Pole or the French Canadian, who deliberately rejects this authority is rare; that is why the Catholic vote comes nearer to being swung by ecclesiastical influence than that of any other Church; and why the outstanding Catholic prelates in the United States, Gibbons, Farley, Hayes, Mundelein, were men whose opposition no president was likely to seek and whose counsel he was usually glad to welcome. After all, a cardinal in Baltimore or Boston has links, through the Vatican, with interests of importance to America which spread all over the world.

The imperfect fusion of the Roman Catholic Church with Americanism follows, of course, from its theory of the universal claim to sovereignty in this world upon which it is built. It is, in some sort, an *imperium in imperio,* for it seeks to build a kind of citadel for its members, entrance into which marks them with an ethos that is permanent. To this end it builds its separate school system, its special training colleges, its special universities; while its School of Diplomacy in Georgetown University at Washington has shown a remarkable power of infiltration into the Department of State in the federal government. It is also fair to say that there is a special Catholic world of literature and of scholarship, the atmosphere of which is permeated by principles and attitudes which a non-Catholic American would have some difficulty in understanding. To all this must be added the vital fact that the Roman Catholic Church stands alone in America in its complete exclusion of laymen from any effective share in the making of its decisions. A Roman Catholic industrial magnate may be asked for advice upon financial matters, or be urged to contribute to the Church funds; but he has no kind of say in the disposition of its properties, the appointment or promotion of its priests, the character of its doctrine or its teaching. It is not an unfair comparison to say that the Catholic laity in America are compelled to play the part of privates with no hope of promotion in the great army of the Church; the commissioned ranks are reserved, without challenge, for its priesthood. No other Church would venture to impose so complete a status of subordination upon its members; nor has any retained, by virtue of the discipline this implies, so full a respect for the priest from the members of his Church as one can find in the Roman Catholic communities in America.

In this aspect the Roman Catholic Church is not only sharply distinguished from other American Churches; it is also felt to be so sharply distinguished by the ordinary citizen. Unlike any other Church, it is the Roman Catholic Church in America; it is not the American Roman Catholic Church. I do not mean for one moment that the overwhelming majority of its members, clerical and lay alike, are not as loyal and devoted Americans as the members of any other church. Undoubtedly they are. But there is still in them some hardly definable quality which gives their loyalty and devotion a permanently different perspective from that of the others. That has emerged, in recent times, in their attitude to the Soviet Union, to Mexico in the last generation, and to Republican Spain. In each case the opinion of American Catholics was set in a frame of reference notably different from that in which the opinion of any other denomination was set. Even if American Catholics are dubious about the wisdom of the policy for which their hierarchy decides, they are less inclined to overt criticism of it, still less to serious opposition, than would be the case with Methodists or Baptists or Unitarians. It is as though some impulse from the *Republica Christiana* of medieval times makes the relation of the individual Catholic laymen to secular policy tinged always with the recollection that there was a time when positive law derived its validity from its conformity with a Divine Law of which the Roman Pontiff was the appointed guardian.

The Roman Catholic Church, I have suggested, is in America, but it is an American Church in a sense quite different from that of any other denomination. It must, nevertheless, apply the body of its social teaching to an American community in which the great mass of its members are poor men and women dependent wholly upon the sale of their labour power for their living, a much smaller number who enjoy the relative comfort and security of a solid bourgeoisie, and a very small number who, like Thomas F. Ryan in the last generation or J. J. Raskob in our own, are among the outstanding wealthy men of the time. The Church in America, from the Encyclical *Immortale Dei* of Leo XIII in 1885, through its related pronouncement in the *Sapientiae Christianae* (1890), the *Quod Apostolici Muneris* (1878), and the *Libertas* (1888), down to the Encyclical *Quadragesimo Anno* (1931) of Pius XI, which was itself both a salute to, and a modernization of, the *Rerum Novarum* (1891) of Leo XIII—the Church possesses a body of directives which it is the business both of its priests and laymen to apply in concrete detail to the situations they occupy; with, of course, the overriding principle of interpretation that, in the last resort, the validity of any particular application is a matter upon which the finding of the Church itself, that is to say of the Supreme Pontiff at Rome, is conclusive and final.

Here, once more, the Roman Catholic Church in America differs from other American Churches in having a wide-reaching and authoritative code of social action. There is, of course, a considerable range of variation in the inferences drawn from the code; some Catholics of high eminence made it the basis, for example, of their warm support for the New Deal of Franklin Roosevelt; while others see no incompatability between its principles and membership in that Liberty League the aim of which was nothing so much as the destruction of the New Deal. It is, indeed, extraordinarily difficult to find a single, unchallengeable, meaning in the code; and it is still more difficult to know what authority it possesses over the minds and actions of Catholic laymen. It is clear that it condemns any social system built upon laissez-faire; but it equally condemns socialism and communism. It is emphatic in its approval of private property; but it agrees that certain undefined forms of property must not be left in private hands. It urges employers to pay a just wage related to family responsibility; but it warns the worker not to press for a wage which would inflict injury upon his employer. It appears to approve co-partnership and profit-sharing; there are certain passages in the Encyclical *Quadragesimo Anno* which appear to the outsider to bestow a somewhat cautious blessing upon the corporate state in its Fascist form, as with its prohibition of strikes and lockouts and the provision for compulsory arbitration; it recognizes the need to organize the workers, but having its suspicions of the ordinary unions, perhaps because they act as a source of socialist ideas, it prefers "Christian" trade-unions under episcopal encouragement. It emphasizes throughout, naturally enough, that it is to the improvement of individual character under the inspiration of true religion that the only road to a just social order can be found.

The problem for the outside observer therefore becomes a

complicated one. There are many Catholics in the United States who belong to either the Socialist or the Communist party; there are, of course, many hundred thousands who not only belong to what Pius XI called the "neutral" trade-unions, but would resent profoundly any attempt to lessen their strength by introducing into the industries where the "neutral" unions operate the competitive element of "Christian" trade-union; and over the major sector of American industry, trade-unionists, whether Catholic or non-Catholic, would bitterly resent any attempt to introduce the habits of the corporate state. Nor is this all. It is patent that there must be a large number of Roman Catholic employers who pay their workers less than a living wage; nor is there any evidence to suggest that either co-partnership or profit-sharing experiments are more frequent among Catholic, than among non-Catholic, employers. Whether the Roman Catholic Church improves the character of those, employers and workmen alike, who accept its teachings raises questions which do not admit of any quantitatively precise answer. It is notable that the rate of crime is higher among professed Roman Catholics than among members of other religious denominations, but this, obviously, cannot be attributed either to the principles or to the influence of the Church to which they belong.

What is, I think, beyond all doubt is the fact that the Roman Catholic Church as an organized institution exercises a conservative, even a deeply conservative, influence in all matters of social and economic importance. This is the outcome of its emphasis upon faith, and not works; of its distrust of radical movements it cannot control; and of its historic dislike of any strong central authority with which it is not in special alliance. It is deeply suspicious of any extension of the federal government's power; that has led it, for example, to be one of the outstanding opponents of the Child Labor Amendment. It has rarely spoken forthrightly about outrageous practices by employers, such as were revealed in the findings of the La Follette Committee on Civil Liberties. The educational standards in its schools and most of its colleges do not compare with even the average standards of those maintained by the states or by private endowments such as Harvard or Yale. It is far more anxious when an attack on parochial schools is threatened than when it is shown that the rate of illiteracy is higher, and the school-leaving age lower, in the Catholic Church than among other Churches in the United States. It continues to set its face firmly against birth-control. As the refusal to allow Bertrand Russell to teach mathematical philosophy at the College of the City of New York, on the grounds that he was an unfit person, made clear, even in a neutral institution the Church will use its underground influence to interfere with academic freedom; while the McMahon case at the Catholic University of Notre Dame is an interesting example of the perturbation of the hierarchy at the possibility that a "modern" outlook was creeping into the institution. Nor is it easily possible to dismiss as unimportant the difficulty other Churches encounter in securing official co-operation with the Roman Catholic Church on issues on which interdenominational co-operation between Protestants has been found to be simple and straightforward.

The short way of summarizing the position is, I think, to say that as an organized institution the Roman Catholic Church shows less direct interest in the problems of the time, save as they touch the interests, and especially the economic interests, of the Church, than any religious organization of comparable importance. I doubt whether its religious leaders feel inwardly anything like the strain that an observer can find in the writings of men like Reinhold Niebuhr, or the long line of his predecessors who go back to the seventies and eighties of the last century. No doubt the Roman Catholic Church can claim one intellectual giant in the field of social analysis in the person of Orestes Brownson; but it is important to realize that all his work of serious stature was done before his conversion. Men like the famous Father Hecker, a century ago, worked hard and nobly at the task of aiding individual men; there is a sense in which he can fairly be described as the American Vincent de Paul. No one can fail to respect the devoted effort of Monsignor Ryan in the last generation, to work out a Catholic social philosophy which would put the Church squarely on the side of large-scale social reform. I do not think it can be said that he succeeded, and I suspect his influence was greater outside his own Church than it was within it; in any case, it would be difficult to argue that he had got much beyond the position of Theodore Parker, or as far as mild Christian Socialists like Gladden and Rauschenbusch were prepared to go.

If one tries to get at the root of the Roman Catholic attitude to contemporary life, there emerges at once an issue of fundamental importance. By making the conduct of the individual in its relevance to his salvation far more significant than the material standards of the environment in which he lives, and by insisting that the state power is a neutral agency concerned with a social welfare regarded as common to all citizens, the Roman Catholic Church insists that the men who operate this power, no doubt in an imperfect way, reach out beyond the bias and partiality from which few of us are able to escape. Out of this comes the principle that, subject, of course, to ecclesiastical approval, the Catholic layman must broadly live by the Scriptural injunction that "the Powers that Be are Ordained by God," where he wishes to depart from this command the Church is at hand to tell him of his obligation. All of which amounts to saying that while the philosophy of the hierarchy is, in the main, the beatification of the *status quo,* a doctrine that rarely brings it into conflict with the business man's normal philosophy, departures from this norm will be authorized by the authorities of the Church rather than by the clergy in conjunction with the laity.

21

~>>K<<~

Evelyn Waugh
1949

from *"The American Epoch in the Catholic Church"*

~>>K<<~

In many respects, Evelyn Waugh, a distinguished novelist and satirist, is in the tradition of critical English visitors. There is much in American life he finds not to his liking. But his weapon is satire and his attacks on American foibles have made few enemies—laughter and anger are unlikely companions. His visit to California in 1947 resulted in *The Loved One,* a classic indictment of American burial customs. In 1948, Mr. Waugh came to America for an extended lecture tour. The following year he wrote for LIFE (September 19, 1949) "The American Epoch in the Catholic Church," a serious, perceptive and friendly appraisal of the Catholic Church in America, is reprinted here by courtesy of LIFE Magazine (℗ Time Inc.).

~>>K<<~

"A. D. or B. C.?" How often among the monuments of the Old World the dazed sightseer asks this question, interrupting the guide's flow of dates! How often he wearily leaves it un-asked! One hundred A. D. or 100 B. C.; a span of two centuries; what does that matter, one way or the other, compared with the huge, crowded interval between then and now?

For most people the birth of Christ is a chronological device, used beyond the bounds of Christendom in Delhi and Moscow; a dateline as arbitrary as the meridian of Greenwich. It is not even accurate, for Christ was born four or five years before the traditional date. From time to time politicians have sought to impose an exploit of their own—the first French Republic, the Fascist March on Rome—as a more notable event from which to number the years. The old calendar came back for reasons of convenience rather than piety. But the Christian, when he dates his letters from the Year of Our Lord, is affirming his Faith. He is placing the Incarnation where for him it must always stand, in the center of human history. Before that Year of Grace man lived in the mists, haunted by ancestral memories of a lost Eden, taught enigmatically by hints and portents, punished by awful dooms. The Incarnation restored order. In place of his bloody guilt offerings man was given a single, complete expiation; in place of his magic, the sacramental system, a regular service of communication with the supernatural; in place of his mystery cults, an open, divinely constituted human Society in which to live and multiply. All his history from then onwards, seen through Christian eyes, all the migrations of peoples and the rise and fall of empires, comprise merely a succession of moods and phases in the life of that Society, the Church Christ founded.

In this deep perspective it seems that in every age some one branch of the Church, racial, cultural or national, bears peculiar responsibilities toward the whole. Vitality mysteriously waxes and wanes among the peoples. Again and again Christianity seems dying at its center. Always Providence has another people quietly maturing to relieve the decadent of their burden. To a Christian of the Fourth Century the seat of authority at Rome must have seemed almost on the frontier; France, Spain and Germany were crude, missionary countries while all that was subtle and gracious in the Faith flourished in the Southern and Eastern Mediterranean. For him it was barely possible to conceive of a Church which had lost Constantinople, Alexandria and Carthage. To Louis XIV the Faith of those places belonged to remote history. He could not think of Christendom without France. Yet in less than a century France was officially atheist. Challoner, the saintly Catholic leader of 18th Century England, would have thought it a preposterous forecast that the grandchildren of his dim, disheartened little flock would see the bishops restored and the religious orders flourishing again in every county. So the battle continues, one that can never be lost and may never be won until the Last Trumpet. No loss is impossible, no loss irretrievable, no loss—not Rome itself—mortal. It may well be that Catholics of today, in their own life-time, may have to make enormous adjustments in their conception of the temporal nature of the Church. Many indeed are already doing so, and in the process turning their regard with hope and curiosity to the New World, where, it seems, Providence is schooling and strengthening a people for the historic destiny long borne by Europe.

Hope and curiosity. At first sight, hope is subdued by many features of American history and psychology. Indeed it could be quite plausibly argued that the people of the United States were resolutely anti-Catholic. Although most of the great adventures of exploration in the new continent were made by Catholics, the colonists (except Maryland) were Protestants whose chief complaint against their mother country was that she retained too much traditional character in her Established Church. School textbooks do not make much of the fact, which research abundantly proves, that it was the Quebec Act, tolerating popery in Canada, quite as much as the Stamp Act and the Tea Duties, which rendered George III intolerable to the colonists. The Constitution-makers little thought that in separating Church and State they were laying their country open to the prodigious Catholic growth of the 19th Century, and in 1948 the Supreme Court has shown in the McCollum case that the phrase may be interpreted to the Church's injury. In foreign policy, when religious questions were involved, America has usually supported the anti-Catholic side, particularly where she is most powerful, in Mexico. President Wilson did nothing to oppose the disastrous anti-Catholic prejudices of Lloyd George and Clemenceau in 1919.

Moreover the individual qualities that are regarded as particularly characteristic of Americans, their endemic revolt against traditional authority, their respect for success and sheer activity, their belief that progress is beneficent, their welcome of novelties, their suspicion for titles and uniforms and ceremonies, their dislike of dogmas that divide good citizens and their love of the generalities which unite them, their resentment of discipline—all these and others are unsympathetic to the habits of the Church. Mr. Geoffrey Gorer has discerned deep in the American soul a psychopathic antagonism to paternity and all its symbols; Catholics call both their priests and their God, "Father." The language of the Church is largely that of the court; her liturgy was composed in lands where the honorific titles of royalty were accepted naturally and it abounds in phrases which sound strange on republican and democratic lips. Many pages could be filled with instance of this kind proving on paper very cogently that America can never play an important part in the life of the Church. It would be a fatuous exercise for already at this moment Catholics are the largest religious body in the United States, the richest and in certain ways the most lively branch of the Catholic Church in the world.

Fifty years ago it even looked as though America might soon become predominantly Catholic. That hope, or fear, is now remote. Immigration from Catholic Europe has dwindled, peasant stock has lost its fertility in the cities, conversions, as far as I could find, barely keep pace with apostasies. Humanly speaking it is now certain that the Church is stabilized as a minority, the most important in the country, but subject to both the advantages and disadvantages of an unprivileged position. There is a paradox inherent in all her history that the Church, designed in her nature to be universal, remains in most places a minority. We are inclined to think that from the age of Constantine to that of Luther there was a single, consistently triumphant, universally respected authority and to wonder why, in fact, she made such poor use of her opportunities. In fact, of course, the Church has always been at grips with enemies inside or outside her body, has never enjoyed that serene rule her constitution expects, has repeatedly suffered disasters from which it seemed barely possible she would recover. Her position in America cannot be understood unless her previous history is kept always in mind. From time to time, from place to place she has been in hiding; and she has been on the throne. In America her problems are less simple. There she is firmly grounded in a neutral, secular state.

The United States does not form part of Christendom in the traditional sense of the word. She is the child of late 18th Century "enlightenment" and the liberalism of her founders has persisted through all the changes of her history and penetrated into every part of her life. Separation of church and state was an essential dogma. Government, whatever its form, was looked upon as the captain of a liner, whose concern is purely with navigation. He holds his command ultimately from the passengers. Under his immediate authority the public rooms of his ship are used for religious assemblies of all kinds, while in the bar anyone may quietly blaspheme. That is the ideal relationship between ruler and ruled, between the individual qua citizen and the individual qua immortal soul, as conceived by doctrinaire liberals of the period when the United States was founded. Men required and tolerated very little from their government. The realm of "private life" was large and inviolable. And the division of Church and State is feasible only under those conditions. Today in most nations the analogy between state and ship has broken down. In some places the captain has developed the mentality of Bligh of the *Bounty;* in others the passengers have been more or less willingly pressed into the crew; all are continuously occupied in keeping the ship running; the voyage is no longer a means to an end but an end in itself. As the State, whether it consists of the will of the majority or the power of a clique, usurps more and more of the individual's "private life," the more prominent become the discrepancies between the secular and the religious philosophies, for many things are convenient to the ruler which are not healthy for the soul.

The tragic fate of Europe is witness to the failure of secular states. But America through the unique circumstances of her growth has so far been proof against this decay and is thus the center of hope even for those who are most critical of her idiosyncrasies.

These idiosyncrasies are now the object of boundless curiosity. A generation ago they caused mild amusement as the eccentricities of a likeable but remote people. Today they are studied as portents of the development of the whole Western world. Catholics in particular study them, for it is a necessary consequence of the universality of the Church that she should develop marked superficial variations in her different branches. The Mass as offered in, say, St. Patrick's in New York or in a Tyrolean village or in a Franciscan mission in Africa, is barely recognizable by the uninitiated as the same sacrifice. Mr. Aldous Huxley, no fool, writes in *Ends and Means*: "Christianity, like Hinduism or Buddhism, is not one religion but several. A Christian Church in Southern Spain, or Mexico, or Sicily is singularly like a Hindu temple. The eye is delighted by the same gaudy colors, the same tripe-like decorations, the same gesticulating statues; the nose inhales the same intoxicating smells; the ear and, along with it, the understanding are lulled by the drone of the same incomprehensible incantations, roused by the same loud, impressive music. At the other end of the scale, consider the chapel of a Cistercian monastery and the meditation hall of a community of Zen Buddhists. They are equally bare. . . . Here are two distinct religions for two distinct kinds of human beings." Only a very learned man can be quite as hopelessly and articulately wrong as that. Any altar boy could tell him that the "incantations" of the Mass are identical whether in Guadalupe or Gethsemani, Ky., and are comprehensible or not simply so far as one understands Latin. The action is comprehensible to any child who has attended catechism. Cistercian incense smells the same as Jesuit. There is high farce in his picture of a homesick Andalusian in India frequenting the rites of Juggernaut in preference to the more severe devotion of the mission church.

But it is palpably true that each culture gives an idiosyncratic local flavor to its church.

We differ most, perhaps, in our notions of reverence. I have seen a procession of the Blessed Sacrament in Spain which the people applauded by exploding firecrackers under the feet of the clergy. It was done with genuine devotion but to a Northern mind the effect was disconcerting. In the same way it strikes Europeans as odd that Americans find the voices of film stars on the radio an aid to saying the rosary. American manufacturers of "religious goods" offer many ingenious novelties, including a "rosary aid," which records each "Ave" on a dial with a sharp click, and a plastic crucifix which, I was assured, had the advantage that you could "throw it on the ground and stamp on it." But I remembered that in France I had seen children eating gingerbread Madonnas. All these observations add to the charm of travel. But there is also "flavor" of a more philosophic kind.

Europeans are very anxious to catch the American flavor for they believe that in two or three generations it will predominate. They ask countless questions about it and get some very misleading answers, for one can find instances to give color to almost any generalization. I saw both in London and Chicago the Italian film *Paisan,* one incident of which portrays, with fewer anomalies than usual, the life of a small Franciscan community in a remote mountain district. Three American chaplains arrive there and are warmly welcomed. It transpires that only one is Catholic, the other two being respectively a Protestant and a Jew. The friars are disconcerted and impose a fast on themselves for the conversion of their non-Catholic guests. In London the audience was mainly non-Catholic but its sympathy was plainly with the friars. In Chicago the audience was composed mainly of Italian speakers, presumably Catholics of a sort, and to them the friars seemed purely comic. It would be easy to generalize from this contrast that American Catholics care little for doctrinal niceties or the ascetic life; that they exalt the natural virtues above the supernatural, and consider good-fellowship and material generosity the true ends of man. That is, in fact, just the kind of generalization which is current in Europe. Yet at that very time Boston was being torn by theological controversy, a contumacious Irish priest proclaiming damnation on all heretics and the authorities reaffirming the possibility of salvation outside the Church in the orthodox terms, which are generous but strict. And all over the country monks and nuns were quietly going about their business of the Opus Dei, singing their office and living by medieval rules, in just the fashion which excited laughter in a Chicago theater.

The two chief impressions which I brought home from America were, first, that there is as great variety there between the outward forms of Catholicism as can be found in Europe; and second, that Catholicism is not something alien and opposed to the American spirit but an essential part of it.

To enlarge on these two propositions. In vast areas of what is now the United States, Catholicism was in colonial times the established religion. It was loosely established and in most of those areas now survives mainly in picturesque, ruined or restored, missions. Only three states can be said to have a strong, continuous Catholic tradition—Louisiana, Maryland and New Mexico. In the first of these the Church has never known persecution or even discouragement and over a length of time that is not an entirely healthy condition. Catholics need to be reminded every few generations that theirs is a challenging creed. In no European country have the faithful been subject to so enervating a toleration as have the inhabitants of New Orleans. It is therefore not surprising that they take their faith easily and sentimentally, with some skepticism among the rich and some superstition among the poor, of the kind that was found in France before the Revolution. It is one of the Devil's devices to persuade people that their religion is so much "in their bones" that they do not have to bother; that it is in rather poor taste to talk too much about it. Marital confusions, the material advantages of secular education, the mere lassitude induced by the climate, keep many from practicing their religion. There is a strange shrine there, unrecognized by the clergy, where the decoration and forms of prayer are Catholic, to which the colored people resort for cures and favors. There is witchcraft in New Orleans, as there was at the court of Mme. de Montespan. Yet it was there that I saw one of the moving sights of my tour. Ash Wednesday: warm rain falling in streets unsightly with the draggled survivals of carnival. The Roosevelt Hotel overflowing with crapulous tourists planning their return journeys. How many of them knew anything about Lent? But across the way the Jesuit Church was teeming with life all day long; a continuous dense crowd of all colors and conditions moving up to the altar rails and returning with their foreheads signed with ash. And the old grim message was being repeated over each penitent: "Dust thou art and unto dust shalt thou return." One grows parched for that straight style of speech in the desert of modern euphemisms, where the halt and lame are dubbed "handicapped"; the hungry, "underprivileged"; the mad, "emotionally disturbed." Here it was, plainly stated, quietly accepted, and all that day, all over that lighthearted city, one encountered the little black smudge on the forehead which sealed us members of a great brotherhood who can both rejoice and recognize the limits of rejoicing.

The history of Maryland has been different. Catholicism was never established there as an official religion as it was in the French and Spanish colonies. The state was founded by Catholics as a place where they could practice their religion in peace, side by side with Protestants. The peace was soon broken and the Church persecuted and subdued. But it survived and emerged at the Declaration of Independence in much the same temper as in England at the Catholic Emancipation Act.* The old Catholic families of Baltimore have much in common with

---

* In 1829 the last of the restrictive laws passed against Catholics after the Protestant Revolution of 1688 was removed, restoring to them most of their civil rights and liberties.

the old Catholic families of Lancashire. The countryside round Leonardtown has the same tradition of Jesuit missionaries moving in disguise from family to family, celebrating Mass in remote plantations, inculcating the same austere devotional habits, the same tenacious, unobtrusive fidelity. That peninsula between Chesapeake Bay and the Potomac is one of the most fascinating areas for the Catholic visitor, and one of the things which inspires him most is the heroic fidelity of the Negro Catholics. The Church has not always been a kind mother to them. Everywhere in the South, Catholic planters brought their slaves to the sacraments, but in the bitter years after the Reconstruction few whites, priests or laity, recognized any special obligation toward them. Often they could only practice their religion at the cost of much humiliation. Some drifted from the Church to preposterous sects or reverted to paganism, but many families remained steadfast. Theirs was a sharper test than the white Catholics had earlier undergone, for here the persecutors were fellow members in the Household of the Faith. But, supernaturally, they knew the character of the Church better than their clergy. Today all this is fast changing. Catholics are everywhere leading the movement to make amends and in another generation, no doubt, those scandals will seem to belong to the distant past. But in the effort to forget them, honor must never be neglected to those thousands of colored Catholics who so accurately traced their Master's road amid insult and injury.

Except in Louisiana and Maryland, Catholics form a negligible part of the *haute bourgeoisie* of the country clubs and social registers. Most of them, Irish apart, grew up to the sound of foreign languages spoken by parents or grandparents in the home. Some, in the Southwest, are survivors of Spanish colonization; most descend from the great waves of immigration from central and southern Europe. To the newly arrived immigrant his Church is especially dear. It unites him in prayer and association with the home he has left; it is a social center where he meets his own kind; it is a refuge full of familiar things in a bewildering new world. But the second and third generations have no tender memories of Europe. They have been reared on tales of oppression and squalor from which their parents courageously rescued them. They want to be purely American and they develop a raw and rather guilty resentment against the Old World which, I think, explains the loud Sicilian laughter I heard in the Chicago cinema. There is a temptation to identify the Church with their inferior station; to associate it with the smell of garlic and olive oil and grandfather muttering over the foreign language newspapers; to think of it as something to be discarded, as they rise in the social scale, as they discard their accents and surnames. Some, of course, do so. It is rare to find formal apostates, but occasionally parents who have ceased to care about their religion have their children brought up by Episcopalian or Baptist, in the belief that it gives them a better start in life and that, anyway, it is the child's business to choose for himself later on. But not often: it is one of the prime achievements of the American Catholic clergy that they have reconciled those first stirrings of a new loyalty with the ancestral faith, and Europeans should remember the problem that had to be solved before they look askance at the cruder expressions of nationalism which get quoted.

The Irish, on the other hand, present a precisely contrasting problem. They have never suffered a prick of shame in avowing their origins. Indeed the further they move in time and place from their homeland the louder they sing about it. Should they ever return they would be shocked by the cynicism of their Dublin cousins. The problem with the Irish is to guard them from the huge presumption of treating the Universal Church as a friendly association of their own, and that problem has not been solved. In New York on St. Patrick's Day, among the green carnations first invented by the Irishman, Oscar Wilde, for quite another significance; in Boston on any day of the year; the stranger might well suppose that Catholicism was a tribal cult. Only when he comes to study American hagiology does he learn that other races have their share in Pentecost. To the European it seems that the Irish have been led to betray their manifest historical destiny. When Englishmen in the last century founded a review which was to be for Catholics what the *Edinburgh Review* was for rationalists, they called it the *Dublin Review*. When there was a project for a national Catholic University, Newman went to Ireland. Had Ireland remained in the United Kingdom, Dublin would today be one of the great religious capitals of the world where Catholics from all over the British Empire resorted for education and leadership. That splendid hope was defeated by the politicians. What Europe lost, America has gained. The historic destiny of the Irish is being fulfilled on the other side of the Atlantic, where they have settled in their millions, bringing with them all their ancient grudges and the melancholy of the bogs, but also their hard, ancient wisdom. They alone of the newcomers are never for a moment taken in by the multifarious frauds of modernity. They have been changed from peasants and soldiers into townsmen. They have learned some of the superficial habits of "good citizenship," but at heart they remain the same adroit and joyless race that broke the hearts of all who ever tried to help them.

It is one of the functions of an upper class to remind the clergy of the true balance between their spiritual and their temporal positions. In most Catholic communities in the United States, so far as there is an upper class at all, the clergy themselves comprise it. From one year to another they never meet anyone better informed or more elegant than themselves. The deference with which they are treated on purely social occasions would tend to spoil all but the most heroic humility.

The presbyteries of Mr. Harry Sylvester's *Moon Gaffney* and Mr. J. F. Powers' *Prince of Darkness* are not mere literary inventions. Reading those admirable stories one can understand why there is often a distinct whiff of anticlericalism where Irish priests are in power. They are faithful and chaste and, in youth at any rate, industrious, but many live out their lives in a painful state of transition; they have lost their ancestral simplicity without yet acquiring a modest carriage of their superior learning or, more important, delicacy in their human relations, or imagination, or agility of mind. To them however, and to the Germans, must go the main credit for the construction of the Church in America. Without them the more sensitive Latins and Slavs would have at first huddled together in obscure congregations, then dispersed and perhaps have been lost to the Faith. The Irish with their truculence and practical good sense have built and paid for the churches, opening new parishes as fast as the population grew; they have staffed the active religious orders and have created a national system of Catholic education.

This last achievement is indeed something entirely unique. Without help from the State—indeed in direct competition with it—the poor of the nation have covered their land with schools, colleges and universities, boldly asserting the principle that nothing less than an entire Christian education is necessary to produce Christians. For the Faith is not a mere matter of learning a few prayers and pious stories in the home. It is a complete culture infusing all humane knowledge. It is no doubt true that some branches of specialized scholarship can best be learned in the vastly richer secular institutions. The Catholic colleges do not set themselves the aims of Harvard or Oxford or the Sorbonne. Their object is to transform a proletariat into a bourgeoisie; to produce a faithful laity, qualified to take its part in the general life of the nation; and in this way they are manifestly successful. Their students are not, in the main, drawn from scholarly homes. Many of them handle the English language uneasily. The teaching facilities are still dependent on European recruits for many of the refinements of learning. But, when all this is said, the Englishman, who can boast no single institution of higher Catholic education and is obliged to frequent universities that are Anglican in formation and agnostic in temper, can only applaud what American Catholics have done in the last hundred years. It is a very great thing that young men who are going out to be dentists or salesmen should have a grounding of formal logic and Christian ethics. "Prove syllogistically that natural rights exist"; "Give the fundamental reason why usury is wrong"; "What is the difference between soul and mind?"; "Give and explain a definition of sacrifice"—these are questions chosen almost at random from the examination papers of a Jesuit college.

I have heard it said that American adolescents tend to "learn the answers" parrotwise without much speculation. This was not the impression I formed in talking to them, but even if it were so, they have learned something which most Europeans ignore. It is a great gain, while the memory is active, to store up formulas. Experience will give them life and later, when he is confronted with a problem, phrases from his college days will come into a man's mind with sudden vivid importance. I noticed this enormous advantage which religiously educated American adults enjoy over their more learned fellows from the secular universities. With the latter, when discussions become general, one got the impression that outside their particular subjects everything was shapeless and meaningless. Nuclear fission threatens material progress; they apprehend this and are at once in despair. What are they here for if not to participate in a benevolent scheme of evolution? It is a question which only the God-fearing can answer. The Catholic remembers the phrases of his youth, which at the time, perhaps, seemed a mere combination of words to be memorized for the satisfaction of an examiner, and suddenly the words have topical significance. He can tap at will the inexhaustible sources of theology.

This fine work of education is, at the moment, somewhat precarious. In America, as elsewhere, the independent schools are in the position of a poker player among men much richer than himself who are continually raising the stakes. The apparatus of education is becoming exorbitantly expensive. The Catholic colleges cannot long hope to compete with the State in providing the engines of modern physical science. There is moreover a powerful group in the nation who openly aspire to uniformity as to something good in itself. I met many anxious Catholic educationalists, but I left with confidence that those who have achieved such stupendous feats in the recent past will somehow triumph over their enemies.

There is no doubt that the Catholic colleges maintain a remarkably high standard of duty and piety. The holy places of Notre Dame are crowded before a football match. The number and frequency of communions are startling to a European. The habit thus inculcated often continues through life as any visitor to any church can recognize. Every soul in his traffic with God has his own secrets. A youth who is inarticulate in conversation may well be eloquent in prayer. It would be an intolerable impertinence to attempt to judge. What is plain to the observer is that throughout the nation the altar rails are everywhere crowded. It is normally from just such a deep soil of popular devotion that the fine flowers of the Faith grow. The Church does not exist in order to produce elegant preachers or imaginative writers or artists or philosophers. It exists to produce saints. God alone knows his own. Without doubt lives of deep, unobtrusive sanctity are being lived in all parts of the U. S., but it is true that the American Church up to the present time has produced few illustrious heroes or heroines. Archbishop Cicognani in his *Sanctity in America* lately collected 35 brief biographies of men and women of eminent holiness who worked in the U. S. Of these, 31 were foreign-born and foreign educated. Of the four natives none, it may be noted, was of Irish extraction. Two, Catherine Tekakwitha, the Indian, and Mother Elizabeth Ann Seton, the foundress of the Sisters of Charity, were converts. Bishop Richard Miles, the Dominican of Tennessee, was a zealous and devoted pastor and administrator. One, Sister Miriam Teresa Demjanovich, was a teaching novice. None was a pure contemplative.

The contemplative life is, of course, only one form of the Christian life. It is a matter of observation, however, that the health of religion in any place and age may be fairly judged by the number of contemplative vocations. Until recent years America has a poor record in this matter but lately there are signs of change. The case of Thomas Merton has aroused wide interest but he is merely one, unusually articulate, representative of a wide and healthy movement. New Trappist houses are being established, postulants for Carmel exceed the accommodation. Man is made for the knowledge of God and for no other purpose. Where that purpose is recognized there will always be found many who seek Him in the cloister, from which grace spreads to an entire people.

The Church and the world need monks and nuns more than they need writers. These merely decorate. The Church can get along very well without them. If they appear, it is a natural growth. They are not much in evidence in America at the moment and the well meant attempts to produce them artificially by special courses of study seem to me unlikely to succeed. A more fruitful source of such luxuries is the variety of interests which Catholics have developed—the small magazines devoted to the liturgy, to social studies, to the translation and explanation of foreign literature and so forth; the works, for example of *Commonweal* in New York, of John and Mary Ryan in Boston, of John Pick in Milwaukee; the Grail movement in Cincinnati; and the Sheil School of Social Studies in Chicago. There is a fermentation everywhere. Space is lacking to examine all these movements in detail but something more must be said of the Grail.

In a homestead, unhappily named Grailville, Loveland, 30-odd girls at a time, of widely different social origins, are being intensively trained in the "lay apostolate." Their life is in startling contrast to the ideals of the advertisement pages of the women's magazines. Strenuous rural pursuits, periods of silence, plain dressing, liturgical devotion prepare them for life in the world as wives or workers. Their number is minute, as was the number of the first companions of St. Ignatius who set out to reclaim Europe in the 16th Century. It is seldom in gigantic rallies and conventions that great ends are achieved. There are the mustard seeds of the parable.

I mentioned a second conclusion: that Catholicism is part of the American spirit. I do not mean that it lacks enemies. Recently there was an attempt to ban specifically Christian Christmas carols from a score of public schools in Brooklyn. The shops all over the country seek to substitute Santa Claus and his reindeer for the Christ Child. I witnessed, early in Lent, the arrival at a railway station of an "Easter Bunny," attended by brass band and a posse of police. Just as the early Christians adopted the pagan festivals and consecrated them, so everywhere, but particularly in the U. S., pagan commerce is seeking to adopt and desecrate the feasts of the Church. And wherever the matter is one for public authority, the state is "neutral"— a euphemism for "unchristian."

I mean that "Americanism" is the complex of what all Americans consider the good life and that in this complex Christianity, and pre-eminently Catholicism, is the redeeming part. Unhappily, "Americanism" has come to mean for most of the world what a few, very vociferous, far from typical, Americans wish to make it. The peoples of other continents look to America half in hope and half in alarm. They see that their own future is inextricably involved with it and their judgment is based on what they see in the cinema, what they read in the popular magazines, what they hear from the loudest advertiser. Gratitude for the enormous material benefits received is tempered with distaste for what they believe is the spiritual poverty of the benefactor.

It is only when one travels in America that one realizes that most Americans either share this distaste or are genuinely unaware of the kind of false impression which interested parties have conspired to spread.

The Christian believes that he was created to know, love and serve God in this world and to be happy with him in the next. That is the sole reason for his existence. "Good citizenship," properly understood, is a necessary by-product of this essential task, but more and more the phrase has come to mean mere amenability to the demands of the government. At present the state makes few exorbitant demands in America, but there are Americans, resolutely opposed to the mechanisms of communism and fascism, who yet exalt this limited conception of "good citizenship" as the highest virtue, and regard the creation of a homogeneous society as the first end of statesmanship. In this popular neutral opinion, Catholics, Protestants, Jews, atheists, theosophists and all the strange sects of the nation differ only in the rites they practice, or do not practice, in certain buildings for an hour or two a week. This is pure make-believe. They differ hugely in morals, social custom, and philosophy of life— in fact in all the things they value most highly. The neutral secular state can only function justly by keeping itself within strict limits. It is not for a foreigner to predict how long the government of the U. S. will resist the prevalent temptation to encroachment. He merely notes admiringly and gratefully that hither-to the temptations have been largely resisted and also that the constitutional separation of church and state does not, when temptation offers, guarantee the confined welfare of any particular, minority, religious body.

The Catholic holds certain territories that he can never surrender to the temporal power. He hopes that in his time there will be no invasion, but he knows that the history of his Church is one of conflict. If his rulers force him to choose between them and his Faith, in the last resort he must choose his Faith. And because in his heart he knows this, he tends to be conspicuously loyal whenever he can be so with a clear conscience. A great French churchman of the 18th Century could write without embarrassment: *"Le Roi, Jésus-Christ et l' Eglise, Dieu en ces trois noms."** Similarly many American prelates speak as though they believed that representative, majority government were of divine institution, and the lay American Catholic insists more

* "The King, Jesus Christ and the Church—God in three names."

emphatically on his "Americanism" than do Protestants or atheists of, perhaps, longer American ancestry.

There is a purely American "way of life" led by every good American Christian that is point-for-point opposed to the publicized and largely fictitious "way of life" dreaded in Europe and Asia. And that by the Grace of God is the "way of life" that will prevail.

22

>>｜<<

D. W. Brogan

1950

from *"The Catholic Church in America"*

>>｜<<

D. W. Brogan, Professor of Political Science at Cambridge University, England, has achieved a large measure of non-academic fame by his brilliant efforts to interpret America to Englishmen and to Americans. Not since de Tocqueville have we had a more sympathetic or perceptive student of our national life, customs and characters. Born in Glasgow, Scotland, Mr. Brogan studied at Glasgow University, Oxford and Harvard. Both in books—notably *The American Character*—and in magazine articles he has presented the fruit of his almost continuous scrutiny of the American people.

This article, "The Catholic Church in America," was first published in *Harper's Magazine* (Vol. 200, no. 1200) May, 1950. It is used with permission of *Harper's Magazine* and the author, the copyright owner.

>>｜<<

I

In the year 1948, the people of North Dakota, in a referendum, voted to prohibit teachers engaged by local school boards from dressing as they chose. This piece of sumptuary legislation was directed at the nuns employed in some overwhelmingly Catholic areas of that state. A month or two later, Hollywood issued its latest travesty of *The Three Musketeers* in which the villain, the Duc de Richelieu, was also deprived of his customary dress which would have revealed to possibly indignant Catholics the fact that he was a cardinal. (It would not necessarily have revealed that he was also a priest and bishop, theologically more important facts.) These two scraps of news illustrate the ambiguous position of the Catholic Church in America. It is highly suspect; it may at any moment be the victim of hysterical legislation and it is, at the same time, a very powerful lobby whose real or assumed interests and feelings are to be cultivated to absurd lengths by anybody, political or commercial, that has to do business in those areas where the Catholics are numerically strong— that is, in every big city of the United States outside the South.

Looked at from one point of view, the Catholic Church is in danger of as much repression as the Constitution allows; looked at from another, it is a danger to the Constitution and the American way of life. Neither picture is true. No essential Catholic rights are, so far, in danger; neither is the Constitution nor the American way of life. But that such illusions should be widespread, that Catholics and Protestants should each be busy looking under the bed for murderously inclined enemies, is proof that there is something odd if not wrong in the position of the most numerous body of American Christians.

And the first cause of this ambiguity can be stated simply. The United States is a Protestant country; this seems a platitude but it is much more than that. It is not that the majority of Americans are adherents, more or less active, of Protestant churches, it is that the historical background, the historical traditions, the folkways, the whole national idea of the "right thing" is deeply and almost exclusively Protestant. There are exceptions to this rule but they are not important. Saint Augustine, the Catholic survivals in Maryland, fragments of New Spain in the Southwest, these are merely specks in a vast landscape where, at all times since white settlement, the religious tone has been set by Protestantism. That the Catholic Church in the United States is the largest organized denomination or that it is the richest and most important branch of the Catholic Church are important but, in this context, irrelevant facts. What is the relevant fact is that the Catholic tradition is new, exotic, suspect. André Siegfried a long time ago advised French Protestants and Jews to leave anticlerical campaigns to the French "Catholics" and always to remember that for those anticlericals "the curé is part of the furniture." The Catholic Church in America is much richer, has more members, and, in many ways, is more powerful than the Church of France, but the priest is most certainly not a part of the American furniture.

The consequences are important and often neglected. It means that, despite their numbers, American Catholics in public controversy suffer from two handicaps. They use the language of American controversy clumsily and their non-Catholic audience does not often make much effort to discover what they are saying.

Then the absence of a Catholic past in America has quite important social and political results. It is possible for millions of Americans to have the most naïve ideas about Catholics, when they have not absurd and hostile ideas. Even in a statistically overwhelmingly Protestant country like Norway, there is a Catholic past which is part of the national inheritance and a writer like Sigrid Undset found a natural audience that Willa Cather had not got for her tales of the American Catholic past. Catholic life in New Mexico and Quebec was not quite as foreign as the rituals of the Indians so admirably described by Edmund Wilson, but it was very foreign. In Scotland, there are the Catholic heroes of the national past. In divided countries like Germany and Holland, it is necessary for both parties to accept, in some degree, the religious heroes of the other side. But in America this is not necessary and so it is not done.

There is, for example, comparatively little curiosity about Catholic doctrine and Catholic organization. (The success of Thomas Merton's books may mark a change, but may mark no more than the appeal of the totally exotic.) Despite Hollywood, a priest is a strange and possibly sinister figure; monks and nuns are even more suspect. I remember a leading Chicago educa-

tionalist expressing his horror at the discovery made at the funeral
of a Catholic high school principal that he had been a "secret
monk" all those years. It was obvious that the deceased had
been a "tertiary of St. Francis," which no more made him a
monk than being a member of the Epworth League made a
Methodist layman a bishop. And it is worth remembering that,
for millions of American Catholics, the critics of monks and
nuns, the objectors to their robes and religious names, are liable
to be regarded as the spiritual and possibly fleshly descendants
of those Americans who burned down the Charlestown convent
and made Maria Monk a best seller. True, the mendacious Miss
Monk got most of her readers, I suspect, from people who read
her confessions instead of *Fanny Hill,* as they drank highly
alcoholic medicines instead of whiskey, to combine sanctifica-
tion with pleasure. But a Catholic layman, or even a bishop or
priest, may suppress his irritation with some activities of the
religious orders of men and women when he recalls the earlier
American Protestant obsession with sins of the sisterhoods.

Another result of the newness of Catholicism in America
is the sense of superiority on one side and inferiority on the other
that it breeds. Just as Thomas Sanction has rightly said, "every
white man is at heart a sahib," there is a sense in which every
American Protestant tends to regard American Catholics as
intellectually, socially, and religiously inferior—and the American
Catholic as a rule is not sure enough of himself to be indifferent.
Sometimes this may take merely social forms—but in a country
with fluid social movement like America, the "merely" is out of
place. It is with genuine surprise that many Americans (Catholic and Protestant) learn that in England, for instance, being
a Catholic can be very smart. I can remember the indignation
of a Boston friend of mine who was startled that the late Marquess of Hartington had married a daughter of Joseph Kennedy,
when I pointed out to her that, from the point of view of English people who cared for such things, the difference between a
Cavendish and a Cabot was so great that the difference between

a Cabot and a Kennedy was invisible. And one reason, I am convinced, why the serious character of *Brideshead Revisited* was not appreciated in America was the double difficulty of taking seriously the religious scruples of fashionable people and of finding them to be Catholics. So that much less convincing *cas de conscience, The Heart of the Matter,* was much more what a Catholic novel *ought* to be.

The average American is very familiar with the idea of a Catholic cop (though not with such sensitive ones as the hero of Graham Greene's novel), but not with Catholic noblemen. Of course, this social distinction is not absolutely universal. A member of an old Maryland Catholic family is at home in Rome in a way that Henry James might have envied and studied. But by and large, American Catholics are neither accepted nor feel themselves accepted as Americans whom other Americans treat as being totally equal. And that the distinction is religious is, I think, made manifest by the acceptance of very bogus "Scotch-Irish" pedigrees proffered by people whose Protestantism (sometimes fairly recent) saves them from being classified as "Micks."

In practically every part of the United States, the Catholics are newcomers, what Charles Maurras used to call "*métèques,*" and so there is a constant strain caused by their growing strength (for if they are no longer growing in relative numerical strength, they are growing in wealth, political and social power, intellectual stature, and pretensions). Inevitably, the majority more or less consciously resent this growth, both on simple grounds of human dislike of what is strange and on the more defensible ground that American society would be more united if all these Catholics would "Americanize" themselves—an idea which, when examined, means cease to be Catholics or become really *American* Catholics—and that in turn means, again, cease to be Catholics, for the word and the institution mean that there is something wider and more important than being an American: being a member of the Church Universal where there is neither

Jew nor Gentile nor even American and non-American. The tension is natural; it will last. At times it seems to increase in force, at others it diminishes, but it never disappears.

The prosperous and prospering American Catholic has often a chip on his shoulder as has the prosperous and prospering American Jew. Each thinks and thinks rightly (the Jew with more reason as a rule than the Catholic) that it is likely that he will, from time to time, suffer social slights and exclusions because of his origin, that at best he will get kindness, not justice.

More important is the intellectual touchiness of the American Catholic. If the intellectual weakness of the educated European Catholic is conceit, the weakness of the American Catholic is a defensive feeling that while, of course, he is right, he can't quite make the other side take that claim seriously, much less accept it. Thus in Paul Blanshard's book, a great deal of his argument for changing American Catholicism is simply a plea for resuming the Reformation, for converting the benighted Catholics from their superstitions. In Europe, it would be recognized that whatever other possibilities of religious change are open, a resumption of the Reformation, the acceptance of Protestantism even in its most "enlightened" forms (in fact least of all in its enlightened forms) is not one of them. Having survived the sixteenth century, the Catholic Church will not go over to the heirs of Calvin or Luther now, nor will its members—whatever triumphs the heirs of Voltaire and Marx may have before them. There is in the American Protestant attitude to Catholicism the old assumption that "there is a religion of all sensible men," which mere mental laziness, ignorance, false pride keep Catholics from accepting. Here American Protestants are merely human; there is an admirable comic description of that attitude on the other side in Stevenson's *Travels with a Donkey;* but the simple denizen of the French abbey had behind him all the prestige of sixteen hundred years. In America, the Protestant has behind him all the local equivalents of papal prestige and power. The Catholic feels it and is touchy.

But he is touchy for another reason. When he is asked to be tolerant, to accept advice from friendly exterior critics, a good many ancestral ghosts walk. The dominant group in the American Church is the Irish and when they are lectured on the beneficent results of the Reformation, they reflect that the results weren't beneficent for them. They are (if provoked) likely to ask that Protestant massacres in Ireland as well as Catholic massacres in Europe be remembered. They may recall that the Catholics, the Quakers, and, some would hold, the Mormons are the only denominations in America who have produced religious martyrs *in America*—and they don't mean martyrs at the hands of the Iroquois, but at the hands of the triumphant Puritans of Maryland.

In more modern times, too, the American Catholic, of Irish or German origin, is not necessarily impressed by the rebukes offered by liberalism. If religious intolerance is absolutely wrong (which is what the *liberals* say), then it is wrong as an accompaniment of revolution in Mexico and Russia; and when that persecution was going on in Mexico, or when it is going on now in Lithuania, one might expect (if one were naïve enough) impassioned protests from the run-of-the-mill liberal. If they have been made, they have been *sotto voce;* at any rate, few American Catholics seem to have heard them. The liberal, lay or cleric, does not seem to this American minority to come into court with clean hands. There may be doubts and ambiguities as to the Catholic position, but there are or should be none as to the liberal or modern Protestant position. Their duty was and is to affirm their faith in religious liberty in Lithuania and Vera Cruz, as well as in Spain or Italy. That no doubt means quarreling with allies and defending enemies, but what of it? Nor has the consistency of the liberals been surpassed by their foresight or understanding of the modern world. Indeed, looked at from the outside, the readiness with which the American liberals have followed their hearts, not their heads, with tragic or comic results, would suggest that modesty or even timidity would become them better than the naïve assumption in 1950 of the old justifiable complacency of the youth of John Dewey or H. G. Wells.

II

The most important result of the Protestant character of American life is the general failure to understand the parochial system. The characteristic of the parochial system in Europe has been, for many centuries, the existence in each community of one officially or popularly recognized ordinary representative of religion, the parish priest, the parson, the minister. The recognition of this representative was normally a joint decision of Church and State. But it was not always so. The State might give official recognition to one representative of religion, while the population gave recognition to another. Thus in Ireland, the "Church of Ireland" rector was hardly ever the uncontested representative of divine things for the great majority of the people of his parish. In most cases he was an unsuccessful rival of the Catholic priest, in some, of the Presbyterian minister. So in Scotland the parish minister recognized by law was often the head of a small group of people in a community whose real spiritual chief was a Free Church minister or, in some parts of the Highlands and the northeast, a Catholic priest. The same thing was and is true of parts of France, Holland, Germany, etc. But in most European countries, the parochial system represented a condition as well as a theory. In Norway, Pastor Manders had no rivals who needed to cause him worry. In nearly every community there was a church officer who was as much part of the pattern of life as the local doctor, postmaster, or schoolmaster. You might not like him or respect him, but there he was. If you wanted the comforts of religion, you went to him as you went to the local doctor to be vaccinated or to the local postmaster to buy stamps.

In parts of the United States this system has existed; in smaller areas it exists still. In Virginia, in South Carolina, the Anglican parson played this role in Colonial times. In other places the Dutch Reformed minister played the part. More important, all over New England the minister filled this role. But in by far the greater part of the present United States—and in nearly all parts of the present United States even where there has been in the past a parochial system—the mere idea of the parish system is unknown. There are places in Louisiana where the priest plays the role of a parish priest; there are areas in Indiana, for example, where the priest plays among the German settlers there much the role that a priest does in the Rhineland. There are places like Lawrenceville where the Presbyterian church has the position of the Presbyterian church in a small Scottish town. But by and large, the American unit of church organization is the congregation, that is, a group of people united in wanting a special type of religious aid and comfort, not a group of people resorting to a territorially determined agency of religious services. And alone among important American religious bodies, the Catholics cling to the parochial system, with consequences often ignored by Catholics and nearly always ignored by their neighbors—and by their ecclesiastical competitors.

There is, of course, nothing especially sacred or immutable in the parish system. French Catholics are even now discussing, with a good deal of passion, the proposition that in great industrial areas at any rate, the parish has seen its best days and that a Christian "cell," which may be in fact a congregation in the American sense, alone can win back the pagan masses of Paris to Christ and the Church. But in America the Catholic parish is the unit, and in most areas it is the only unit of its kind.

How does this affect the relationship of American Catholics with their fellow countrymen, especially with that minority of Americans who are active members of organized religious bodies? It leads to a great over-estimation of the power of the American Catholic clergy, to a political temptation to cultivate their good will, to delusions of grandeur among the clergy and episcopate, and to a grossly exaggerated fear of Catholic clerical power among politicians and among hostile and, sometimes, envious Protestant ministers. It is easy to see why this mistake is made. The politician or the minister sees crowds pouring into the local Catholic church, crowds going to a series of "services" on a Sunday morning when the ministers of the community are each fighting an often losing battle with the attractions of golf or the inertia bred by a hangover. *If* the Catholic church were a Protestant church, such crowds would be proof positive of the personal weight and power of attraction of the minister. Sometimes that attraction is much to the credit of the minister and the congregation; sometimes as in, say, Fort Worth, Los Angeles, and Minneapolis in fairly recent times, it was to nobody's credit— from a "liberal" point of view. The Protestant church may be full because the minister is Harry Emerson Fosdick; it may be full because he is Elmer Gantry. But the Catholic church may be and, usually, is full because it is the only Catholic church in a defined territory and its crowds prove no more about the abilities, the character, or the popularity of the parish priest than do crowds in a post office.

Of course, in a big city, it is not quite so simple. Many people may go to mass at a smart church run by the Jesuits or Paulists or Dominicans rather than to the local parish church, but that is an exception. The parish system is the norm and it underlines the fact that the Catholic priest is a priest and not a preacher. He is a professional man carrying out functions that he alone can carry out. He is not a performer building up an audience. Of course, certain well organized Protestant churches, especially the Methodists, have a modified version of the parish system, but they cannot impose the monopoly position of the Catholic parish priest. (I know one southern hamlet, too small to be called a village, in which there are two Methodist churches, as well as one Presbyterian church.) But the average American does not see that the priest is a professional man with the local "franchise"; he sees him as a preacher making friends and influencing people by preaching, visiting, by all the arts winning men to God or the Devil. So the priest is given credit for far more influence than he need possess and is compared with a popular and really influential minister, when often a closer parallel is with the local manager of Bell Telephone system.

The functional, impersonal, official character of the parish priest is seen at a higher and more baffling level (for the Protestant) in the Catholic bishop. For the priest has to please the bishop, while the bishop, roughly speaking, has to please nobody. No doubt he has important, i.e., rich, laymen to coax for funds; he has to obey, in final matters, the Pope; but by and large he is his own boss. This is so well known that there is (I am told) an English Catholic joke according to which his priestly friends tell a new-made bishop, "You'll never eat a bad meal or hear the truth again." The last is probably an exaggeration, but what is certain is that a bishop does not have to justify his authority often enough. No doubt (I am not privy to the secret discussions of any hierarchy) his brethren on the episcopal bench tell him home truths, but that is about all they can do. In his own diocese he isn't arguing, he is telling them, them being his priests. But he has, in practice, also to tell his laity, over whom he has far less control, and non-Catholics over whom he has none, directly at least. But the habits of uncontested command are not really suitable for public discussion—as is made only too obvious by many episcopal pronouncements from Cardinal Spellman downward. Of course, some of the lapses in episcopal tact and manners are due to the American habit of conducting delicate controversies at the top of one's voice. And the public manners of Bishop Oxnam and Monsignor Sheen suggest that among bishops the habit isn't confined to Catholics and that among Catholics it is not confined to bishops. If Cardinal Griffin and Monsignor Knox, Dr. Newton Flew and Dr. Donald Soper don't feel the need to shout, it is not their Catholicism or Methodism that explains their conversational tone, but their life in England, where even religious shouting is thought to be bad form.

Manners apart, it is a pity that Catholic bishops, singly or collectively, have not learned that more moderation in the use of adjectives would secure a better hearing, or even a hearing. For, whether they know it or not, a great deal of what they say goes with the wind as fast as they say it, as far as the average Protestant is concerned and, sometimes, as far as the average Catholic is concerned, too. Cardinals and bishops don't realize this, for like prominent ministers and rabbis they are favored people, newspapers give them space, automatically, though sermons and other ecclesiastical pronouncements must outrank editorials for the place of the least read section of newspapers.

III

It is a pity, for it means that there is far less *discussion* of religious questions in America than is desirable *if* there is to be public discussion, a question not to be settled out of hand, as Dr. George N. Shuster has pointed out. As he said, the "pot will bubble if the fire is fed" and whatever the motives of the feeders, the result is not likely to aid Americanism, or to do more than create toil and trouble.

Look, for example, at the controversy over banning the *Nation* because of Mr. Blanshard's articles. Nothing could, at first sight, seem more obvious than that the New York school authorities are wrong and that the *Nation* and the embattled liberals are right. But important questions should not, even in the atomic age, be settled at first sight. And second sight provokes second thoughts. The *Nation* has not been suppressed; Mr. Blanshard's book did not meet, in publication, anything like the difficulties that, for so long, prevented discussion of Christian Science. But the New York school authorities decided that the taxpayer's money should not be used in circulating a magazine which so deeply offended the parents of so many tens of thousands of school children and, of course, so many hundreds of thousands of voters. It is no adequate answer to say that Catholics should not be offended, that Mr. Blanshard is honest, careful, and public-spirited. I have no doubt he is all these things. I have no doubt that he is innocent of any conscious desire to hurt or shock, but he hurt and he shocked and I don't see how any reader, with any power of sympathetic imagination, can fail to see that he must hurt and shock. Many of the points made by Mr. Blanshard seem to me valid, others, at any rate, well worth discussion; others reveal a curious conviction, more fitting for a congressional committee than for a serious controversialist, that when a thing has been described as un-American, the case is settled. (It would be pardonable for instance to think that it was in Canada, that priest-ridden country with its church schools paid for out of taxes, that the Ku Klux Klan, the Dies Committee, Murder Incorporated, and other odd features of modern life flourished.)

But even if Mr. Blanshard never made any mistakes, or if he revealed a passionate desire to reform Catholicism in Catholic terms, even if he were a Lamennais or a Bernanos, there is a good case against circulating articles like his through the public school system—and a good reason provided by the main claim made by the defenders of that system like Dr. Conant. The claim is that the public school system is the main maker of American unity (and the parochial school system an enemy of American unity). The first claim is, I think, undoubtedly true, the second highly plausible. It is as makers of a national ethos, as the creators of an American attitude, that the public schools, at all grades, make their best contribution; and that contribution is so great that it more than makes up for their notorious weaknesses as educational institutions in the old and, possibly, obsolete European sense.

But if they are to fulfill this function, then certain other functions of a complete educational system must be abandoned; they must not raise questions that destroy the unity. Thus, in France, no defender of the lay school in theory (the practice was somewhat different) justified critical discussion of Catholic doctrine in the public schools; to have done so would have totally justified the setting up of a rival school system by the Catholics. I think the New York school authorities were right, as they would be right in refusing to circulate a magazine giving a correct but hostile account of the ritual practices of orthodox Jews in the Bronx (or of Mormons in Utah). *Toute vérité n'est pas bonne à dire,* a wise maxim most certainly applicable in a system whose main business is to find the common denominator on which, alone, a people so diverse in origin as the Americans can unite. And if Mr. Blanshard or his friends believe that they are really contributing to American unity by polemics of this kind, well, as the Duke of Wellington said to the man who said he believed he was Mr. Smith. "If you can believe that, you can believe anything."

There is another point. One of the most important sections of Mr. Blanshard's book deals with medico-legal questions on which official Catholic teaching is different from that of most non-Catholic doctors. I think that Mr. Blanshard has made one or two very important and valid points, but he also raises some questions about which it would be gross impertinence to say that he has not thought deeply, but on which it is, I think, fair criticism to say that the deep thought is not visible in the book.

For instance, it is easy to push a Catholic onto the defensive by asking what rational defense there can be for a doctrine that forces a doctor (and a husband) to let a woman die when she could be saved by killing a fetus that, in no possible way, could live. The Catholic defense, if it is to be made, will have to be made at a much higher level, that this life is unimportant and that in the sight of God the mother and the fetus are of equal value. The effectiveness of this defense will depend on how deeply the Catholic believes this and I am sure Mr. Blanshard is right in asserting that many young American Catholic women do not at all accept this view of their unimportance in this world. But there are other questions involved; should a mother be saved at the cost of a fetus that could live? If so, why? Because the mother is more valuable? How do you know? Because the mother and father have the right to decide? One could go on; one could recall the notorious fact that many abortions are performed to save trouble, not life, that one of the makers of the modern liberal mind defended infanticide, the killing of fully delivered children whose presence embarrassed their (unmarried) mothers. But it will be objected that these are absurd projections of a humane attitude. Maybe, but Catholics are not rationalists. They agree with Cardinal Newman that it is not "a slight benefit to know what is needed for the proof of a point, what is wanting in a theory, how a theory hangs together, *and what will follow if it be admitted*." There's the rub, what could follow might be Auschwitz, the extermination of Jews and Gypsies. And on the principles of what may be called statistical morality: if that is what the majority wants, it is all right. If it isn't, again, why not?

These are questions that should be raised if controversies of the type started by the *Nation* are to be encouraged in schools. Does anyone think that boys and girls of the dating age need no guidance (I mean intellectual, not dogmatic) on these points? Does anyone doubt that if these controversies are to be fostered in the educational system, a Catholic parent is fully justified in keeping his children away from the public schools and that he has a real grievance if he is taxed to support a school system in which things he feels most sacred are open to teen-age discussion, with no more leadership than the teachers are trained to give in these matters—which is none?

I have said that Mr. Blanshard makes some valid points. I think, for example, that it is scandalous (as far as it is true) that Catholic nurses should be encouraged to dodge their duty of getting patients the religious comfort they want. If a Catholic nurse is to behave in this way, she has no more place in a public tax-supported hospital system than a zealous Quaker has in West Point.

There is another question that is implicitly raised and which is of considerable political importance. This is the degree to which clerical authority is effective in these matters. It is far less effective than it looks on paper, which, I am sure, is not a secret from the clergy. And there are two reasons for that. One is that Catholic moral theology is much more rigorous than the modern world will really stand. Problems like those raised by Mr. Blanshard were not important in the old days when the mothers couldn't be saved anyway—and when their opinions were not asked. But we live in a world of feminism and of science. Many women's lives can be saved and women are now well out (in America) of their old docile acceptance of masculine authority (perhaps they were never in it anywhere).

Then the Church, in its official organization, is a masculine body. The most popular saint of modern times is a woman, but Sainte Thérèse of Lisieux could be a saint but not a priest. The woman's point of view is not, in fact, automatically present in the minds of the bishops or of the Roman congregations. (And final decisions are made in Rome, where women have not yet attained the freedom of American women.) In addition, the questions raised by abortion, birth control, etc., are questions in which clerical opinion is necessarily exterior. Priests or nuns dedicated to perpetual continence are in a strong position in preaching to boys and girls the beauty and propriety of pre-marital chastity. But they are in a weak position preaching to married couples about problems of which they know nothing at first hand. The priest gets less help from his professional textbooks than is often thought, for they are written from the outside in a curious rabbinical spirit of mechanical regulation. When one considers that a main charge against the Catholic Church has been its readiness to be all things to all men, the way in which it insists on asking for trouble over questions like these suggests deep conviction—and the passion with which the campaign against the legalization of birth-control in Massachusetts was conducted suggests both passion and panic. For it is impossible to believe that the bishops of Massachusetts do not know that contraception is as widely practiced in that state as in any other, or that the Bishop of Hartford does not know that (so I am told) it is perfectly easy to buy contraceptives in Connecticut.

Why then do they fight for such formal victories? For the same reason as the Methodists of Oklahoma defend formal prohibition of alcohol in that state: not that it does much to cut down the consumption of booze but that it is a public testimony against sin. So, too, it is unlikely that the Catholic leaders in France and Italy who have campaigned against public brothels think that their disappearance will notably increase morality; but the state will not be an open partner in it. This is a respectable attitude but when it leads to such excesses of political pressure as have been seen in Massachusetts, it is an expensive attitude, breeding that lay dislike of too much clerical interference which has cost the Church so much, especially in Catholic countries.*

Catholic zeal over the suppression of indecent books, opposition to easy divorce, the importation of Irish sexual prudery and Puritanism may, in the not very long run, do the Church as much harm as the antics of Bishop Cannon and his kin did American Protestantism. People may laugh at an official who believes that a man who has committed fornication is unfit to be an American citizen (page Dr. Kinsey), but they may cease to laugh if the Church really manages to impose its standards on the average sensual man and woman.

There is a danger here of worldly hypocrisy. A great many books, plays, films are, in fact, designed to stimulate sexual desire and give sexual pleasure, activities that on good New Testament authority are gravely sinful. A great deal of anti-clericalism in all countries comes from men whose pleasure is interfered with. "Don't forget," said that wise man, Élie Halévy, "that Molière would have disliked Tartuffe even more if he had been sincere." It is not clerical hypocrisy that annoys, it is clerical sincerity, if you like, clerical fanaticism.

What the Catholic bishops are fighting is the growth of forces in American life that make the maintenance of the old Christian standards of sexual morality increasingly difficult.

* Two recent investigations (both made by Catholics) have shown that although the Catholic birth rate in England and Scotland is higher than the average, it is not much higher and it is lower than the general birth rate of a generation ago.

The formal increase in the membership of all churches, the support given to organized church activities by business, by the press, cannot conceal the fact that in one most important field of human conduct, the standards defended and imposed by all orthodox Christians for two thousand years are on a losing defensive in America (and of course elsewhere). So the Catholic bishops try to call in the secular arm, but the secular society does more harm than any amount of censorship and moral policing can do good. After all, it is not the movies, the burlesques, the sexy historical novels that do most to weaken the old folkways; it is advertising. But advertising is business and so sacred. I am convinced that if the manufacture of contraceptives were economically as important in Connecticut as divorce is in Nevada, the Catholic leaders of the state would be as impotent to destroy the business as Senator McCarran is to shut down the divorce mills of Reno. It is not unnatural that the bishops should lunge about wildly, doing their cause more harm than good, but they are discussing or, at any rate, talking about an important problem which few people really want discussed candidly. They make nuisances of themselves, and, as censors, are often markedly naïve, but Christians should not worry about the sneers of the world. "To the Greeks foolishness" is a living text today. And though one might never think it, Bishop Oxnam and Cardinal Spellman have more in common than either has with the most enlightened agnostic liberal. Cardinal Spellman at least knows this.

IV

What separates them? Partly an old Protestant tradition, partly an older Catholic tradition. Protestants naturally regard the Church of Rome with some of the feelings with which a good American regards England. It is his mother or it is the pit from which he was digged or it is both, even at the same time. And quite apart from theological principles, the Catholic regards the Protestant as a truant. If he comes home all will be forgiven, but he must come home first.

Then the richest and most important branch of the Catholic Church is, as I have said, forced to exist in the most Protestant country in the world. And its high command is in a country where it is quite natural to think of Protestantism as a passing fad. It is difficult to go to Rome and not to feel that, or not to recall, with more amusement than anything else, the fantastic project to erect a vast Methodist building on the Janiculum (I think) that would have put St. Peter's in the shade, a dream of the days when American Methodism was riding high, wide, and handsome to political disaster, as American Catholicism may be doing now. It is another ground of friction that the effectiveness of papal authority is exaggerated, like the extent of the infallibility claimed for the Pope. The centralization and uniformity of Catholic authority is more on paper than in reality. The central bureaucracy is muscle-bound and the belief that the Vatican is preternaturally shrewd in its estimates of world affairs is a romantic dream. The record of the nineteenth century shows that. Yet Catholics in America have to take the rap for bigotry or folly in Spain or Latin America, while northern Protestants need accept no responsibility for southern serpent handlers, or American Protestants in general for the latest news of barbaric race pride plus vaunting Protestant orthodoxy in South Africa.

There is not, perhaps, a great deal that American Catholics (or anybody else) can do to induce a sense of proportion and decency in Spanish bishops, but they could do something. They are so important to the Church that a firm explanation to the Vatican of the harm done in America by Spanish intolerance might do good. And it might be made, *if* reproaches to American Catholics for their palliation of intolerance were made as candidly and as charitably as they have recently been made in England by Dr. H. G. Wood.* But, alas, they are not likely to be made in that tone as long as the fact that friction is natural and incurable is not accepted, on both sides, with more clarity; or until it is accepted that no Christian Church can give uncondi-

* *Religious Liberty Today.*

tional allegiance to any state, and that no state, however Catholic—Ireland or Portugal or the France of St. Louis—will ever give, or should ever give, the clergy all they claim. The outsider may laugh or be surprised (though he should not be surprised; it is a long time since it was said, "How these Christians love one another"). But even the outsider, the pagan, if he is a patriotic American, or a foreign wellwisher like myself, should regret that so much American time and temper are being spent in sterile controversy, that the need for tolerance—and its high price—are not yet fully accepted in Jefferson's country.

It is right however to point out that one kind of tension is sometimes confused with another. For not only is there a permanent tension over the Catholic question, there is an old American anti-clerical tradition which, at any given moment, comes into play against the body of clerics that seems to be making most of a nuisance of itself. It is an old tradition; it goes back to colonial Virginia and colonial Massachusetts. It is represented by some of the greatest names in American history. Patrick Henry against the parsons; Benjamin Franklin against the Quakers (yes, there can be Quaker clericalism); Jefferson against the "priests," by which he meant the orthodox ministers of New England. Twenty-five years ago, it was the Protestant evangelical clergy, especially in the South. Then "liberals" sought allies among the Catholics to fight the Methodist Board of Temperance, Prohibition, and Public Morals. Now, though not quite so clearly, the animus of the anti-clericals is directed against the Catholic hierarchy. But it could be directed against any clerical interference that really riles the average man. It is not to be confused with the anti-Catholic animus as such though, at this moment, they may be hard to distinguish.

V

It was, I believe, Robert Louis Stevenson who said that Carlyle talked as if telling the truth were as easy as playing blind hookey. Many people talk as if religious tolerance were as easy, in theory and practice, as playing gin rummy. It isn't. It is, of course, easy to tolerate beliefs and practices that do not interest or affect you at all. At this distance, few of us are upset about oddities of religious practice in Tibet. It is easy, too, to be tolerant of beliefs that differ in minor ways from your own. Modern Presbyterians can tolerate, with ease, modern Congregationalists. You may even put up with eccentricities of people formally in union with you, though you may doubt their sanity or loyalty. (The history of the Church of England in modern times suggests that this is a strain, too.) But the real test of your devotion to tolerance comes when you tolerate beliefs and practices that you think imbecile, dangerous, immoral, disgusting, or disloyal. If you do not tolerate such beliefs and practices, then you are not being tolerant. If you do tolerate them, but resentfully and reluctantly because you have to, you may practice toleration but you don't feel tolerant.

But that means that many people, perhaps most people, don't really believe in toleration? Of course it does; most people don't. As Justice Holmes pointed out, there is nothing unnatural in suppressing beliefs that you think you know to be wrong and dangerous—*if* you have the power. A great deal of toleration has grown up in the modern world just because people hadn't the power. You may refuse to persecute because the cost of even successful persecution to the winners would be too great; it would cause a civil war which, even if you were sure of winning it, would be a political disaster (the argument that led to Catholic Emancipation in the British Isles in 1829). You can abandon persecuting measures because they are a source of national disunion, as Bismarck did when he accepted defeat in the *Kulturkampf*, not because he thought it was wrong, but because he thought it was proving politically too costly. You may, when the whole question is rather academic, abandon formal legislation against a small religious minority in deference to world opinion and to the irrelevance of the legislation, as Sweden has recently abandoned its anti-Catholic legislation. (I have deliberately chosen examples of Catholics benefiting by these courses of conduct since they will be more of a novelty to the average reader.) You may, as the French *politiques* probably thought in the sixteenth century, regard both sides and all the questions involved as irrelevant to the problem of ruling the state well. These are pragmatic reasons for being tolerant and are probably the reasons that, in fact, animate most people who are tolerant as a result of reflection and not as a result of mere authoritative teaching of national slogans without any corresponding reflection, the kind of teaching given in many American public schools.

But even if you are convinced that you are right, if you think that, in your case, Holmes's reference to the once fighting creeds that have lost their power has no relevance, you may still be tolerant on another and higher ground, that to coerce a man into denying his most important convictions about the nature of the universe is the most odious crime a state can commit. (Normally this means forcing a man to adopt one religion and abjure another, but I have chosen different words to cover the case of atheist martyrs, of whom there may have been some.)

It is only the last doctrine that really fortifies you against all the temptations that assail the man of good will at the sight of human folly. For, of course, orthodox Protestantism is no guarantee for and orthodox Catholicism is a guarantee against the complete toleration of the religious or the anti-religious follies of our neighbors. It must be a very convinced devotee of the doctrine of private judgment who has not had doubts when he has contemplated the religious pages of the Los Angeles press on Sunday mornings! It must be a very trusting believer in the good sense of the common man who does not occasionally share Renan's doubts about the right of the average man, brought up in a Catholic society, to reject so admirably articulated a system of doctrine as that provided by the Church. (I hasten to add that I know that Renan also said that the typical anticlerical, M. Homais, was right all the same.)

Toleration *is* difficult, much more difficult than the average writer about it thinks. Was it for example intolerant for the East India Company to suppress *suttee* and *thuggee,* two religious customs treasured by Hindu orthodoxy, but regarded by Westerners like Bentinck and Macaulay as forms of murder? It might be argued that all the English rulers of India were doing was to prevent Indians murdering other Indians under cover of religion. But what of a widow who desired to be burned alive on her husband's pyre? Macaulay had no doubts. Toleration or no toleration, it was not allowed. A Christian who thinks that suicide should be penalized can agree with Macaulay. But a believer in complete religious freedom or in the complete freedom of moral choice is in no such simple position.

Is it intolerance to ban Christian Scientists from exercising authority in universities with medical schools? The late Lord Lothian, a great public servant with all the normal qualifications, was not elected chancellor of the University of Edinburgh because he was a Christian Scientist and therefore, it was said, would be out of place as formal head of a university whose greatest glory was its medical school. Had Lord Lothian remained a Catholic, he might also have been defeated, since it might have been held that his religion disqualified him from being head of so eminently Protestant an institution as the University of Edinburgh. But that argument could not be used in barring a great learned Catholic nobleman from the lord rectorship of Glasgow University whose founders, a pope, a king, a bishop, were all Catholics. Nevertheless the third Marquess of Bute who, in addition to all his other qualifications, was a great benefactor of that university, was not elected lord rector because he was a Catholic. That was, I think, intolerance of a kind that Catholics are more inclined to remember than are the members of the dominant sects in the English-speaking world.

Orthodox Judaism, orthodox Calvinism, orthodox Catholicism, orthodox Liberalism (there is such a thing), all involve spectators in considerable pain, moral or intellectual. But tolerance involves submitting to these exhibitions of human weakness;

humor involves suspecting that you, in turn, are a cause of tears, temper, or laughter, in other people. It involves Mr. Blanshard's putting up with scapulars (although it does not involve preventing critically-minded Catholic laymen or clerics from pointing out to the marketers of scapulars the dangers of scandal). It involves Gentiles' controlling their astonishment or irritation at certain aspects of Jewish ritual. It involves Catholics' controlling their impatience at what they think is often the betrayal of the Christian cause by Protestant divines barely recovered from fellow-traveling. It involves, in fact, that very difficult art or attitude, tolerance. A parable from a most acute critic of America and of American Catholic life, the late Mr. Dooley, may make the point. He was asked why there were so few divorces in his part of Chicago. He replied that in the Archey Road, when a husband and wife found that they simply couldn't go on living together, they went on living together. No political union is a marriage of totally true minds, but it is a marriage all the same. Americans, of religion or none, will have to go on living together and they had better begin by learning the minor social arts that make it possible.

23

⟶⟩⟩❬❬⟵

Raymond L. Bruckberger, O.P.

1950

from *One Sky to Share*

⟶⟩⟩❬❬⟵

There is more than a little truth in the generalization that English visitors to America have been inclined to be antagonistic and French visitors to be friendly. Certainly the writings of Father Raymond L. Bruckberger, a French Dominican, would not belie this thesis. An enthusiastically friendly visitor, Father Bruckberger is a priest of many and varied talents. He was a fighter in the French Commandos, Chaplain General of the Resistance groups and chaplain of the French Foreign Legion in the Sahara Desert; he has written and directed films and is the author of several books, including a memorable fantasy, *The Seven Miracles of Gubbio*. He came to America in 1950. The journals he kept were later published under the title, *One Sky to Share*. These passages are from this book and are used with permission of P. J. Kenedy & Sons and Father Bruckberger, holder of the copyright.

⟶⟩⟩❬❬⟵

JUNE 5, 1950

I have been here for more than two weeks, and I have said nothing of the community that has welcomed me. Clearly, monastery life is theoretically the same everywhere, and nothing is more like a Dominican community in one place than another Dominican community somewhere else. In that sense, though I change my country, I never change my home, like those experienced travelers who always stay in the same Palace Hotels in Paris, London, Constantinople, Buenos Aires, Sydney, or Los Angeles.

The Dominican community in which I find myself is young, very young. There are thirty-five novices, an impressive number when you consider that they are destined for only one of the three Dominican provinces in the United States (and the newest of the three—only ten years old!), and that the novitiate is renewed each year. Moreover, forty more are expected by the month of September. They are charming and look even younger than they are—a trait common to the Nordic peoples. Not one speaks French, but since they are polite and friendly, they all smile when they encounter me. For me, that is the most important thing, perhaps even the most fundamental part of the dialogue without which no social life is possible.

In religious circles in Europe, it is believed, or claimed that life in American monasteries is lax. I have not found it so. Quite the contrary, in fact. The order of the day is different, but just as strict, and I must say that I have never seen a religious community more faithful to the Divine Office and to the common observances. There is really a fine atmosphere of contemplation, of prayer, and of joy. The recreation periods are incredibly animated and joyful; I have never laughed so hard, and I often feel as if I were seeing a very funny American movie. That is my life in the monastery that is without doubt the most beautiful modern monastery in the world.

I was surprised—I am used to it now—by the alert rapidity and the lusty vigor of the recitation of the Office. It is a real clamor mounting up to God, the proclamation of young and vigorous hearts, perhaps like an Indian war chant. I wonder if in this, too, the Americans are not right, if it is not their way that is in the true medieval tradition, rather than the ridiculous preciosity of the Gregorian chant sung in such and such a celebrated monastery in France.

In front of me in the choir there is a young Negro novice. Again I wish I were an artist so that I might paint that beautiful ebony face startling against the brilliant white of the Dominican habit. I cannot watch unmoved that young man at prayer: his proud and modest air, his oval face with lowered eyes and strong, regular features, expressing the candor and primitive vigor of his soul. An extraordinary visage of inner purity and the intense tranquility that comes from God. How I wish there were a great saint in the United States, Dominican and Negro; a saint such as St. Francis of Assisi who could inspire a whole generation of youth and create in this country spiritual forms as universally intelligible as the music of Harlem: sainthood in blue. There as elsewhere, the Church solves her problems from above, and without speaking of them. That is because at her heights she no longer has a problem. Her only thought is to give; to all, to give everything, to give with open hands.

At my window I stand above the little esplanade in front of the chapel and the entrance to the monastery. Every morning at the same hour a superb Buick glittering in the sun comes to a stop for a few minutes. It is the postman making his rounds.

JUNE 8, 1950 * CORPUS CHRISTI DAY

This morning I was present at High Mass, and at the Corpus Christi procession that always stirs me. Here it is less beautiful than it was in my old monastery in France, because here there is no cloister. Nevertheless, it had a charming simplicity. These Americans have a way of accenting the Gregorian chant which makes of the liturgy almost a military ceremony. I like that. And always the details that surprise and amuse no one but me. During the procession two novices were taking photographs. Under the ceremonial cope that I wore, I had put on a magnificent surplice of nylon. Why not?

WINONA * AUGUST 31, 1950

Yesterday, on the day of St. Rose of Lima, a Dominican and the first American saint, there was a reception, and thirty-six novices took the habit. From the altar where the Prior was seated out to the door where the families were massed, the floor of the chapel was packed. Thirty-six young Yankees asked admittance into the ranks of the Dominicans at the hands of the Castilian noble of Visigoth blood, blond and blue-eyed, who seven centuries ago founded his first monastery at Toulouse. What human institution can glory in such antiquity and such universality, based on authentic legitimacy? It is evident that the ceremony in all its detail, even to the short discourse read by the Prior, goes back to the origins of the order.

How well drawn the contract is, how carefully all precautions are taken in advance, so that in the future there can be no cause for complaint. . . . The language is not in the least sentimental, not the language of piety, but rather the tone of a Commando officer who calls his men together at the bivouac:

> Is it quite understood that you are all volunteers? I warn you for the last time that you may never come back. In any case it will be too late in a minute and anyone who hesitates can expect the treatment he deserves. Do you all agree? O. K., forward march, single column behind me. . . .

When one allows himself to talk like that to young men, he must not afterwards lead them to pick wildflowers. It is then, and only then, that they would have the right to complain of deception:

> . . . And when you have accomplished all these things perfectly, even then you will suffer tribulations, reproaches, humiliations, all of which you will have to bear with patience. However burdensome these ordeals may be, they have a great recompense: eternal life, which I promise will unfailingly come to you from God, if you observe what I have just said. Will you, then, insofar as it is possible, observe all that I have said to you? If you answer yes, it is the Lord who has begun, it is He who will complete the task!

Thus spoke the Prior to the thirty-six baseball players who listened on their knees, looking at him unwaveringly as a liegeman might have looked at his rightful lord.

Then the vestiture. For all the simplicity of the Dominican habit, it takes a long time to dress thirty-six novices one after another, and the choir endlessly repeated the admirable strophes of the *Veni Creator*. Each one, transfigured in his new uniform of white tunic and black cloak, came back to kneel in his place. I attentively watched their faces, made more youthful by the habit of the Order; they had precisely the grave and intent expression, with the half-pout of the lips, which every baby has when he bravely tries to take his first steps alone.

Finally the *Te Deum* was sung. At the end of the long ceremony in the delightful chapel, which seems to have been brought from Italy in the Liberty ships of victory,—then, in spite of the sacredness of the place, the American temperament burst out. As the ceremony dictates, the friars and the senior novices were placed in a double row in the center of the chapel from the sanctuary to the door. The newcomers in Indian file—the expression is very appropriate here—went from one to the other and gave the accolade, the "kiss of peace" which I have seen so perfectly done in the Benedictine monasteries of France. This is where America overflowed the boundaries of the ceremonial: the boys behaved rather like young puppies bumping each other about. In front of me one novice, a senior novice, smacked his fist lightly in the ribs of the friar he had just embraced. He repeated the performance with each one. Behind, among the joyful families, a young girl was nearly in tears from the effort of trying not to laugh. It was difficult to refrain from laughter. Never had the Negro embraced so many white men.

I have always noticed that in Europe such a ceremony is lightly veiled in sadness. Our old races love the world too much. But doubtless God prefers those who laugh as they give.

OCTOBER 10, 1950

I have tried to put young American artists on their guard against servile and gross imitation of French artists, whose greatness I nevertheless admire profoundly. How could I not warn young American scholars against the insidious propaganda of the French teachers of the "new theology"? I hate their false prestige and their lack of intellectual integrity. It is just there that I think their inferiority complex plays a nasty trick on young American scholars. They are too easily charmed by all that comes from France. I do not understand why. When one talks with American professors of theology or philosophy, one discovers that their minds are just as good as French minds, and that they are as capable of making their own philosophical systems. What is more, the rectitude of their intellectual conscience naturally preserves them from the casuistry of a fronde. Besides, here the authority of the Pope is not a meaningless phrase.

Nothing, however, is sadder to read than an American Catholic review of theology or philosophy. Not that the published articles are inferior, far from it, but they are nearly all translations or else signed by names not American. In Christian theology and philosophy, America is almost mute. Such silence and such absence of published thought are very serious, for in this field a great country like America cannot be replaced by anything or anyone. Especially since her theologians and her philosophers would bring to the common dialogue the vigor, integrity and straightforwardness that are characteristic of the best of America.

What causes this lack? Too much work. In a country where there is so much to do and to build, where audiences are avidly receptive, any Christian theologian or philosopher is overburdened the year round by the harassing task of teaching and more especially of preaching in all its forms. To a European it is inconceivable that excellent professors of theology should have sixteen to eighteen hours of classes a week. How could they possibly have any time to think or write? And moreover on Sundays and during vacations they must go off in all directions to preach. It is not the "new theology" of our French theologians which should fascinate young American scholars and clergy, but the working conditions of the French theologians who write books because they have the time to do so.

It is a serious situation, particularly serious in a country that understands perfectly the need of time for research in other fields. All the time necessary is available to those who engage in atomic and physiochemical research, in designing and testing planes, and in scientific medicine. It is not uncommon for a great university to pay full salaries to several professors and then leave them entirely free of classes so that they may write books or pursue their own studies. The results are here: America has many of the best physicists, the best chemists, the best civil engineers, the best doctors, in the world. If the same methods were applied in theology and philosophy, I have no doubt that America would have some of the best theologians and philosophers in the world. The men are here: you meet them, you talk with them, you feel their quality. They are here, but they have no time.

God and my readers will bear witness that I love America. If I were given three wishes that I thought important for the glory and the greatness of this country, one of the three would surely be the foundation of a Thomist Institute for advanced theological and philosophical studies, headed by a score or so of excellent young professors who would have to teach only two or three hours a week and whose job it would be to write and publish articles of a scientific character.

24

Eric von Kuehnelt-Leddihn

1950

from *"America Revisited"*

Eric von Kuehnelt-Leddihn is not exaggerating when he describes himself as a commuter to the United States. Born in Austria, he spent most of his youth in seeing the world, taking time out to earn his Ph.D. at the University of Budapest. He has taught at Georgetown, St. Peter's, Fordham and Chestnut Hill and has addressed the students of most Catholic colleges in this country on one of his frequent lecture tours. Politically, he is a rarity, proudly proclaiming the virtues of monarchism. He has written a variety of books, including a detective story, and articles by him appear regularly in English and American magazines and newspapers. When not lecturing he lives with his family in a Tyrolean mountain village. This article, "America Revisited," appeared in *The Catholic World,* January, 1950 and is reprinted here by permission of *The Catholic World.*

The average American has always considered the foreign lecturer a mixed blessing; especially the suave, titled British lecturer with an Oxford accent gives the impression of being an agent for alien interests. Although I am neither suave nor British I started on my own lecture tour of the United States last year with a certain hesitation because the message I was anxious to convey was far from popular or even reassuring.

Let me recount the presumptuous findings of a man who,

to all practical purposes, has become a commuter between the Old World and the New.

My first visual impressions upon arrival spell the word opulence. Of course, Switzerland and Belgium also bask in their wealth, but their scale is so very much smaller. The United States, moreover, has been considerably "dolled up" since 1947; the busses, the trains, the stores and even the homes have new services, new installations, new paint, new features, new small luxuries. After the severe regime of 2,150 calories *per diem,* the chocolate flavored banana split has its magic attraction and I gained, after my three months of breath-taking hurrying and scurrying, no less than twenty-three pounds.

But these are mere externals. The mood of the country I found changed in few respects because the "Great Awakening" as to the danger from the Soviet East had taken place just before I left the States in 1947.

Even so, I met some individuals—and a great many of them were Catholics—who combined strong political uneasiness with a curious form of subconscious Marxism. After I had given a lecture on crucial European problems in a large American city a group of businessmen discussed the matter with me. They were visibly unhappy about my antiquated views and one of them intimated that I had produced a brilliant, but long-haired college-professor talk which shirked the real issue. All the difficulty, according to this gentleman, came from the callous indifference of members of the European upper-class toward the common man whom they failed to keep happy with ice-cream cones, shiny automobiles and refrigerators.

Upon my remark that man does not live by bread alone and that there are autonomous ideas which have to be reckoned with, I caused even more dissatisfaction, and was asked to explain the essence of world history in a nutshell which, of course, I could not do. "Well, then I'll tell you," came the answer. "History is nothing but economics." "Are you a Catholic?" I inquired. "Yessir! I'm a daily communicant." Were it not for his religious convictions the good man would have made an excellent research director in the Marx-Engels Institute of Moscow.

There is not only too much general belief in the economic interpretation of history even in the best informed circles, but also the facile conviction that most countries' ills could be cured by the sole application of the social gospel. Too often one is not only faced by the effort to escape from the tragic, but also from the irrational which, whether we like it or not, does stalk the world. Poverty, misery and penury are by no means always the forerunners of Communism, and the fact that ideas can run away on their own legs, is frequently ignored.

Bulgaria, a country with a well-balanced agrarian distribution, always had its fill of Communists and Bohemia-Moravia belongs in the same category, nor does Communism among well-to-do French peasants make much sense. It is for this and other reasons that the otherwise admirable and vitally important enterprise, the European Recovery Program, will in itself not be able to lick Communism. Nor will Stalinism dissolve through reading of the Sears-Roebuck catalogue over the "Voice of America."

The Church in the United States is making enormous strides in many fields. Some of them are invisible to the naked eye, others are expressed in brick and stone. The vast majority of majestic buildings standing either isolated in the landscape or planted on the periphery of towns and cities are at least in some fashion serving Catholic activity. They may be colleges or orphanages, hospitals, old peoples' homes or high schools, convents, monasteries or other centers. There are also extensive additions to buildings already erected: the convent schools have new labs, the colleges new libraries, the hospitals new operating theaters, the monasteries new chapels.

This alone should discredit the European myth of the "dollar-loving American"; generosity and love of money do not mix. It is either/or. And the liberality of the American Catholic is really startling.

Progress since 1945 has been remarkable and the Church

is slowly leaving her imprint on the face of the country. The building activity is not the whole story because one sees Catholic books issued by secular publishers in secular bookstores; Catholic films in secular movie houses made by very secular companies; Roman collars and nuns' habits are met with frequently on the streets and the Church emerges—whatever the views of the Bible Belt—as a definitely American institution.

More than that: in the eyes of the agnostic and indifferent masses she appears to be the most concrete expression of religion. And last, but by no means least—the Church is also rapidly making the social grade and that in a competitive society with a subconsciously Calvinist attitude toward the hierarchy of earthly values, is of no mean importance.

Yet the stranger often wonders what reactions this growth must cause among those who are not of the faith. That there is a steadily increasing resentment which unites Protestants and "indifferentists" nobody who engages in endless nocturnal discussions in a Pullman smoker can doubt. To what extent these feelings will continue to rise it is impossible to foresee. The old accusation of "loyalty toward a foreign potentate" has, of course, disappeared and the old mixture of fear and snobbish contempt has turned into an uneasy envy.

There is the general consensus that the "use" the Church makes of the sacrificial obedience and the enthusiasm of her followers is not "fair": Catholics take their religion "too seriously"; they contribute too much money; those terrible nuns teach for a pittance in the parochial schools, etc., etc.

There is one thing which baffles me in the field of Catholic educational policy and that is the greater stress laid on the parochial grade schools than on the high schools. In order to underwrite the present order one must be convinced that the years of childhood are more important for the formation of a personality than those of adolescence—a position which is allegedly Jesuitical but curiously Freudian.

To the outsider it would seem wiser to concentrate on the

last two years of grade school and on the secondary education, not to mention the colleges. That such an adjustment might cause a minor earthquake in the Catholic educational system nobody will doubt. It would be a plain disaster for a lot of public grade schools—though a well-deserved retribution for the financial treatment of religious education which is without parallel in countries west of the Iron Curtain.

Taking into consideration the often heroic efforts to provide Catholic education it doubtless seems presumptuous for a European to find fault. (The Dutch Catholic educational system, much larger than the public or Protestant one, rests entirely on payments which the Dutch government is *privileged* to make.) But if American Catholics have not recognized more fully the important role and the enormous responsibilities which Divine Providence has placed on their shoulders, their Catholic institutes of higher learning are probably to be blamed for this shortcoming.

The burden which has been placed on the shoulders of American Catholics is indeed colossal; they represent the largest single religious unit in the most powerful nation of the world, and their faith, moreover, embodies not only Truth but is a living link between the two hemispheres, a role for which Protestantism with its national Churches and a mere thirteen per cent of the Continental population is patently unfitted.

American Catholics should therefore conscientiously cooperate in the supranational efforts of the Supreme Pontiff, whose title— *"Pontifex Maximus"*—means actually "Highest Bridgebuilder." The Catholic colleges and universities of America teach primarily the eternal verities of the Church, just as do Fribourg, Louvain, Milan and Nijmegen, but in the very next category they are almost exclusively institutions for the education of young Americans for an American way of life in the American fashion with an exclusively American outlook. (Imagine Louvain trying to make "typical Belgians" out of their students or Fribourg teaching "the Swiss way of life"! They would become places of higher learning of a purely *local* significance.)

Upon reflection it should be evident that owing to the indivisibility of the Common Good extending over the whole earth we Catholics are citizens of the world *before* we are citizens of any particular country. We should bravely acknowledge the fact that some of our avowed enemies on the left have handled much more cleverly their stolen goods—supranationalism, for instance—than we our own patrimony! It is precisely in this respect that the age-old accusation against the Catholic of being a second-rate patriot has wrought the heaviest damage.

Today America subconsciously expects from Catholics not a percentual increase in Purple Hearts and Congressional Medals, but a real mediatorship between the Continents through the intellectual, spiritual and material channels of the Church Universal. Dean Sperry of Harvard gave concrete expression to this disillusionment when he wrote that American Catholics have gone too far in their concept of patriotism; and I should like to add that they are leaning over backward in order to demonstrate their unfailing Americanism. This is a historico-chronological mistake, since the fairly legitimate attitudes of 1880 and 1890, once dictated by prudence, have today lost their meaning and purpose.

If American Catholics have failed to explain to their compatriots the perplexities of the Old World's political temperament, their higher schools cannot be entirely exonerated. They have not seriously tried to impart a certain insight into these strange but traditionally so important political forms of the past, nor have they sufficiently described the *via dolorosa* of the Catholic nations which for the past 160 years have been in a state of almost perpetual upheaval, drifting from one crisis to another even more catastrophic.

Instead, they have belittled almost everything grown on Catholic soil, apparently believing in a special outpouring of the Holy Ghost over the Protestant nations. It would be well if American Catholics were to make a serious study of Christopher Dawson and Donoso Cortés (cf. *The Catholic World,*

November, 1949), and the writings of their own Founding
Fathers.

In these matters it is necessary to make a distinction between
men's and women's colleges. It is the latter not the former which
impress the visiting lecturer most favorably, a statement I want
to extend to faculty and student body alike. Here again an er-
roneous type of patriotism is primarily responsible for the situation, which the relatively greater maturity of girls in their late
adolescence can only partly explain.

The smaller Catholic college often labors under notions which
the better non-Catholic institutions have fortunately discarded
long ago, for example, the idea that intellect and masculinity
are incompatible in "God's own country." A credit system for
chapel visits, plus the football coach as a central figure, are not
assets, either spiritually or intellectually speaking.

In addition, some of the teaching orders have a system of
rotation which sends their members every four or six years into
a totally different place with a radically different job. This system
has its spiritual advantages for the teachers but it hardly takes
the intellectual good of the students into sufficient account.

The nuns, on the other hand, have been far more on their
toes; and where the natural gifts were lacking, they have striven
to make up by hard, tenacious, if not heroic work. To lecture
in an American Catholic women's college is almost invariably
a pleasure and the enthusiasm and the intellectual curiosity
one encounters give added strength to the visiting lecturer.

In a Pittsburgh college instead of giving the one planned
lecture, I gave four and did it with real enjoyment. The one
class that I taught I found admirably prepared and the nuns
no less keen than the students. In Albany, Philadelphia, Los
Angeles, St. Louis, Portland, Milwaukee, Chicago, Weston,
Denver, and other places, the story was very much the same.

Of course, what I have said above about men's colleges is
by no means true of all of them. The seminaries which com-
manded my unreserved respect, the Canadian college not far

from Detroit, and the one diocesan college whose delightful and humorous priests entertained me at meals (humor is always a sign of intelligence), I will not easily forget.

It is in the men's colleges also that an inflexible spirit of conformity prevails and this spirit makes itself felt negatively in many another domain. I found it even in Catholic bookstores where the proprietors would not "touch" a Graham Greene, a Bernanos or a Bloy, and would not even handle *The Commonweal* under the counter. The mere fact that I wrote for it caused raised eyebrows.

"Do you really agree with their political views?" I was asked.

"Usually I don't."

"But you still write for them?"

"Yes, why not?"

Increased suspicion, and the mounting conviction that I am a man without principle.

All these strictures, however, are not meant to take an iota away from the real achievement of American Catholics which only the malicious would ignore. Again and again I was cheered by the American readiness and freshness in tackling organizational problems; the old pioneering spirit is far from dead.

One of the lay organizations which impressed me most was the "Te Deum International," with its forty-seven chapters, founded by an enthusiastic Springfield (Ill.) surgeon. His network, featuring dinner and forum talks, covers virtually the whole Middle West. In spite of its isolation it is this part of the nation which is the most refreshing. I have met there intelligent audiences, zealous priests and bishops who with their genuinely Christian urbanity gave the impression of being true successors of the Apostles rather than of the Byzantine emperors.

I admit that the participation of the younger age groups was often sadly wanting, but the curious indifference of young men toward affairs which might disastrously affect their lives is an old American phenomenon which brooks few exceptions save on the West Coast.

Certainly no effort should be spared to reach more Catholic students through the Newman Clubs; since the Catholic universities are at present unable to take care of all their applicants, a disgruntled ghetto-like attitude toward the burning problem of the spiritual welfare of Catholic youth in secular universities, is definitely out of place.

All in all the visiting lecturer cannot fail to be deeply impressed by the efforts of the Church in America. If this article contains more censure than praise, it should be remembered that maturity needs no patting on the back, but on the other hand makes constructive use of criticism. The contribution of American Catholics to the Church Universal is so staggering that no words of mine could change or seriously belittle it. However, the battle for a genuine *rapprochement* between the Old World and the New must go on; we have too much to lose by not standing together to indulge in the luxury of perpetual misunderstandings.

We have to fight especially against the two great and nefarious vulgarities on our respective Continents: the stupid American notion that Europe is a land of degenerate and effeminate atheists who are brooding over a dishonorable past, but are out to "soak" America, and the equally contemptible and nauseating European concept of the United States as a nation of dollar-worshipers, uncouth, shirt-sleeved, hard-boiled manufacturers. We must help the truth to prevail. And finally, let the materialists realize that for us the things that matter are our common sacramental bonds.

25

André Siegfried

1955

from *America at Mid-Century*

André Siegfried, a distinguished French political scientist and
historian was no ivory-tower observer of other lands—he travelled
extensively in Europe and Latin America and was a frequent visitor
to the United States. His lectures, magazine articles and books in
their authentic insights showed the result of his personal investigations. He published two books on the United States: *America Comes
of Age,* in 1927, and *America at Mid-Century,* in 1955. The latter
book was far more critical of American life than his first report and
caused much discussion in the American press.

The following selection is taken from *America at Mid-Century* by
André Siegfried, copyright 1955 by Harcourt, Brace & World, Inc.,
and reprinted with their permission.

The Protestant faith . . . has not failed to invite a certain
measure of reproach as a religion for the Anglo-Saxons, proud
of their respectability, gentlemen of principle and prosperity,
who relegate foreigners and immigrants to a sort of secondary
status from the religious, moral, and social standpoint. It has
also been suggested that, in this orientation toward action, the
essential elements of religion are apt to be lost; the ever-present
preoccupation about results or, one might almost say, human out-
put, does not allow for the significance of the divine transcendence and the spirit of selfless worship; moreover, the desire for

being up-to-date has given certain evangelists a sort of cordial vulgarity which does much harm to the poetry of religion, sometimes even to its essential dignity. Religious-minded people eventually feel that something is lacking. Catholicism has to some extent benefited from these objections, but they have on the rebound brought about certain Protestant reforms that are not without significance.

Catholicism in the United States has always been under a handicap. It is considered a religion for foreigners, aliens even, giving that word its derogatory significance. It is the church of the immigrants, the unassimilated, consequently the humble people low down in the social scale; when the son of a Protestant magnate married a Catholic—what a scandal—his mother would remark, when she went on that occasion to the local Catholic church, on the fact that she had never set foot in it before, except for the weddings or funerals of her servants. It is no exaggeration to say that the pomp of the Roman Church, the splendor of its ritual, the brilliance of its ecclesiastical vestments, and the magnificence of its processions before which the faithful kneel, give to the old-fashioned American the uncomfortable impression of something too exotic for a Protestant country. This impression is reinforced by the fact that the members of the Catholic church belong to national groups not easily assimilated into the American background; besides the traditionally dominant Irish group, there are Italians, Germans, Poles, and French Canadians.

Feeling itself to be kept on the fringe, outside the main axis of society, when its wish is to take part in the national life on an equal footing, American Catholicism is, above all, anxious to become Americanized. Great prelates such as Monsignor Ireland or Monsignor Gibbons, were on the way toward carrying out this program at the end of the last century; and though the immigration of Slav and Latin peoples has retarded this assimilation, it is nonetheless making progress, particularly as the newcomers show extraordinary eagerness to adopt the customs of the New World. If this is carried on, it is with a clear wish to integrate Catholicism in its entirety into American society. It is already a Church that has adapted itself to the national environment; it is proud of its wealth, of the size of the churches it has built, of the modernity and comfort of its schools and convents. Its priests, well-fed, living in well-heated houses, accustomed to travel by sleeping car, must feel a sort of condescending pity for their poor European colleagues. Their contribution to the religious thought of the world is negligible, but they have a feeling of power which, moreover, does not fail to cause some anxiety in Protestant circles, long accustomed to having the monopoly of influence.

Catholic action in the United States, therefore, belongs to the national environment, but, though essentially American, it has its own particular moral and religious aspect. Catholicism is particularly active in the defense of family life, far more so than the Protestant faith. It is un-American in the firm stand it takes against birth control sterilization. It also runs counter to American policy on the subject of separate schools, claiming for its educational establishments subsidies that are surely contrary to the constitutional principle of Church and State. The existence of a religious minority that receives orders from a foreign pope, and, moreover, an Italian, is more and more a source of annoyance to the Protestants, who, faced with an indubitable increase in Catholicism, are taking up the anticlerical arguments so familiar in France. But in the United States the attitude is anti-Catholic rather than anticlerical.

If such anxiety is arising, it is because Catholicism has made progress since World War I. The general level of social standing among Catholics has risen, but there have also been numerous conversions from Protestantism. To what are these due? The austerity of the Protestant form of worship draws some Americans away from the severity of the reformed church to the more poetic ritual, in which the mystical side of religion is more fully developed. According to Sinclair Lewis, the monotony of the daily life of the little townships of the West is broken only by two events which open its windows toward a conception of the infinite: the passage of the train and the Catholic Mass. As everywhere in the world, the dispersed nature of the Protestant church makes men eager for discipline, ready to appreciate the strength of a church founded upon authority. I believe that the Catholic Church has made progress in the United States because of its excellent organization, the efficiency of its particularly active clergy, its indefatigable propaganda, and the intelligent pressure that it brings to bear upon politicians. It must be added that the higher birth rate among Catholics naturally swells their numbers.

Statistics indeed show a considerable increase in the number of Catholics, which will soon be more than thirty million, but there has been no increase in the proportion of Catholics as compared with total population. The growth of their influence cannot, however, be denied, and this influence marks a new phase in the history of the country. They form a substantial minority, ready to make its voice heard and to put forward ideas that cannot be said to be in line with the basic doctrines of the United States. A religion founded on authority, which refuses to recognize the exclusion of religion from public schools and is not resigned to the principle of separation of Church and State, forms what is virtually a foreign element in the national life. There is no question of not recognizing its place in the community, but this recognition creates difficult adjustments and grave political differences.

This does not mean that the patriotism of the Catholics is in any way inferior to that of their older-established or assimilated fellow citizens. The patriotism of the latter is Anglo-Saxon—and naturally Protestant—in concept. That of the Catholics amounts to a loyal and even passionate attachment to the American way of life and a sincere feeling of gratitude to the country that has made this life possible. The nationalism of the United States was formerly exclusively Protestant, like that of the Ku

Klux Klan, but it is now possible for a Catholic nationalism to exist, no less exclusive, but possessing other lines of defense: one has only to think of Senator McCarthy.

The ever-growing claims of the Catholic minority have aroused a new spirit of anti-Catholicism among the Protestants. All the arguments of French anti-clericalism have reappeared, with a freshness of approach which they have now lost in France. The pope is a foreign sovereign, and it is scandalous that Americans should follow his dictates when they vote. The Roman Hierachy is incompatible with the American Constitution; Rome has not abandoned the idea of conquering America: *Caveant Consules!* When in 1951 President Truman wished to appoint an ambassador to the Vatican, he met with Protestant opposition of astonishing violence; pastors denounced the measure from their pulpits as an intolerable scandal, an insult to the Protestant character of the nation, and innumerable lists of signatures confirmed their protests. The depth of this reaction must not be misunderstood; it represented instinctive defense on the part of a religious monopoly which has ceased to exist.

Catholic thought has nevertheless exercised its influence in the very heart of the Portestant world. The Catholic ritual exerts evident attraction, not only in High Church Episcopalian circles, where the churches positively overflow with stained glass, crosses, incense, candelabras, candles and sumptuous priestly vestments, but also in the churches of the reformed tradition, where today there is an esthetic preoccupation which contrasts strangely with their early asceticism: the Baptist church entrusted by Rockefeller to Harry Emerson Fosdick is partly based on Chartres Cathedral, with chapels commemorating great men such as Lincoln and Pasteur; and a desire for elegance is widespread among most of the denominations. But this must not be mistaken for a return to Catholic practices, for the intention is exclusively esthetic without bearing on the form of worship, except in the case of the Episcopalians. There are, however, signs of a more strictly religious conception of religion, an indefinable weariness of a form of Christianity so practical as to become matter of fact, and the reintroduction into worship of the spirit of adoration, with emphasis on the altar rather than exclusively on the pulpit. The Federal Council of the Churches of Christ has instituted a "section of worship." The idea of divine transcendence, long eclipsed by the eighteenth-century idea of God pervading the universe, reappeared under the influence of Karl Barth, and, though its influence is now somewhat on the wane, there is definitely a greater interest taken in theology. These tendencies, reflecting the influence of analogous European movements, mark also an infiltration of Catholicism which does not, however, penetrate down to the roots of the Protestant faith.

26

Arturo Gaete, S. J.

1956

from *"The Paradox of North American Catholicism"*

In January, 1959, the national Catholic weekly *America* made editorial mention of an article about American Catholicism which had recently appeared in a leading Latin American weekly, *Revista Mensaje*. It was written by Arturo Gaete, a Chilean Jesuit, who had spent four seminary years in the United States. Said *America:* "If the hundreds of seminarians who now each year come from Latin America to this country for their studies analyze us as sharply and as sympathetically as has this visitor, then our two continents are far closer today than they have been in past decades. Past gaps in mutual understanding are gradually but surely being filled in by visits back and forth between the two halves of our hemisphere. At any rate we are no longer total strangers to each other." Father Gaete's article is translated from *Revista Mensaje* (vol. VII, n. 73, Oct., 1958, and n. 74, Nov., 1958), a monthly magazine published by Chilean Jesuits of the Centro Bellarmino in Santiago, Chile.

Among the nations of the West, the one which holds the most surprises for Latin Americans—both pleasant and unpleasant— is the United States. Although the French are really more different from us than we suspect, we are nonetheless able to find our bearings in France; and in the vast dimensions of German culture, long before we are really capable of understanding it, we manage to distinguish certain fundamental lines and can

213

begin to appreciate the differences which will exist between the Germans and ourselves, and the Austrians and the Swiss as well. But the American keeps us off balance for a long time. Nor is this just a casual disconcertment but one which rises out of the very essence of our relationship with him. We are doubly confused when confronted with the American Catholic, being baffled with both his Americanism and his Catholicism. It is not a question of dislike. On the contrary, the visitor no sooner disembarks in the United States than he finds himself enfolded in an atmosphere of American Catholic charm which is without equal. This first impression is so commonly experienced as to be basic; the disconcertment follows and presupposes this first impression.

Man always tends to evaluate his present experience of things and people in the light of his past experience. If a young man talks to an adult about a personal problem, frequently the adult needs very little detail in order to understand difficulties and to explain to the young man with great clarity the nature of a problem he could understand but obscurely. The young man's admiration knows no bounds: "I had only to tell him one or two things and he knew the rest," he will say. The "rest" is precisely what the adult has personally lived through, or experienced vicariously through the lives of others. First he found a common denominator from his own experience and used it to enter and solve the young man's problem on the supposition that it runs parallel to his own.

The same thing occurs when we come in contact with another nation. Encountering the American, we are surprised from the beginning with his extraordinary sense of charity. I have known many charitable men, from every part of the world, but never an entire nation except for the United States. This sympathy which the American spontaneously feels for the needy is a rare phenomenon in history and I do not know if it has ever been adequately explained. In France one is greeted courteously and warmly with *"Enchanté!"* But since the French are extremely busy people, after a short while one notices that the enchantment has cooled sufficiently to permit a convenient exit. On the other hand when the American says, "Very pleased to meet you," or simply, "It's wonderful having met you," he is actually sincere. The word "wonderful" is used frequently in the United States. At the Eucharistic Congress of 1941 in one of the assemblies held in the Municipal Theater of Santiago, an American representing the Catholic Youth Movement was asked to address the assembly. He began his speech with the words, "My smashing friends." To us this was amusing since in such a situation we would have expected simply, "My dear friends." He was only attempting to translate "wonderful friends," which is commonly used as an opening line in the United States, where it would not seem at all amusing. In our experience with charitable people we have always observed that they possess a number of other related characteristics. We find the American is a charitable person and automatically assume that he is also endowed with these other characteristics. And it is here that our surprise begins because, although he is unquestionably charitable, he does not hold true to the pattern of our associations. For instance, we see that his solicitude for the needy and the underdog takes a different track when there are race barriers to be crossed. An eloquent case in point is the attitude of the Catholic of the southern states with respect to the Negro. In many parishes in these states Negroes are made to sit in the back of the Church during Mass; in others, they are relegated to a gallery on a second floor. Nor can a Negro use the same Confessional as the whites—they have their own; even when it comes to the reception of the Eucharist, the Negroes must receive after the whites. A southern woman once said to me: "If I see that a Negro goes ahead of my child to Communion, right there and then I shove him out of line." Here is the height of paradox; separation in the very act of receiving the Holy Sacrament of Communion!

But let us not be so quick to change our admiration to scorn. The situation is much more complex than it seems, and even now things are changing for the better. In the Church of St. Alphonsus in Woodstock, Maryland, for example, the pastor, wanting to breach segregation, decided that Sunday Mass would henceforward be served by a white and a Negro boy (he had difficulty putting the idea into practice, however, since it was virtually impossible to find Negroes able or willing to serve Mass under such conditions).

The purpose of these examples is not to pass judgment on the state of American Catholicism—whether it is good or bad— but to show the sort of thing which gives rise to the sense of alienation which it engenders in us. This impression is received not only by Latin Americans, but by continental Europeans who visit the United States, as well. When we travel in Europe we certainly see things which are surprising to us, but our overall reaction to the broad aspects of French and German Catholicism is not one of alienation. In the examples set forth above, the thing which keeps us from understanding why such a paradox can exist is our lack of knowledge of the peculiar history of the southern United States. Those who have read Margaret Mitchell's novel, *Gone with the Wind,* or who have seen the movie of the same title, would discover at least the beginnings of an explanation.

Compared with current thinking in Europe, the theological ideas of the American clergy and most literate laymen seem conservative. It is, however, a peculiar kind of conservatism. In Europe, if someone is conservative in theology, he tends to be conservative about every aspect of religion. Or if he is liberal, to be consistently liberal. But here again, the American Catholic jars our traditional understanding of these things. For in the United States it sometimes happens that men who are extremely conservative in most matters will at one and the same time be more liberal than Europeans on others. For instance, the American Catholic's—to us—liberal conception of the question of Church-State relations.

The same sort of thing can be noted in American Catholic political thought. With regard to internal questions, one can see them embrace positions which we call "leftist," without this in the least preventing them from holding strong "rightist" views on international relations. Here again we are surprised: the terms "left" and "right" are applied frequently by ourselves and by Europeans to all sorts of things, with a comfortable sense of consistency. A person is to the right or to the left in everything—in his opinions, in his politics, almost even in his temperament.

A paradox is a strange phenomenon, something which runs opposite to the ordinary, and American Catholicism seems to fill the definition perfectly in the eyes of the European and the Latin American. And vice versa, to American eyes, Europeans and Latin Americans are a strange sight at first glance. But the paradox is not absolute; it represents only the first stage in our understanding of a reality which has been structured in a different fashion from our own. Thus in the case of the American Catholics it is necessary to take more than immediate impressions into account. We must live among them on a day-to-day basis and come to understand why things happen the way they do. Since the base of the paradox stands rooted partly in the American way of life and partly in the structure of American Catholicism as it has evolved in this way of life, to understand it, it is necessary to know both American history and the history of American Catholicism. Since it is impossible to undertake the whole of American history we will concentrate on some basic facts in the history of American Catholicism and see how they have shaped its present existence.

One basic historic fact of great consequence is that at the beginning of the last century, when we in Latin America were gaining our independence there were scarcely any Catholics to be found in the United States. The seventeenth-century settlers who colonized the Northeastern region were Puritans fleeing English persecution. They had come to practice their own religion and were not willing to admit any other. The Southeastern territory was colonized by nobles who, in the majority, were Anglicans. The only English colony which was Catholic in its origins was that of Maryland, founded by Cecil Calvert, second Lord Baltimore. But a revolution in 1689 was to confirm the rule of a Protestant majority. At the beginning of the seventeenth century, Rhode Island and Pennsylvania were the only colonies where Catholics had religious and civil rights. A few Catholics had migrated and those few had generally been persecuted; thus, it is not at all strange to find that when the new country proclaimed its independence, Catholics formed only an insignificant group.

In 1956, according to the *Official Catholic Directory,* the Catholic population of the United States had increased to thirty-three million. Where did they come from? And this brings us to a second basic historical fact about the Church in the United States: it is composed of immigrants who arrived in great masses in a relatively short period of time. A series of events in Europe combined to bring this phenomenon about. In 1840 the famous "Potato Famine" drove hundreds of thousands of Irish away from their homes and across the Atlantic to settle in the big cities along the Eastern coast of the United States. They were always accompanied by a priest, who assumed both the temporal and the spiritual leadership of the expedition.

Between 1840 and 1870, political upheaval, the *Kulturkampf,* and the promise of cheap and fertile land combined to cause many German farmers to migrate to America. Once they arrived they settled in or around the big cities of the mid-west—St. Louis, Chicago, Cleveland, Milwaukee. Later came the Southern Italians, and the immigrants from Eastern Europe, particularly the Polish and the Austro-Hungarians. All of these groups, in marked contrast with the first and settling immigrants, were Catholics. In fact, to be Irish or to be Polish also meant to be Catholic.

A third basic fact: the immigrants were looked upon as

inferior and were relegated to the lowest place on the American social ladder.

A fourth factor was that the immigrants maintained a sentimental but not a political tie with the lands they left behind them in Europe. Politically and socially they were "protestant" with respect to Europe, since they left because they were unwilling to accept the limitations of the place assigned them there and came looking for another and better world. The first generation of immigrants found themselves in a hostile land, where everything was strange, including (except for the Irish) the language. The rupture with the "Old Country" was virtually complete. The trip over was long and expensive and the immigrant had quite frequently stripped himself to the financial bone to make it. The majority were illiterate, frequently without any friends or relatives with them. Understandably, they felt like men without a country.

The fifth fundamental historical fact necessary to appreciate the peculiar nature of the Church in the United States is that these immigrants almost universally experienced the natural and most urgent need to flock together, to belong again, to something they understood. This something was the Church, incarnated in the presence of the priest. Aside from the spiritual benefits to be offered, the priest was in most cases the only educated person in the group; he was the only one used to exercising authority. He had dealt with problems in Ireland or Bavaria and he was able to deal with the problems presented by the new land. He was also a forceful and effective link with the past—not with the political system the immigrants had left, but with their villages and customs, their songs and dances. And the Church, with its great feeling for tradition, was quick to realize that these human values should be conserved and integrated in the American way of life. Many immigrant-born practices survive even today—the St. Patrick's Day parade up Fifth Avenue in New York is a prime example. On 183rd Street in the same city I have seen the famous procession which the Italians present in honor of our Lady of Carmel. They still gesticulate and express their devotion openly with true Mediterranean spontaneity, as if for a few hours they were back in Naples: some take off their shoes, others walk on their knees, some pin dollar bills to the Virgin's clothing. Those of the first generation—and there are many of them yet—still make their confession in Italian. *"Sono tante settimane dopo l'ultima confessione,"* they would tell me, and I would reply in English, which they understood perfectly, and which they used every day in the course of business. But since they never managed the language perfectly, they prefer to talk to God in their native tongue, the better to put their most intimate thoughts.

With a history so different from that of Latin America and Europe, we begin to understand why the American Catholic seems so different. We are used to seeing the Church identified with the very fabric of society, growing quietly and slowly at its own rhythm. New arrivals—whether by immigration or by birth—are absorbed gently into a well-organized system. In the United States just the opposite took place: the immigrants found themselves as isolated as if they had suddenly been set down in a desert—both they and their religion were strange, and utterly cut off from the world.

It is from this that a final fact emerges. The Catholic communities of Europe or Latin America embody all the strata of society, and all of society's problems. The Church in Europe included both kings and commoners, farmers and mechanics, country-folk and urban dwellers—with all the natural tensions between these groups continuously in play; it also was used to the struggle between Church and States and to the confrontation of Faith made by science and rationalism. Europe and Latin America have lived through these problems and their consequences. The American Catholic of the past century has simply not been exposed to anything like this. His experience was very simple—priest and people. It is something we know nothing of and it is what makes it difficult to understand American Catholicism today. Because, although things have changed considerably, it is from this point that they began.

* * *

There is an archetectonic style of churches, very common in the United States, which well symbolizes the sociological reality of American Catholicism. These edifices have two floors. You ascend to the second by two exterior staircases on the front, and two others at the sides. The Church is located on the second floor; on the first floor you find the offices, parish club rooms and dance-hall. In the United States one comes down from Benediction to the dance, or one goes up from the dance to Benediction with the utmost of naturalness. This unexpected association is surprising to us, because in Latin America as in Europe, entertainment and religion have traditionally followed separate roads. The place for social life was the Court, the feudal castle, the dance-hall or the club—in any event, not the parish. In the United States the newly arrived immigrants had none of these places for entertainment at their disposal, and the pastor immediately foresaw the necessity for some form of entertainment and thought it best for this diversion to take place under the auspices of the Church—in fact as well as symbolically.

We might be tempted to ask what place a priest has at any dance, even a family affair. In the United States the thought enters no one's mind. For the priest is the one who organized the dance in the first place. Not only parishes, but Catholic colleges and universities sponsor dances, which are frequently advertised in the diocesan newspapers.

The priest takes charge of everything. To begin with, he has to be on hand to greet people—for he issued the invitations. He has to see that the microphone is working properly, that the musicans are on hand in the proper numbers and that they are given occasional refreshments, that the girls are all being danced with in the proper spirit of "Catholic Action." In some places there is a moment in the course of the evening when the orchestra plays a predetermined tune, and everyone stops for a moment of prayer; and then the band plays on.

The parish was not only a place for worship and entertainment, but an employment agency and a labor union headquarters, as well. The priest stuck out his fists and his neck to protect the rights of his parishoners. If you have seen the film *On the Waterfront,* you have seen a priest portrayed in a role that still exists today. Another function of the parish was to function as an education center. Many immigrant groups, especially the Polish and Germans, wanted to conserve both their Faith and their language and saw that if their children attended the public schools both might well be lost. For public school teaching was, of course, presented in English, and set against a background atmosphere that was at first Protestant and later determinedly secular. Thus, the parochial school system was born and went on to become an amazingly vigorous part of American Catholicism. With time, these schools gradually lost their exclusively national characteristics and became a truly effective means of integrating later immigrants into the American way of life.

It is still the opinion of the vast majority of American Catholics that there can be no substitute for a Catholic school education and that they must bear the cost. It is an accepted feature of American Catholic life that every Catholic parish—or at least, every group of parishes—must have a school which children can attend without prohibitive expense.

Perhaps I can best illustrate this attitude of conviction with an example. I was supposed to celebrate Mass and deliver a sermon one Sunday at Our Lady of the Rosary Church in New York City. When I arrived in the sacristy before Mass, the pastor said to me: "Don't worry about the sermon, Father, I'm going to preach it." And during the Gospel I saw him mount the pulpit carrying a thick account book. His sermon, in substance, was that he had consulted with a firm of architects who told him that the cost of building the proposed new school would be $1,200,000; he had calculated that the parish (everyone took this to mean the parishioners) could afford to pay $200,000 a year toward such a sum; this left a loan of $1,000,000 to be secured; he urged the parishioners to give generously and to try to surpass the yearly quota of $200,000. If so, they could considerably shorten the twenty-five year loan payment period and save a great deal of interest. He documented all these figures from his account book, justifying them carefully in a business sense. What he did not try to, or have to, justify at any time during the sermon was that the parish needed a new school and that the parishioners were going to have to pay for it.

It is interesting, too, to note how money for such projects is actually collected. It is via the famous envelope system. At the beginning of the year a packet of fifty-two envelopes is given to each family in the parish by the simple expediency of placing them in the pews for each wage-earner to take home of his own accord. Each subsequent Sunday they bring one of these envelopes to Mass with $5, $10 or more enclosed. The envelopes are properly addressed with the name of the donor and the sum enclosed. A list is then posted in the church's bulletin which tells who gave how much during the week. This process may seem strange but it is not really so surprising when you remember that Catholics in almost all communities were a despised minority, looked down upon for their faith, their language and economic inferiority. This naturally engendered a "ghetto" mentality which convinced them better than any preachments, that they had to make common cause in order to survive and to show that they could still be Americans without sacrificing their religious beliefs. They saw the church as their own property, not as a building belonging to the priests. They were all poor, but together they could build churches, schools, clubs—all theirs.

Another result of this "ghetto" mentality is the American tendency to view every aspect of Catholic life as a single sacred lump. To criticize anything about the parish was to criticize the

Faith, and what in Europe or Latin America might be regarded as healthy criticism, inspired by sincere apostolic motives, may well be fiercely resented by American Catholics.

Some years ago, a Chilean came to study in an American Catholic University; in the courses in religion and apologetics which he attended he was argumentive, reading that attitude as one proper for a student wishing to get at the core of the truth; if the instructor's counterargument did not seem valid, he would politely say so. After a while, however, he noticed that his attitude was neither shared nor appreciated by his fellow students. They wanted the class to provide them with ready answers with which to squelch anyone who criticized the Church. The debates and delays caused by the Chilean simply exasperated them. This situation is changing, though, and rapidly.

It is this attitude, too, which helps to explain why there are so few Catholics in the field of science and research and why Catholic universities compare so unfavorably with the so-called "Ivy League" schools—Harvard, Yale, Princeton, Columbia, and the rest. A Catholic professor used to say: "The father of an average student at Harvard is a former student of Harvard, Princeton or Yale; the father of an average student at Fordham, is a bus-driver or a policeman." Recently, one of the most renowned theologians in the United States, Gustave Weigel, S. J., called similar attention to the dearth of Catholics entering or excelling in science and research. But I must be careful not to invite false conclusions in making this point. Considered against the great numbers of scientists in the United States, the Catholics are few, but these few are still far more than the Catholic communities of Latin America can claim; likewise, though Catholic colleges and universities on the whole are inferior to major universities in the United States, they are still superior to the Catholic universities of Latin America. And I say "on the whole" because in particular disciplines, some American Catholic universities compare quite favorably with even the best universities of the United States.

I regret that the limitation of space makes it necessary to pass over in silence so many admirable aspects of the American way of life which have made possible the growth of such a vigorous Catholic community. Catholics owe very much to the fact of being Americans. We would have to say something, for example, regarding the relations between Church and State, and about the climate of political tolerance that exists in religious matters. In the spiritual life of the American Church there is much that deserves unqualified praise. There is the splendid sacramental tradition: the churches filled to the brim every Sunday of the year; the fact that the overwhelming majority of American Catholics go to Confession and Communion at least once a month; the splendid social contact within the Catholic community—in a given parish almost everyone knows everyone else and all know the pastor or one of his vicars personally due to the priests' practice of visiting every home in the parish at least once a year, and especially in times of personal need. We must also admire the enterprising spirit and firm grasp of reality possessed by the American Catholic. In the United States there may be fewer ideas than there are in Europe, but there is also less distance between these ideas and their realization. The French write about many admirable things but once these have been published in a book the interest in them usually declines so that their realization is a long time in coming, if ever. Nor is this all that is deserving of praise. What American Catholics have accomplished in the educational field in less than a century, and what they have done for the foreign missions in less than fifty years is truly remarkable, and more so if you know their beginnings. In both of these areas the labor of the Sisters must be recognized as one of the supporting pillars of American Catholic life; gentle and pious, they yet know how to cope with the modern world.

Nothing that has been accomplished by the Church in the United States would have been possible without the greatest possible generosity—generosity with money and generosity of self. The number of Catholic charitable institutions document the first sort of generosity; the thousands of vocations which flow from the United States each year are liberal proof of the second kind. It has been less than a hundred years since the Italian, German and Belgian Jesuits were coming to the United States as missionaries. Today, one out of every four Jesuits in the world is an American.

In conclusion, permit me to recount a personal anecdote. Some years ago, on the evening before I was to leave the United States, one of my colleagues invited me to have dinner at his house. There I met his father, whom I will call Mr. Brian, and who could be described as an old Irish farmer, one of those simple and straightforward men who put one in mind of Nathaniel, the Israelite, in whom God found no deceitfulness. After dinner, Mr. Brian took me aside and we sat on the sofa to drink a Coca-Cola.

"I am an uneducated man, Father," he said. "who barely knows how to carry on a conversation, as you can see. I have worked hard all my life; I know how to read and write and very little else. But my pride lies in my sons and what they have accomplished: Pat is a Doctor of Theology; Bob a Doctor of English Literature; and Jim a skilled mechanic (the one who earns the most money in the family—$150 a week)."

I think that the story of the Brian family is highly representative of what I understand of American Catholicism. If I had to sum it up in a few words I would use "Immigration" to describe the past, "Generosity and Courage" for the present, and "Problems" for the future, because that theologian, the professor of English and the mechanic, when he becomes rich, each springing from a common background but moving away from each other in separate orbits, are going to generate a whole new set of complications.

I would like to end where I began. I referred to the attitude of Southern Catholics towards the Negro and mentioned that we should resist our impulse to pass judgment but rather use it as a key to try to penetrate to the meaning behind it. The American Catholic shares in all the defects and virtues of his countrymen. Each man must be judged as an individual. It is not fair to reproach Peter that he has less mathematical talent than John; on the other hand, we can reproach him directly for not having made use of his own God-given artistic talents. Something similar happens with countries. Let us not reproach American Catholics for their bad taste in building churches. The immigrant has more pressing problems than esthetics. In solving the task that confronted them, American Catholics have performed admirably. Mr. Brian left his sons established. The work was simple but very hard. Bob has educated himself, Pat has travelled; and the problems which now face them at home and abroad are infinitely more complicated. We shall see what they do about them.

27

≫⫸⫷≪

Christopher Dawson

1958

from *"Catholic Culture in America"*

≫⫸⫷≪

Christopher Dawson, pre-eminent English historian, came to America in 1958 as the first Charles Chauncey Stillman Professor of Roman Catholic Studies at the Divinity School of Harvard University. The author of many noted studies of Christian culture and of the impact of religion on the Western world, he had long been interested in American life and is a sympathetic reader of American literature. He was asked to assess Catholic culture in America for the twentieth anniversary celebration of the Thomas More Association in Chicago, and his observations, which follow, are reprinted from the June–July, 1959, issue of *The Critic* (copyright 1959 by the Thomas More Association).

≫⫸⫷≪

The problem of Catholic culture in America is one of the vital issues of our time and one which has been the subject of the most diverse opinions and judgments. The Catholic Church is the most ancient institution in the Western world with the longest history and the most unbroken tradition behind it. Yet in this last age it has produced a new growth which has sprung up unexpectedly on an alien soil and in an unfavorable climate, but which nevertheless shows most remarkable signs of vitality. If it continues to grow as it has done during the last hundred years it is going to change a lot of things not only in America but in the world at large. And therefore it deserves the study not only of Americans but of all Catholics and, most of all, of Catholic historians.

What makes this development so paradoxical is that it is, so to speak, the by-product of the social and political expansion of Protestantism in the New World and that today the influence of the Catholicism of Protestant America has come to outweigh the importance of the Catholicism of Catholic America. From the beginning, from the time that Columbus landed in the Bahamas, the Catholic Church played a leading part in the discovery and settlement of America and this not only in South America but in the North also—from Florida to California and from the mouth of the Mississippi to the Great Lakes. But all these centuries of effort and missionary achievement did not create the American Church that we know. The conquerors and the explorers, the missionaries and the converts represent one side of the Catholic history in the New World, but it is the other side that is responsible for everything that we think of as American Catholicism and that side is represented by the Church of the Catholic immigrants who entered the purely Protestant culture of the English colonies and the States that were their successors, gradually creating a diaspora, a network of Catholic minorities throughout the whole of the United States. This movement extended with the western advance of the American nation and as it advanced it incorporated and swallowed up the older Catholic communities which owed their existence to the other older movements of French and Spanish origin.

The one exception to this process was the little colonial Anglo-American Church of Maryland. Its numbers were never large and throughout the colonial period its existence depended entirely on the ministry of the Jesuits of the English province, of whom some 186 came to America in the first 140 years of Maryland's existence. But its importance is out of proportion to its size, since it provides a vital historical link with the native English tradition of Catholicism and with the native American tradition of English culture, and at the time of the Revolution it gave Catholics a modest share in the foundation of the United States through the participation of some of its representatives like the Carrolls.

Apart from this narrow thread of historical continuity with the English colonial past, American Catholicism owes everything —even its existence—to the immigrants—first to the French who left Europe and the West Indies at the time of the Revolution, then to the Irish and the Germans and finally to the Poles and Italians and Czechs and Hungarians and Ukranians who continued to swell the tide of foreign migration until the age of the World Wars.

Of all these elements it was the Irish that were the most important both from the religious and the social point of view. In spite of their intense loyalty to Ireland and to one another, they were the element that adapted itself most rapidly and completely to the American way of life and they brought with them from their native land that tradition of solidarity between priest and people which has been the common characteristic of American Irish Catholicism.

Many of the features in American Catholicism which distinguish it from continental European Catholicism are really as much Irish as they are American. In Europe there was, generally speaking, an alliance between the Church and the Catholic State, and between the clergy and the conservative ruling class. But the Irish immigrants had brought with them from the old country a profound distrust of the Protestant government and usually an open hostility to it. And on the other hand there was a close social alliance between the common people and their priests who were of the same blood and class and culture and who had taken the place of the ruling class as the social leaders of the people. Thus the democratic character of American Catholicism which is the first thing that strikes the foreign observer is not entirely a product of American conditions, but owes its basic character to its Irish inheritance.

It is true that this Irish tradition underwent profound changes in America. It lost its native language and with it the rich inheritance of Gaelic peasant culture. But this was the necessary price that the Irish had to pay for their successful adaptation to American society, since the fact that they were English-speaking gave them a great advantage over all the other immigrant groups. At the same time they transformed themselves from a peasant class into an urban proletariat, and they did it so thoroughly that in the course of the nineteenth century they became the predominant element in most of the great American cities. By carrying out this revolutionary process of social transformation, the Irish created the new social pattern of urban Catholicism which was adopted by almost all the subsequent immigrant groups with the exception of the Germans. These later immigrants—Poles, Italians, Czechs, Hungarians, Lithuanians and Ukranians—were, like the Irish, uprooted peasants who became city dwellers in the New World and who found in the life of their Catholic churches and parishes and schools the moral protection and the element of spiritual continuity which enabled them to survive in their new environment.

This is perhaps the most important factor which distinguishes the social tradition of American Catholicism from that of the Old World. In Europe it was the peasants who remained most loyal to the Church and who provided probably the greatest number of religious vocations, while in the great cities the Church had to face the growing opposition of the forces of anti-clericalism and irreligion. But in America the situation was just the opposite. The whole strength of the Church lay in the cities—especially the great cities of the East and Middle West—while the rural districts, apart from the areas of German settlement in Northern Ohio and elsewhere, were solidly Protestant and in many cases maintained all the anti-Catholic prejudices and delusions of the past. This situation was all the more significant because the earlier American culture was predominantly a rural one. When the movement of Catholic immigration started the American urban civilization did not exist. American Catholicism has grown up with the American cities, so that the place of Catholicism in modern American culture, which is now an urban one, is even more important than its numbers and its dates of origin would lead one to suppose.

In spite of this, we must admit that throughout the nineteenth century, and indeed down to the age of the World Wars, the social prestige and the culture achievements of American Catholics were very modest. Catholics were an underprivileged, disregarded minority and the Catholic Church was the Church of the poor and the strangers. All through the middle decades of the century Catholics were exposed to a campaign of misrepresentation and abuse which sometimes, as in Boston and Philadelphia, reached the pitch of open persecution in the burning of churches and convents. Yet in spite of it, the progress of American Catholicism went on without a break. Unpopularity and lack of privilege may have been unfavorable to the development of an intellectual culture, but they strengthened the social solidarity of the Church and the loyalty of the Catholic people to their religious leaders. In the midst of economic hardship American Catholics built up their own social and educational institutions until the American Church became the most highly organized and well equipped religious body in the United States.

Under these circumstances it would be ungenerous to reproach American Catholicism for not producing scholars and philosophers and men of letters. It was the Church of the poor, and the starving Irish peasants who fled from the famine or the uneducated peasants from Central Europe who came to America to work in the mines and factories could not hand on a tradition of Catholic intellectual culture that they had never possessed. Everything had to be built up from the foundations and the present state of Catholicism in the United States is a proof of the greatness of their effort and the solidarity of their achievement. By the end of the nineteenth century, under the leadership of Cardinal Gibbons, American Catholicism had established its position securely as an integral element in the life of the nation and American Catholics were becoming increasingly aware of their strength and of the new opportunities which were being opened to Catholicism by the civilization of the New World.

Hence the spiritual and intellectual leaders of American Catholicism—men like Father Hecker, the founder of the Paulists, the famous Archbishop of St. Paul, John Ireland, and Bishop Keane, the first rector of the Catholic University—were foremost in the advocacy of American ideals and the defence of the American way of life. They held that the freedom of Anglo-Saxon institutions was in practice more favorable to the progress of Catholicism that the outmoded patterns of the European Catholic state and that the democratic Catholicism of the New World was destined to be the Catholicism of the new age. But this optimism proved to be somewhat premature. It provoked a controversy between conservative and liberal Catholics both in America and Europe which resulted in Leo XIII's letter to Cardinal Gibbons condemning "opinions which some comprise under the name of Americanism" with special reference to Eliot's life of Father Hecker, which had been the center of controversy, especially in France.

It was a strange and inconclusive controversy, since the Americanists of America, as represented by Archbishop Ireland, denied that such opinions had ever existed among them, and the Americanists of France, like the Abbe Klein, described Americanism as a theological phantom. The confusion arose from the fact that the Americanists were no theologians and the anti-Americanists knew very little about America. The fact was that a new Catholic society and way of life had emerged as an integral part of the great new American democratic civilization, sharing the same characteristics—the same weaknesses and the same strength. It was a living reality, not a theory. Where its critics and admirers both went wrong was in attributing it to an ideology that it did not possess. For there was in fact no such thing as Americanism; there were only American Catholics. It was not until ten or twenty years after the Americanist controversy was over that

American Catholicism began to acquire full cultural consciousness.

For it was only after the closing down of European immigration after the First World War that the barriers which separated the immigrants from the native American were overcome and real social and cultural unity between the two elements in the population was finally achieved. The results of this have become increasingly visible since the end of the Second World War, and this finds expression in three different directions. First, the Catholics have ceased to be regarded as Irish Americans and they have become simply American Catholics—and this was just what Cardinal Gibbons and so many of the Catholic leaders of the past had been aiming at. Secondly, Catholics have gained a new economic and social status. They are no longer an underprivileged proletariat, as they were more or less throughout the nineteenth century, and have become largely a middle class community. This involves a certain loss, since the fact that the American Church was predominantly the Church of the poor was a source of spiritual strength from the religious point of view. But seen in relation to American culture, the achievement of economic success is such an important source of social prestige that it was difficult for Catholics to take their full share in American life without it. And thirdly, the last twenty years has seen a great advance in Catholic education and a growing awareness of the importance of intellectual values and of the need for a Catholic culture.

This was the greatest weakness of American Catholicism in the past, owing largely to the lack of economic opportunity and to the lack of any cultural tradition among most of the immigrant groups; even today it is commonly said that Catholics do not take their proportionate share in the intellectual life of the nation. But against this we must set the remarkable achievements of American Catholic education—three and a half million children in the elementary schools, 700,000 secondary school pupils, and 300,000 students in universities and colleges—a record of voluntary effort which I believe has no parallel elsewhere in the world.

No doubt the results on the level of higher intellectual culture are disappointing, but so they are in American secular education where the vast expenditure of money and effort over the last thirty years has not produced a corresponding advance of higher culture. But the creation of this massive educational system is in itself a great achievement and it should be regarded as the necessary condition and preparation for the American Catholic culture of the future. The fact that Catholics are now demanding a higher standard of cultural achievement as we see in books like Msgr. John Tracy Ellis' essay on *American Catholicism and the Intellectual Life* and Professor O'Dea's book on *The American Catholic Dilemma* is itself a sign of progress, and it seems to me as certain as anything can be that Catholic higher education is bound to advance and expand until it changes the whole aspect of American Catholic culture. For as education reaches a certain point of development, it opens up new and wider cultural horizons. It ceases to be a utilitarian parochial effort for the maintenance of a minimum standard of religious instruction and becomes the gateway to the wider kingdom of Catholic culture which has 2,000 years of tradition behind it and which is literally world-wide in its extent and scope. The name of this Association to which I am speaking today (The Thomas More Association) shows that American Catholics are fully aware of this tradition—that they feel that they can claim fellowship and spiritual relationship with a man like St. Thomas More, who in a different country and in a remote age stood for exactly the same cause and the same tradition of culture for which they stand today.

In the past, owing to adverse circumstances, American Catholics were deprived of this cultural heritage and forced to exist as outsiders on the periphery of a dominant Protestant culture. Nevertheless they were the legitimate heirs of a much richer cultural inheritance than anything that American Protestantism knew, and now that they are free to enter their inheritance, they will ultimately be able to exert an increasing influence on American thought and culture. It is obvious that this is an infinitely more important issue than the questions of political influence—if there is any chance of a Catholic being elected President and so on—questions which have a certain journalistic appeal but which only touch the surface of Catholic life. It is the cultural issue that is the vital one, for it is only by a communication of culture and the meeting of minds that it is possible to make Americans realize the true nature of Catholicism and the real significance of Catholic values. Throughout the greater part of the nineteenth century it is safe to say that American Protestants knew less than nothing about all this. What they thought they knew was a caricature—a stereotype imposed by centuries of religious controversy and prejudice. And even today this state of ignorance is by no means fully dissipated, as one sees by the big sales achieved by Mr. Paul Blanshard's books only a few years ago.

Now it is easy to understand, if not to forgive, the misunderstandings which inspired the Know-Nothing movement a century ago. The New Englanders for instance had their own highly developed regional culture, based on the old Puritan tradition and the new Unitarian ideology, and it was natural that they should resent the incursion of vast hordes of uneducated Catholics, speaking what was almost a strange language and worshipping, so to speak, strange gods. But all this is ancient history. The descendants of the immigrants today are as American as the descendants of the Pilgrim Fathers, and the American Catholics of the present age are an educated people who have learned to adapt themselves to the American way of life without sacrificing their own religious and intellectual tradition. It is true Catholics are still a minority—far larger and stronger and better organized than many Catholic majorities in the Old World.

Why then do we not possess a higher intellectual prestige and a stronger cultural influence in this country? It must surely be because Catholics have not yet learned how to use their latent cultural resources. If the thirty or forty million Catholics in this country were aware of their cultural strength, there is no power in the land that could equal them. The only conclusion we can draw is that American Catholicism is a sleeping giant, or perhaps rather that it is a giant that has not yet learned to speak. As our recent critics have pointed out—and they are for the most part friendly Catholic and American critics—we are still inadequately represented in proportion to our numbers in the world of scholarship and learning, and perhaps even more in the intermediate world of public information and communication—the world in which American public opinion is formed. No people is more susceptible to these influences than the American—they are like the Athenians of St. Paul's time, ready to listen to any new idea, even though they do not agree with the views of the speaker or the writer; so that there is in America today a field for the communication of Catholic thought which offers a great opportunity for the action of a lay apostolate.

Now it is the main burden of criticism in the books to which I have referred that we do not possess a lay intellectual class which can take advantage of this opportunity. Here again it is easy to explain the deficiency by historical causes. The system of American Catholic education was created by the clergy and at first higher education was mainly concerned with the education of priests. It was inevitable that this should be so. The Church had to have priests, while there was no lay educated class that had to be taken into account.

But that is now a thing of the past. The Catholic universities and colleges have been producing an educated laity for a considerable period and there is no reason why Catholic laymen should be treated or should regard themselves as an underprivileged intellectual class. Nevertheless there is always a certain time lag in educational development, and the clerical orientation of Catholic education in the past continues to affect the American cultural pattern so that the Catholic laity still find it difficult to assume a role of cultural leadership.

I believed it is only a matter of time for this state of things to be rectified. American Catholicism has overcome such tremendous difficulties in the past, in the age when the foundations of our modern educational institutions were laid, that the difficulties of the present are trifling in comparison. Indeed, an optimist might suggest that today it is not so much a question of overcoming difficulties but rather of taking advantage of the new opportunities that are offered to us. In the past the question was one of bare educational survival in a non-Catholic society and Catholics had no time for developing the latent resources of Catholic culture; but now the Catholic laity are awakening to the riches of their cultural inheritance and the non-Catholic world is more ready than ever before to listen to what we have to say on the subject, if we can speak to them in the right language.

American Catholics have one great advantage which is not shared in anything like the same degree by others—they are members of a universal society and they can draw freely on all that is being thought and written by their fellow Catholics elsewhere since we are all members of one another. Now one of the most striking features of Catholicism today is the renaissance of theological studies which has been developing during the last twenty years—most notably in France but not in France alone. Unlike the theological revivals of the past, this movement is not confined to the clergy but has met with a great response from the lay public. My friend, Dr. Frank Sheed, has done a great deal in England and over here also to stimulate this movement and to show how every intelligent Catholic, even if he has no specialized training, can take his share in it and become, so to speak, theologically literate. Now we have this very comprehensive series—*The Twentieth Century Encyclopedia of Catholicism*—which is published here in English by Hawthorn Books. This series is a comprehensive attempt to cover the whole field of Catholic culture from theology and philosophy to literature and art and its purpose is to put this universal range of knowledge at the disposal of the educated Catholic layman.

This is a remarkable indication of the interest that is being shown today in Catholic culture. And it is not the only sign. There is also the publication of the numerous paperback series which represent a kind of cultural revolution, and though most of them are not Catholic, Catholic classics are very well represented in them. For instance, one can buy editions of the English and Spanish mystics for under a dollar as well as the Venerable Bede's *Ecclesiastical History of the English Nation* and Newman's *Grammar of Assent.* I do not know who reads these books; someone must do so or they would not be published. This means that the layman possesses far greater opportunities for self-education than in the past and there is some reason to suppose that he is taking advantage of these opportunities and that Catholic culture is being spread all the time under the surface by this silent propaganda of classical literature. In addition to this there are the Catholic literary reviews and magazines—publications like *The Critic* and *The Sign* and *Jubilee,* which have taken on a new lease of life in recent years.

And finally there are movements on a deeper spiritual level, like the liturgical movement and above all the revival of the contemplative life in the new American Trappist or Cistercian communities. And this is perhaps the most hopeful sign of all, since the contemplative life is the standard of Catholic higher culture and the source from which the intellectual and spiritual life of the whole Catholic body is nourished and sustained.

And so I believe that the prospects for Catholic culture in the United States are more hopeful than at any time in the past. No doubt very much remains to be done, for the movements of which I have been speaking are minority movements within a minority community. These minority movements still have to penetrate and leaven the existing Catholic mass culture. Until they have done this, American Catholicism cannot speak to America with the full force of its thirty million voices. But that time will surely come. For the creation of this great American Church out of nothng in the midst of a society that seemed as remote from Catholicism as any society in Christendom was not the result of human planning or design. It is God's work, not man's, Who has made for Himself a new people in the New World out of exiles and the disinherited for whom there was no place in the Old World. This new Catholic people has grown together until it has become one of the greatest Catholic bodies in the world. We cannot believe that this historical process will stop at this point. As American Catholicism matures, its culture will increase in richness and depth, and it will acquire the new powers of communication and self-expression which are inseparable from a mature culture. American Catholicism is certainly called to play an increasing part in the life of Christendom and perhaps on the stage of world history, and if the men of this generation play their part, we can look forward to an advance of Christian culture which may change the outlook for Western civilization.

28

~>>)«<~

Norman St. John=Stevas

1959

from *"The Catholic Church in America"*

~>>)«<~

Norman St. John-Stevas is an Englishman who has achieved fame as a legal authority, a political correspondent and the holder of somewhat unconventional opinions. Many of these opinions are to be found in *Life, Death and the Law,* his discussion of the relationship between law and morals in England and the United States. He has shown particular interest in the problem of obscenity and during the English court proceedings against *Lady Chatterly's Lover* he was a defense witness for the D. H. Lawrence novel. A Catholic, Mr. St. John-Stevas is accustomed to finding himself in disagreement with many of his fellow Catholics, both in England and the United States, on morality and the law. His comments on American Catholics appeared in *The Sign,* March, 1959, under the title "The Catholic Church in America." They are reprinted here by permission of the author.

~>>)«<~

When I arrived in New York, just twelve months ago, my mind, like that of every tourist, was filled with thoughts of the sight-seeing and new impressions that lay ahead. I longed to ascend the Empire State Building, to walk along Fifth Avenue, to see the lights of Broadway, to visit the Metropolitan Museum, and to stroll (before dark) through Central Park. And since I had been assured so often and overwhelmingly that New York was not the United States, my imagination leaped ahead, with intoxicating visions of Henry James' Boston, the green and pleasant countryside of Virginia, the rolling wheatfields of Kansas, and far-off, hilly San Francisco.

What I had not bargained for, even in fancy's rosiest flights, was the greatest assembly of Catholic prelates and dignitaries that I had ever seen in my life, despite ten visits to Rome. Yet there they were, the day after my arrival, gathered in the Yankee Stadium to honor Cardinal Spellman on his jubilee. In an arena which I associated vaguely with baseball, hot dogs and Coca-Cola, I found five Princes of the Church, more than one hundred bishops, innumerable monsignori, and a host of clergy, religious and laity presided over by the Delegate of His Holiness the Pope. The strength of the Catholic Church in the United States, its visible and overflowing vigor, was thus my first impression of American Catholicism. It has remained an abiding one.

Later the same day, I was taking tea—an unforeseen but very welcome amenity—in a New York drawing room, where I was introduced to a charming, white-haired priest, with whom I had a lively conversation and whom I took to be a member of the archdiocese. He turned out to be a Carthusian, the founder, in fact, of America's first Carthusian Monastery! I would not have been surprised to meet a film star in New York but a Carthusian prior was definitely not on my provisional engagement calendar. Here was another aspect of American Catholicism, in striking contrast to the elaborate pomp of the morning's ceremony. Here was a symbol of the intensity of the country's spiritual life.

These were my first two impressions of American Catholicism: external strength and inner devotion. Subsequent experience has deepened both impressions. Around them I would like to arrange some further thoughts and reflections on the Church in America.

Everywhere I have traveled in the United States, save in the deep South, I have been deeply impressed by the visible signs of Catholic vitality and growth. From New England to the Pacific Coast, cathedrals, churches, schools, great universities, hospitals, monasteries, and convents, all testify to the vigor of Catholic life. Can this, one asks oneself, be the "immigrant" Church, which less than two hundred years ago had only a few thousand adherents in the whole United States? (Only in the South, in Tennessee or North Carolina, have I found conditions that reminded me strongly of the rural English Church, struggling against material odds in a semi-hostile environment.)

These buildings erected by the Church are more than graven images. They are centers of activity which must be unparalleled in the contemporary Catholic world. Hardly a day passes without my opening the New York *Times* to read about some Catholic endeavor or some controversy in which Catholics are involved. Whatever one thinks of the Catholic Church, whether one loves or hates her, she cannot, in the United States, any longer be ignored.

But here I come to my first point of criticism. No outside observer can fail to feel how much of Catholic activity in public life appears to be negative in character. One day a Catholic doctor will be denouncing contraceptive devices with impassioned invective. The next day, a monsignor will be condemning an immoral film. The third day, a speaker at a Communion breakfast will be calling for a crusade against evil literature.

The primary role of the Church is not to condemn the world but to redeem it, and the danger of overdenunciation is a cutting off from the very world the Church exists to save. The modern world is full of evil. But, in many ways, it is also a much better world than the world of some centuries ago. All that is good in it, the Church must baptize and make her own. So I should be happier to see fewer denunciations and rather more headlines like these: "Catholic sociologist calls for more aid to underdeveloped countries, more liberal immigration policies into the United States." "Catholic author awarded N. O. D. L. prize for the best novel of the year." "Catholic bishop calls for opening of institute of higher studies."

As an Englishman, and therefore presumably a Protestant,

I hear franker and more candid views about the Church than normally penetrate to more obviously Catholic ears. Constantly, I have been dismayed to find that the predominant attitude toward the Church is one of distrust and fear. Non-Catholics fear that they will be denied religious freedom, that their civil liberties will be compromised, that the Church will be merged with the State, should Catholicism ever become the majority religion of the country.

Some months ago, I attended a conference on "Religion and Society" sponsored by the Fund for the Republic. There the views I had heard expressed in private received striking public confirmation. For a week, a distinguished and representative gathering of Catholics, Protestants, and Jews discussed the different problems raised by religion in civil society. But, whatever the question discussed, only a few minutes were needed for the debate to center around the Catholic Church. In a sense, this was a high compliment, but it had other less pleasing aspects.

It soon became apparent that what outsiders often see when they look at the Catholic Church is not the Church of Christ with her world-wide redemptive mission. They see a huge power structure aimed at the destruction of traditional American liberties. Much responsibility for this rests with mischievous propagandists such as Paul Blanshard. Yet, bricks are not made without straw, and Catholic indiscretions are at least in part to blame. Whoever is responsible, and however complicated the historical and cultural causes of such an attitude may be, the attitude is a fact; it is a major stumbling block to the conversion of the United States and one which American Catholics will ignore at their peril.

It is not that the Catholic Church in America could honestly be described as "Un-American." Indeed, in many ways I believe the Catholic Church is too American, too uncritical of government policies, sharing too many of the national prejudices, including the general aversion for intellectual activities. It is however fair to say that the Catholic attitude to American freedom is, to some extent, confused.

The great majority of American Catholics feel as strongly about constitutional liberties as the next man, but the feeling rests on an unsure intellectual foundation. This is sensed by those outside the Church. All conflicts, said Cardinal Manning, are basically theological. What American Catholics need more than anything else is a clearly worked out theology of religious freedom and civil liberty.

Our late Holy Father, Pius XII, gave a clear lead to the Catholic world in 1953 when he addressed the National Convention of Italian Catholic Jurists. "It is plainly true," said His Holiness, "that error and sin abound in the world today. God reprobates them but He allows them to exist. Wherefore the statement that religious and moral errors must always be impeded, when it is possible, because toleration of them is in itself immoral, is not valid absolutely and unconditionally. . . . The duty of repressing moral and religious error cannot, therefore, be an ultimate norm of action. It must be subordinate to higher and more general guiding principles, which in some circumstances allow, and even perhaps seem to indicate as the better policy, toleration of error in order to promote a greater good." Here in embryo is a whole Catholic theology of toleration which should be developed by American Catholic thinkers, both clerical and lay, and applied to problems of the contemporary scene.

I have highlighted one particular problem, but this raises a wider issue, to which it is closely connected, the contribution of Catholics to the intellectual life of the nation. Never has a branch of Catholicism so rich in numbers and material resources made a smaller contribution to the world of ideas than the Church in America. Practicing Catholics in France, at a rough estimate, can be no more numerous than those in America, but while the French Church is in intellectual ferment, a powerhouse of ideas for the Universal Church, from America comes scarcely a stir. In this respect, even the fragmentary scholarly record of the small and impoverished band of English Catholics makes a favorable comparison.

Many reasons have been put forward to explain this dearth

of Catholic scientists, philosophers, and political thinkers: an immigrant Church, the social make-up of the Catholic body, the concentration on providing elementary and secondary education for an ever-growing population. These are convincing explanations up to a point, but they do not go to the root of the problem.

Basically, I believe there have been few Catholic scholars, because American Catholics have not desired them. By this I do not mean that anti-intellectualism is widely diffused in the Catholic body. The generous patronage extended to foreign scholars would at once disprove this. Rather, because scholarly activity has not been rated highly in the United States, Catholics have been content to be dependent on a European supply. Today Catholics are much more aware of the "decorative" or "prestige" value of distinguished scholars than in the past. Yet, they still think in terms of scholarship for utilitarian or apologetic ends, rather than for the pursuit of truth for its own sake. Until the Catholic body and its leaders accept the idea of the intellectual vocation as the highest (sanctity always excepted) to which either clergy or laity can devote themselves, Americans will continue to lack a flourishing, native Catholic scholarship.

A Church of "egg-heads" is not an especially entrancing prospect, but a Church without them is worse, and this situation will persist until the full ideal of the scholarly and intellectual life, with all its rewards and sacrifices, is put before every Catholic student who is capable of following it. In this respect, American Catholics are failing not only the Church but the nation, for with her centuries-old tradition, her cultural accumulation of the past, her great doctors, philosophers, and thinkers, the Catholic Church should be one of the principal civilizing influences in the United States, but on this inexhaustible treasury she has so far only sparingly drawn.

Whatever shortcomings American Catholics have shown by intellectual mediocrity they have made up for by their devotion to the spiritual life. I wish European critics of American Catholicism could see for themselves the crowded churches, the patient lines outside the confessionals, the packed Communion rails, which, Ireland apart, have no equivalent in what are optimistically called Catholic countries. Wherever I have traveled I have found the same devotion to the Holy Eucharist enshrined in the hearts of the people. To me, this religious fervor has been inexpressibly comforting and encouraging.

Yet I am not uncritical of American devotional practices. Personally I like novenas and other means of "storming heaven at short notice," but they seem to me to have an exaggerated place in American Catholic spiritual life. One can have too much of a good thing. The mind of the Church is expressed principally in the liturgy, but in this, except for a small but vital minority, interest seems to be much too meager. How rarely can one find solemn High Mass fittingly performed, and rarer still is the Church's official music, the Gregorian Chant. The caterwauling that emanates from so many choir lofts is more often an obstacle than an aid to devotion. Where are the Sunday evening services? What has happened to Vespers and Compline, among the loveliest of the services which the Church provides?

Much, however, has been done: missals are used in millions where before they numbered thousands; the new Easter Ritual gives great promise; dialogue Masses are burgeoning; but the goal of a fittingly performed liturgy in every Cathedral city of the United States is not even in sight.

Clerical respect is also a striking characteristic of American Catholic life and is a welcome change from the rancid anticlericalism that has stultified so much of the Church's work on the European continent. Priests move with friendliness and ease among the laity, and, rather more surprisingly, so do nuns. Here, let me pay a tribute to American nuns. I had met very few intelligent, informed women until I visited American convents. The freedom and ease, the lack of self-consciousness, the acceptance of modern life which characterizes American Sisters is something quite new to my experience. One is aware that they are dedicated religious, but also that they are human beings. Reverence for the clergy can, however, be exaggerated and I am disturbed by certain aspects. The deep resentment expressed at any outside criticism of the Catholic clergy and the unthinking support given to a priest involved in public controversy, irrespective of the merits of the case, are not wholly praiseworthy. Perhaps this unwillingness to criticize explains the low quality of preaching in Catholic churches. Draughty appeals to lead more moral lives or catalogues of the Church's material achievements are poor substitutes for sermons based solidly on Catholic doctrine or on the life of Our Lord.

Outside of Chicago, the part played by the laity in the life of the Church seems disproportionately small and out of accord with the modern mind of the Church, with its continual stress on the apostolate of the laity. In the nineteenth century, Monsignor Talbot, a convert Anglican parson, once gave a celebrated definition of the role of the laity: "to hunt, to shoot and to entertain." Things have changed somewhat since then, but too often Catholic laity are content with a passive financial role.

I hope these short notes of mine will not cause annoyance or resentment. They are written in a spirit of humility and with a freedom to which only a "foreigner" can aspire. Self-criticism is essential to progress, but what is a common-place of the interior is not so readily accepted when applied to the Church's external mission.

The responsibility of the Catholic Church to the American nation is a heavy one. As the doctrinal basis of Protestantism dissolves, the moral cosmos fragments with it, and the time is not far distant when the Catholic Church will become the sole institutional repository of Christian values in the United States. Not that the American people are materialist. Quite the contrary, and after my year's experience of the natural goodness and generosity of Americans of every faith and none, I never want to hear that particular accusation again.

Yet it is a reproach to all of us that often enough the sheep look up and are not fed. The daily, faithful observance of God's law in private life is indispensable for bringing souls to Christ. Scarcely less important is a zealous and restless desire to improve our present arrangements, a profound anxiety that everything is being done to cooperate with God's plan for the redemption of the world.

29

> ⇒»⟫⟪⟪

Illtud Evans, O.P.

1962

from *"North America: The Church"*

> ⇒»⟫⟪⟪

Father Illtud Evans, a British Dominican, is the editor of the distinguished monthly review *Blackfriars,* a well-known preacher and writer—*One and Many, Voice of Lourdes* and *Voice of the Holy Land*—a frequent contributor to American and English journals, a regular broadcaster on BBC and a university lecturer. He is noted in the fields of theology, liturgy, religious art and penology. This report, which first appeared in *Blackfriars* (Vol. 43, no. 500) resulted from an extended lecture tour in America. His comments are reprinted here by courtesy of *Blackfriars* Magazine (London).

> ⇒»⟫⟪⟪

The figures of course are formidable. And the European enquirer can be mesmerized by the catalogue of Catholic achievement in the United States: a population now of forty-five million, with 55,000 priests, 170,000 religious sisters (of whom nearly 100,000 teach in schools), 267 universities and colleges with more than 300,000 students, 10,000 elementary schools with over four million pupils, 850 hospitals of every sort in which more than fourteen million patients were treated in 1960. In the same year nearly 132,000 converts were received into the Church.

The statistics matter, if only because they are the staring facts that declare the vitality of the Church in the only way it can be externally measured. They indicate something too, of the astounding generosity of American Catholics, who, with no help from public funds, have built up a system of churches and schools unparalleled in the Church's history. But the Church is not merely a corporation to be surveyed in terms of its efficiency or of the successful image it presents to the world. It is easy for the visitor from an older and more casual society to wonder a little at the signs of a high-powered organization— the discreet hum of the electric typewriters in the carpeted rooms of the chancery offices, the multitude of monsignori bearing their hide brief-cases, the jet black Chryslers—and to see in it all the ecclesiastical equivalent of the sort of business set-up commended by *Fortune* magazine. Unhappily too many observers remain at this superficial level of judgment, which is only to say that the Church uses, as she must, the material means at hand in her temporal mission, here and now.

Nevertheless, the image of the Church as established so firmly in American life, and in a way that Americans readily understand, has its importance. It is a far cry from the Church of the immigrants, for the most part despised as alien, to the Church that has "arrived" to become one of the most characteristically American of institutions. Robert Cross, an astute non-Catholic observer, can even say that "Catholicism has at last become part of American culture." The emphasis here is on "at last," and with justice. Until quite lately the Church's energies were almost wholly taken up with the problems of providing for the vast army of immigrants—nine million Catholics came to America in less than a century—who brought, from Ireland, Italy, Germany, Poland, loyalties of language and tradition that had little in common with the assumptions that formed the accepted American framework.

The Church indeed had few roots in the earlier—and formative—history of the United States. There had been the colonization of Maryland, of course, and the strange, hidden Catholic life of New Mexico and the California missions. And the influence of the French Jesuit missionaries, still to be discerned in Detroit and St. Louis, is not to be ignored. But the evolution

of American institutions found little place for Catholic ideas
or aspirations, and the teeming millions of Catholic immigrants
were readily dismissed by New England intellectuals as a lesser
breed, certainly without the law as understood on Beacon Hill.
It was the great and far-seeing achievement of such men as
Cardinal Gibbons and Archbishop Ireland to prepare the ground
for the establishment of the Church in America as the Church
of America, rooted firmly in a society that was free. Their insistence on the right—and paramount duty—of Catholics to
take a full share in their country's life and institutions can seem
gratuitous now. But they spoke at a time when the Church was
still absorbed in sectional interests, struggling to assimilate its very
mixed elements, and only emerging to defend itself against its
cruder enemies.

It was inevitable that the political attitudes of Catholics should
reflect their national origins; inevitable, too, that the pressure of
anti-Catholic agitation should lead to the formation of caucuses
whose influence is still an important, and often malign, element
in the municipal affairs of such cities as Boston and New York.
It is instructive in this context to remember that President Kennedy was the grandson of "Honey Fitz," a characteristic Boston-
Irish boss. The process of moving up is rapid in American life,
and Catholics, for the most part late starters, are certainly in
the running.

If one tries to analyse the spiritual strength of the Church
in America, the danger is necessarily one of generalizations
based on evidence that can never be adequate. But at once one
can record an impression of robust and uninhibited faith and
of a degree of actual religious practice that has surely no parallel
in recent European experience. It has to be admitted that church
attendance of every sort is at a high level in America. It is a
form of social conformity that is specially important in country
districts and in smaller towns. But the proof of the vigour of
Catholic life is perhaps to be found in such hard facts as the
resilience of vocations to the priesthood and the religious life,

and, most notably, in the popularity—in the true sense—of retreats for lay people. When 300,000 laymen make a closed retreat in an average year and do all the organizing themselves, observing silence with a strictness that has its own virtue in the maelstrom of American life, the usual impression of a bingo-dominated Catholic community, concerned above all with organization, needs to be revised. At Gethsemani, which has acquired its own importance as the monastery of Thomas Merton, who has contributed so profoundly to the spiritual awakening of American Catholicism through his writings, one finds week by week large groups of wholly representative laymen, sharing in the religious and liturgical life of the Cistercian monks. Their presence is in a way more remarkable than that of the monks themselves.

One has the impression that so far the liturgical advances of the last few years have had little general effect on Catholic life. America remains a great country for the novena and the "shrine," and the necessarily Irish tradition of so many of the clergy means that, as in Ireland itself, advance will be slower in some areas than many lay people would like. There are of course some notable exceptions to such a general statement, and the work and publications, for instance, of the Benedictine monks of Collegeville are profoundly affecting the religious life of many parishes and certainly most Catholic colleges throughout the country. But the piety is still characteristically individual in its emphasis, and a glance at most Catholic journals will reveal a strong interest in what one might call pragmatic tests of the Church's life. Nowhere is there such an interest in the moral theologian's role, as the extraordinary debate recently about the right to "defend" a fall-out shelter showed.

It is the achievement of Catholic education that is bound to impress the visitor. In terms of "plant" it is formidable. One scarcely ever visits a school or college where ambitious building projects are not in progress. So far the concentration has largely been on provision for a rapidly growing community, and in any case increasingly large numbers of Catholic students will have to go to "neutral" universities, for the Catholic institutions cannot hope to find room for them. Thus in one large city the Catholic university has 3,000 students, with some eighty priests on the faculty, while the independent university includes 4,000 Catholic students, with until recently only one priest acting as their chaplain and running the Newman centre. This disproportion is a startling illustration of a problem that is going to grow to perhaps unmanageable proportions. In the meantime there has been much self-examination among Catholics as to the results of the education they have and for which they have made immense sacrifices. In particular, Msgr. Tracy Ellis of the Catholic University of Washington, has stressed its disappointing contribution to scholarship in the true sense, but, being a historian, he has shown how inevitable this was in the formative stages of the Church's growth, when energies were wholly concentrated on building up institutions, often isolated as they were from the general stream of American educational advance, and deprived of any sort of aid from public funds.

It is perhaps a matter for debate whether the conception of the Catholic University, providing courses of instruction in all the academical disciplines, is likely to need modification under the stress of present-day needs. The mere cost of such departments as engineering or nuclear physics is itself a difficulty, and it will often happen that the graduate of a Catholic college will in any case do his graduate work of preference in a "neutral" university, whose material facilities are likely to be better. A concentration on the programme of the "Liberal Arts College," preserving humane values which are everywhere threatened by the claims of technology, will remain an essential Catholic contribution to true learning and perhaps ultimately a more valuable one than the attempt at competing in specialist fields. It is odd to find a School of Business Administration as an indispensable part of any Catholic college, but as Father Walter Ong, S. J., has pointed out, the social ability of business in American life, and all its implications in terms of universal optimism, has necessarily affected Catholics as they take an increasing share in American life at all its levels. "The Church feels this milieu is not to be neglected, but redeemed," he comments.

The coming-of-age of the Church as an established feature of American life has of course created much suspicion among those, such as Dr. Blanshard, who see in Catholic advance a threat to the American tradition of tolerance and democratic process. It is ironical that this should be so, for it is in America that a realistic understanding of the Church's function in a "pluralistic" society has been most frankly faced. It is true that there are Catholic groups who find in the opposition to Communism a sufficient justification for the extremes of conservatism associated with the John Birch Society. And the memory of the late Senator Joseph McCarthy is far from forgotten. But it may well be that the providential role of the American Church in 1962 is to present to the world an exemplar of what religious freedom means. The circumstances of their history have required American Catholics to avoid any sort of equivocation in this matter. One recalls the extraordinarily prescient remarks of Archbishop Carroll in 1784, "America may come to exhibit a proof to the world that general and equal toleration, by giving a free circulation to fair argument, is the most effectual method to bring all denominations of Christians to a unity of faith."

It is certainly true to say that the response to the present Pope's ecumenical concern has been prompt and generous in America. "Togetherness" needs no encouraging, and what might be called the Rotary assumptions of American life make contacts, at least at a social level, easy to achieve. The "dialogue" is constantly discussed, but less frequently is it conducted at a high level of intellectual interest, though here one must acknowledge the contributions of such theologians as Fr. Courtney Murray, S. J., and Fr. Gustave Weigel, S. J. In whole areas of American intellectual life, indeed, the Society of Jesus is marked by a combination of sound learning and an awareness of the nature of the Church's intervention in the circumstances of to-day. There are many reasons, of which the recollection, and even the recrudescence, of such crude anti-Catholic campaigns as the Ku Klux Klan, is not the least important—why the Church's concern has seemed exclusively one of defence. Catholics have been notable more for their protests against injustices under which they have laboured than for any radical concern for justice as such. They have been forced too often into the corner of an apologetic that justifies the Catholic opposition to divorce, birth control or whatever it be; their theology has seemed to be more a matter of answering objections rather than of proclaiming the truth.

It has to be admitted—and Americans are the first to admit it—that the intellectual contribution of Catholics to American life, in the sense of applying the resources of their theology to a constructive appraisal of the world in which they live, has been very limited. But, as Jacques Maritain has pointed out, the very newness of the Church's larger mission in America has always to be remembered. Cardinal Cushing recently remarked that not a single American bishop could claim a father who had had a college education. He was of course instancing this fact as proof of the identification of the Church in America with the workers, with those who could claim no privileges. The picture will be very different in a few years time, and already the most universal Irish episcopal names are giving place to many unspellable Polish and Croatian ones.

What sustains American Catholic life above all else is its vigorous optimism. It may be that as yet the deeper implications of the Church's social teaching, the taxing dilemmas that her moral authority must increasingly create in the evolving American scene, have not been seriously faced. And here a certain confusion of political acceptability with religious sanctions can arise, as in the profound suspicion among many American Catholics of "socialization," with the suggestion that even a modest beginning of the welfare state is the high-road to Communism.

The agonizing moral problem presented by the possibility of nuclear warfare is only the gravest of many problems in which the mounting crisis for Christian opinion will have to be realized. And the providential history of the Church in America, with its freedom from the pressures that Governments have so often exercised in Europe, should stimulate a candour and courage which the situation will surely soon need. It would be sad if the pressure to conform to the image of "Americanism" should ever obscure the Church's freedom to instruct the conscience of her children or should limit their choice in following it.

In such matters as racial segregation, the lead given by some American bishops has been admirable, though they have wisely done nothing to countenance the violent seeking of sudden solutions which cannot disperse at once the inherited attitudes that are so often an unconscious factor in the life of the south. And a real sense of solidarity with the sufferings of others in poverty and oppression has been practically expressed in the record of the Catholic Relief Services, which have made more than $800 million available throughout the world since 1943—and this, of course, quite apart from the astronomical aid given by Federal agencies and met by taxation. The plans now being worked out to help in such territories as Latin America—and here Cardinal Cushing has been notably active—call not only for cash but for the personal service of Catholics, many of them laymen and women, and the response has been wonderfully generous.

The hope for the Church in America, as everywhere else, lies in the growing maturity of its laity, aware of a true vocation and not, as so often in the past, restricted to a passive conformity. Here such hopeful signs as the growth of the Christian Family Movement and the lively spirit of the Newman groups match the true needs of the times—and here, increasingly, one may believe that America will begin to assume in the life of the Church at large responsibilities which she has too often evaded. With resources so huge and an enthusiasm so generous, it seems especially sad that American life can superficially appear so trivial, so unaware of the true dimensions of the Church's mission at this point of human history. But the self-questioning that has recently surveyed Catholic education and its contribution to American life is itself a sign of a new and adult awakening. What is needed now is the capacity to communicate to the world beyond the parish walls the hope and justice and above all the charity that the Church commands to redeem society. And one can be hopeful that this will happen, for of the solid spiritual fidelity of the great mass of American Catholics one can have no doubt. They, and all of us, must begin to apply it, to see its total range in terms of a social conscience as well as those of individual perfection.

A NOTE ON THE TYPE
IN WHICH THIS BOOK WAS SET

This book has been set in Granjon, a lovely Linotype face, designed by George W. Jones, one of England's great printers, to meet his own exacting requirements for fine book and publication work. Like most useful types, Granjon is neither wholly new nor wholly old. It is not a copy of a classic face nor an original creation, but rather something between the two—drawing its basic design from classic Garamond sources, but never hesitating to deviate from the model where four centuries of type-cutting experience indicate an improvement or where modern methods of punch-cutting make possible a refinement far beyond the skill of the originator. This book was composed by Progressive Typographers, Inc., York, Pa., printed by Wickersham Printing Company of Lancaster, Pa., and bound by Moore and Company of Baltimore. The design and typography of this book are by Howard N. King.

A unique phenomenon in American life has been the growth of the Catholic Church in this country. The Catholic settler was an unwelcome person in most of the early colonies. Later as the number of immigrants continued to flow into this country, the mood of the country drove these Catholic groups into nationalistic ghettos in the cities. Finally, throughout past decades Catholics in America have not only been accepted but have risen to their present position of some influence and affluence.

THROUGH OTHER EYES is an attempt to restore to the modern reader the misunderstandings, prejudices, and successes in the dynamic growth of the Church in the United States. By recording the impressions of foreign visitors, of literary, religious, or cultural standing, at the time of their visits to the United States in the past two centuries, the editors have provided more than an historical study of the Church as an institution. The eyewitness observations of keen literary or religious minds comprise rare reflections of the historical settings and national moods in which the Church had to struggle for survival and later growth. If it were possible to classify this anthology, it would be more a study of a living organism in American society with all the qualities of an excellent biography. Few historical or statistical sum-